Praise for *The Persuaders*:

'Fierce and timely.

'A work of engaging ... ...tion of
the forces jellifying o... ...mes

'Garvey doesn't pull any punches ... It's hard to stop reading.'
New Scientist

'The author worries, rightly, that in losing the ability to argue and
question intelligently we become more susceptible to the subtle
and unseen skills of powerful persuaders.'   *Financial Times*

**Praise for James Garvey's *The Ethics of Climate
Change*:**

'If you don't yet know why you should be morally outraged about
the present situation, read this book. Calmly, carefully, with well-
marshalled facts and sound argument, Garvey shows us just how
badly the nations of the industrialized world – and the citizens of
those nations – are behaving. He also tells us what we need to do
about it.'   Peter Singer, Princeton University

'Open this book and James Garvey is right there making real sense
to you. A new philosopher doing logic in the world. In a necessary
conversation, capturing you to the very end.'   Ted Honderich,
Universi... ...

THE
PERSUADERS

THE
PERSUADERS
THE HIDDEN INDUSTRY THAT WANTS TO
CHANGE YOUR MIND

JAMES GARVEY

ICON

This edition published in the UK in 2016
by Icon Books Ltd, Omnibus Business Centre,
39–41 North Road, London N7 9DP
email: info@iconbooks.com
www.iconbooks.com

First published in the UK in 2016 by Icon Books Ltd

Sold in the UK, Europe and Asia
by Faber & Faber Ltd, Bloomsbury House,
74–77 Great Russell Street,
London WC1B 3DA or their agents

Distributed in the UK, Europe and Asia
by Grantham Book Services, Trent Road, Grantham NG31 7XQ

Distributed in the USA
by Publishers Group West,
1700 Fourth Street, Berkeley, CA 94710

Distributed in Canada
by Publishers Group Canada,
76 Stafford Street, Unit 300
Toronto, Ontario M6J 2S1

Distributed in Australia and New Zealand
by Allen & Unwin Pty Ltd,
PO Box 8500, 83 Alexander Street,
Crows Nest, NSW 2065

Distributed in South Africa
by Jonathan Ball, Office B4, The District,
41 Sir Lowry Road, Woodstock 7925

Distributed in India by Penguin Books India,
7th Floor, Infinity Tower – C, DLF Cyber City,
Gurgaon 122002, Haryana

ISBN: 978-178578-100-1

Typeset in Minion by Marie Doherty
Printed and bound in the UK by Clays Ltd, St Ives plc

Contents

ABOUT THE AUTHOR

James Garvey works for the Royal Institute of Philosophy and edits *The Philosophers' Magazine*. He has written and edited books on the history of ideas, philosophy, ethics, consciousness and social and political thought – his books have been translated into ten languages. He also writes for *The Guardian*, the *Times Literary Supplement*, the *New Statesman* and the *Times Higher Education*. He lives on a canal boat in London.

'At the end of reasons comes persuasion.'
LUDWIG WITTGENSTEIN

Preface

'The moment we want to believe something,
we suddenly see all the arguments for it, and
become blind to the arguments against it.'

GEORGE BERNARD SHAW

Before I disappear into the footnotes, it might help if I tell you how this started. Five years ago I had the philosophical equivalent of what recovering alcoholics call 'a moment of clarity'. I was in a large, crowded lecture hall in London, listening to a talk given by a high-flying Oxford theologian, and I did something I almost never manage to do. During the question and answer session that followed his talk, I got in an absolutely killer objection. A philosopher behind me swore happily when he heard it. Another sitting next to me smiled, leaned over and whispered, 'You've got him! You've got him in a regress!' Indeed I had.[1]

I won the argument that night, plainly, and to come to the point, it made no difference at all. The speaker didn't change his mind. He took more questions and just got on with promoting his view. It occurred to me then that maybe arguments aren't actually very persuasive. Even really good ones. That's what came to me in my moment of clarity.

This thought was to me a big deal. I've spent a lot of a life picking over arguments, surrounded by philosophers and their books and articles – all of us taking arguments very seriously. I thought that arguments are sometimes how you get at the truth and how you persuade others of the truths you have found. A number of people, both inside and outside the academic world, think so too. That's a large part of what we are all up to in an open society. We present our arguments to one another, sometimes in the public square. We listen, and the side with the strongest reasons is judged right in the end. Those with the best arguments have the assent of all reasonable people, and we move forward together. We've had the Enlightenment. We might stumble from time to time, but that's how things are supposed to go now.

I began to suspect that's not even remotely how things actually go at all. I don't want to overcook the point and suggest that arguments are entirely unpersuasive – but we might well overestimate their hold on us. And I'm not simply saying that quite often brawn trumps brains – that's nearly too obvious to mention. I'm also not being naive, I hope, having only just noticed that human beings are capable of extraordinary irrationality. But I believe there is something newsworthy here, something worrying, over and above all the obvious stuff, something just out of focus, on the corner of our collective vision. Maybe despite how it feels on the inside, good reasons actually have little effect on us, and in fact other forces largely shape what we think. The world we are building together, the lives we are living, the hopes we have and the actions we take – it's all very much what it is because of something other than good reasons. That possibility menaces me more than a little.

If that Oxford don was anything to go by, philosophers weren't much moved by arguments, and if they weren't, I wondered who was.* Was the giving of reasons a waste of time? Was I ever really persuaded by an argument or did I just have thoughts and find good reasons for them afterwards? I did have the experience of hearing an argument in favour of something I didn't believe, and although I couldn't find fault in it, I nevertheless didn't buy it for a second. I thought there must be something wrong with it that I just hadn't spotted yet. I began to worry, a lot, about the real role of argument in an actual human life. All of this wasn't exactly life-changing, but if I wasn't careful I thought I might be in some danger of losing my faith in rationality. I could at least feel it slipping. It was like my worldview had tilted slightly, and now nothing looked quite right.

It did not help as I slouched onto a bus on my way home from that lecture that I found myself thinking of the Marx Brothers' film *Horse Feathers*. There's a musical bit with Groucho playing a professor, cheerfully singing, 'Your proposition may be good, but let's have one thing understood. Whatever it is, I'm against it.' That was the soundtrack in my head that night. 'And even

---

* I think philosophers are persuaded by arguments in a very narrow range of circumstances – see David Chalmers (2015), 'Why isn't there more progress in philosophy?', *Philosophy*, 90.01, pp. 3–31 for a good guess as to why and when. There are at any rate famous philosophical arguments that most philosophers find extremely powerful, nothing obviously wrong with them, but that they still don't find persuasive: Agrippa's trilemma, Berkeley's arguments against the existence of matter, Hume's problem with induction. Even Hume couldn't talk himself into sticking with some of his own conclusions. What hope do the rest of us have?

when you've changed it or condensed it, I'm against it.' I recall feeling slightly ill.

I talked to friends about my experience of winning an argument without persuading my opponent, and they all had similar stories to tell. It happened a lot when talking politics or about a politically charged topic – equally reasonable people with equal access to the facts coming down on opposite sides, unable to see reason in what the other says. I encountered it often when writing and speaking about climate change – what seemed to me to be straightforward, compelling combinations of scientific fact and moral argument seemed to someone else entirely unconvincing, even worthy of ridicule. I knew an environmentalist who was interested in the psychology of climate change denial – so strange was it to him that he thought it must be some kind of pathology. Meanwhile, his green beliefs were likened by those on the other side to a kind of groundless religious fundamentalism. 'Beating them over the head with the facts doesn't work', he said. I imagine those who did not share his view thought he didn't have his facts right. There are arguments about climate change all over the place, but few people are persuaded by them. Something else is going on.

I started thinking about the genuinely persuasive forces out there. If not arguments, what actually does change our minds? What do we find persuasive? When people with money and power and know-how attempt to persuade us, what do they do? Advertisers, politicians, marketers, lobbyists and public relations professionals all seem to be up to something other than giving us good reasons. Is that because giving reasons doesn't work very well, or at least not as well as other persuasive tactics?

What are the dark arts practised by the pros and where did they come from? How did we end up with a world where good arguments are so easily ignored? Has it always been that way or is this some new fact about us? Is something taking the place of reason in public life? What is this shift doing to us, to our minds and to the world that we are building all around us? This book is a start on these questions, all of them raised inadvertently by an Oxford don with implausible views. I'm not sure I should thank him.

I am sure I should thank a number of other people. I'm grateful to many authors who have guided me through unfamiliar territory – those who know the literature will recognise my many debts. Some friends and other interested parties were good enough to read and comment on an earlier version of this book, and many others are owed thanks for different kinds of help. I'm especially grateful to Sarah Balmforth, Mango Benson, H. Skott Brill, Quillian Brogan, Catherine Clarke, Davis Cook, comrades at Crisis, Steve Donaghy, A.M. Ferner, Kim Hastilow, Duncan Heath, *Hei Matau* and crew, Ingrid Honderich, Ted Honderich, Rob Kerr, Ian Lambert, the librarians of Dr Williams's Library and Senate House Library, Justin Lynas, Anthony O'Hear, Marianne Pearson, Dan Pollendine, Ros Ponder, Sophie Robards, Will Robards, Matt Ryan, Stuart Scott, Rowan Searle, Matthew Shepherd, Heather Sillitoe, Ian Sillitoe, associates at the UCLU Jiu Jitsu Club, Olivia Wood, and Judy Garvey in particular for her unwavering encouragement and support.

This book is for V.

The Robin Hood on Butcher Lane

'I find I am much prouder of the victory I obtain over
myself, when, in the very ardour of dispute, I make myself
submit to my adversary's force of reason, than I am pleased
with the victory I obtain over him through his weakness.'

MICHEL DE MONTAIGNE

When George III began his slide into insensibility and
the American colonies were in open rebellion, the
people of London insisted on being completely reasonable
with one another. It all started some years earlier, with a small
group of men who met in a pub called the Robin Hood on
Butcher Lane.[1]

Up the stairs, out of earshot of the clamour of the labourers,
artisans and Strand girls below, they booked a private room on
Monday nights. Notoriously finicky about membership – boors
need not apply – as many as fifteen of them turned up to smoke,
drink and politely beg to differ with each another. They took
sides, for or against any question that caught their attention,
sometimes choosing an agreeably subversive topic, perhaps
objecting to the government's policy towards France's expan-
sion, debating whether Scripture might admit of personal interpretation, arguing the merits of popular books recommending

reform, and enquiring into whether virtue or vice might afford superior pleasures. They took it in seven-minute turns, the time carefully observed by a vigilant factotum. After about two hours of spirited debate, when everyone had had enough, the chair summarised the arguments and brought the proceedings satisfactorily to a close. Although anyone was entitled to speak, some sat quietly and simply listened, enjoying the splendid sound of points eloquently made.

Perhaps an enterprising publican spotted the quiet ones and thought to open the doors to spectators – for a small admission fee of course. By the 1730s, the Robin Hood Society was a going concern, joined a decade later by the Queen's Arms Society, and on it quietly but resolutely went, with just three or four groups scheduling regular debates, ranks swelled a little by budding lawyers, politicians and, oddly enough, actors – all keen to gain experience of speaking in public. But in the winter of 1780, something unexpected happened.

It had the shape of an epidemic centred in the heart of the city, with debating societies springing up around the Robin Hood at first, then fanning out all the way to what were then nearly London's borders. Every neighbourhood succumbed. As far north as Islington, the Summer Lyceum met at Smith's Tea Rooms. In the south, the Theological Debating Society convened in St George's Fields. As far east as Rotherhithe, the School of Oratory scheduled regular discussions in China Hall. In the west, the Black Horse Tavern on New Bond Street was home to the Lyceum for the Investigation of Historical, Political, Literary and Theological Subjects. A newspaper editor baulked at the 'rage for disputation, which has so suddenly spread itself in every part of the metropolis'.[2] Another worried that 'the Disorder is become so epidemical, that we are in Danger of dying a Nation of Orators'.[3]

Seven clubs met in the autumn of 1779, but in a few short months 35 debating societies, catering to every conceivable intellectual taste, shoehorned hundreds of people into taverns, auction houses and dancing halls each night of the week. People of every rank rubbed shoulders in the debating rooms – at least anyone who could come up with entry fees, sometimes not much less than the cost of a pricey theatre ticket. As a patron described it: 'After a dirty walk, we were admitted, through the mediation of sixpence, into a spacious room, well lighted up and uncommonly crowded. The group was one of the most whimsical I had ever seen, and the countenances were in general divided into the *classical*, the *supercilious*, and the *vacant*, and the ranks would have been equally distinguishable, but that our introductory sixpence, like *death* and *stage-coaches*, had levelled all distinctions, and jostled wits, lawyers, politicians and mechanics, into the confusion of the last day.'[4]

Every large venue in the city was given over to 'rational amusements', and every self-respecting Londoner had views about where to go for a good argument. The Robin Hood could now expect 600 attendees a night – as many as 1,200 wedged themselves in for a big event. The largest brains in the country – the likes of Burke, Boswell and Pitt – weighed in.

Competition for custom was fierce. The societies distinguished themselves however they could, specialising in theological questions, political discussion, even sly takes on otherwise mundane matters to do with everyday life. Love, sex, and the proper relationship between a man and a woman were topics regularly revisited. Which is the more contemptible character:

the effeminate man or the masculine woman? Is marriage or celibacy more desirable? Is the love of the intellectual or 'the personal charms' of a woman more likely to induce a man to marriage? Is the 'deliberate seduction of the fair, with an intention to desert, under all circumstances worse than murder'? Can men and women ever truly be 'platonic friends'? A vote was taken at the end of this debate and the matter decided in the negative.

The Temple of Taste offered music, poetry and acrobatics in the run-up to the main event, while the Female Inquisition attracted attention with the potentially titillating prospect of 'fair orators', famous lady speakers whose gifts for argument were matched only by their beauty. Unamused, La Belle Assemblée banned men. Some clubs banned alcohol. Others banned women. One banned women and alcohol.

The better halls were commodious and grandly illuminated by fine chandeliers, with plush sofas and chairs arranged in gradually elevated circles to enable as many as possible to catch sight of all the action. The Lycée François held all its debates in French. For its part, the Carlisle House School of Eloquence encouraged frank debate by permitting speakers to conceal their identities behind masks, sternly warning that 'if any improper behaviour or expression shall be used under the concealment of a masque, the person offending shall submit, at the injunction of the President, to unmask or retire'.

It's easy to imagine these rooms as occasionally rowdy places, packed with eighteenth-century Londoners thrilling to verbal fisticuffs, baying for oratorical blood, but in fact it was incredibly civilised. The chair was expected to keep order, which usually wasn't difficult, as people turned up to hear incisive points made with style and eloquence, not mere knock-about. You can get a feel for it in this letter to the editor of the *Gazetteer*, gushing about a recent debate in the Queen's Arms:

> I was present on Friday evening last, and much pleased was I to observe so numerous an audience assembled, for the laudable purpose of edifying each other, by a search after truth. The question (which related to the indulgence lately granted by Parliament to the Roman Catholics of this kingdom) was discussed with the greatest candour and ingenuity by several gentlemen, long and well known in the society for their eminent abilities as to sound knowledge and real argument. Some new and juvenile speakers made their first essay, and were received with all that warmth of applause which is so fostering to the budding genius, and for which the society has always been remarkable, from its early institution to the present time.[5]

Not exactly bear-baiting is it?

But if it's easy for us to get it wrong when we try to imagine the urbanity of those taking part in London's grand debates, how unrecognisable would our world seem to them? Teleport the members of the Robin Hood Society to the present day, and subject them to a few of our forums for argument and debate: talk shows, reality television, blog posts and tweets, newspaper opinion pieces, late-night radio, hostile interviews, party political broadcasts, electioneering, and Prime Minister's Questions. What would they make of what argument has become? Would they see anything more than shouting back and forth, contradiction, accusation, insult, point-scoring, bickering and smearing? Would they find anything to admire in us at all?

In the end, London's flirtation with rationality did not last long. Largely in fearful reaction to the brewing French Revolution, the debating societies were violently repressed by the government – thugs were hired to break up debates, police constables blocked the doors, landlords were threatened with fines or worse, popular speakers were roughed up, and finally Parliament voted in the Seditious Meetings Act, effectively making public debate a treasonous offence.[6]

When the Robin Hood held its final meeting before being forced to close its elegant rooms, it was a kind of high-water mark in the history of reasoned discussion in the English-speaking world. No doubt we're the beneficiaries of progress along all sorts of intellectual lines, but our Georgian forebears would almost certainly wipe the floor with us in an argument. We wouldn't stand a chance.

What happened to us?

*

As the members of the Robin Hood might have had it, an argument was not merely disagreement. It was two or more people presenting and backing up their positions and then scrutinising one another's claims. If they were on top of things, they would have considered two fundamental features of argument: the logic of the presentation and the truth of the premises therein. Those arguing were expected to respond to points fairly made and accept them when that was where the argument led. It meant that one might change one's view in the light of criticism – and one might even do so gladly, because the essence and aim of a decent argument, for them, was largely the discovery of truth. No doubt the debating halls were sometimes filled with people arguing for the fun of it, for prestige, or for practice, but truth was the highest goal that could be shared by both sides. On a good night, they worked towards that goal together, enlightening one another, to the edification and applause of those in attendance.

When we think of an argument today, we mostly imagine something else entirely: entrenched positions, shouting matches, red faces and the butting of heads. There's rarely give and take, often no conception of one's interlocutor as a person with views up for consideration, no thought of modifying one's position in response to a good point. In fact the demonisation of your opponent is now an excellent and effective tactic, as is the deliberate misunderstanding of his or her claims. We appeal to emotion and authority, distract with irrelevancies, stoop to fallacy if it helps, and ignore good points no matter how well made they are. We stick to our guns, and we seek to undermine each other by any means.

Worries about this sort of carry-on are in the air at the moment. In a recent TED Talk the philosopher Michael Sandel put it bluntly: 'If you think about the arguments we have, most of the time it's shouting matches on cable television, ideological food fights on the floor of Congress.'[7] Much the same point is made, this time with regard to written argument, by Lee Siegel, columnist and editor-at-large for the *New York Observer*: 'The name-calling and yelling on cable TV and the Internet have made us forget [the power of the written word]. Polemic seems to have gone the way of the typewriter and the soda fountain. The word was once associated with the best practitioners of the form: Voltaire, Jonathan Swift, George Orwell, Rebecca West. Nowadays, if you say "polemic," you get strange looks, as if you were referring not to refined argument, especially written argument, but to some sort of purgative.'[8]

Maybe something has happened to us. Contemporary persuasion is now rarely done through argumentation. It now seems to operate mostly outside of reason.

In nearly every hour of your waking life, a lot of people will try to change your mind. Estimates vary from several hundred to several thousand persuasive messages encountered by the average adult each day, and almost none of it consists in giving you good reasons in support of a conclusion. Instead, you'll experience product placement, infoganda, sock-puppeteering, decoy pricing, viral marketing, astroturfing, crowd manipulation, newsjacking, framing, spinning, propagandising, agenda setting, message carpet-bombing, anchoring and the nudging of your choices – all in an effort to affect your beliefs, desires, values, decisions and actions. You are very rarely reasoned with. Instead, you are nudged, anchored and incentivised.

It may well be a profound shift in the way human beings interact with one another. Even if it is, a glance at history will tell you that the picture is nevertheless complicated. We haven't always been entirely reasonable or unreasonable – it hasn't been a slow march out of the darkness and into the light. There have been peaks and troughs – great moments like the days of the grand London debates, and much less reasonable times, perhaps like the ones we're in now.

At this odd moment, to consider just a corner of it, many of those engaged in debates in America about the budget, gun policy, healthcare, abortion, taxation and so on are barely able to speak to one another without anger. Religious debates between new atheists and believers can sometimes consist only in insult and slur. Objections to war in the Middle East are met with questions about one's patriotism rather than reasoned argumentation. Compare this to what human beings have been capable of in the past.

As recently as two hundred years or so ago, Americans with considerably different political opinions and agendas were able to sit down together, engage in something approaching dialogue, and ratify the Articles of Confederation. Dominican friars in the Middle Ages thought it their religious duty to converse with unbelievers, calmly and carefully, to help them see the divine light through civilised discussion. In the eighteenth century, while British soldiers were in action in India, a London debating society invited people to enjoy refreshments, listen to music, and then join polite company in addressing the question, 'Is not the war now carrying on in India disgraceful to this country, injurious to its political interest, and ruinous to the commercial interests of the [East India] Company?' This kind of thing is all but beyond us now.

In pointing to all of this I don't mean to suggest that the past was a watercolour of uniformly rosy rationality. When we think about the attack ads and mudslinging of contemporary political campaigning, for example, it's easy to pine for what we imagine were simpler and better times – bold men holding forth to attentive crowds of modest but reflective townsfolk, running for office on nothing less than the power of their excellent ideas. It's worth remembering that candidates for the US presidency did not actually engage in campaigning until 1840, when William Henry Harrison was forced to make a personal appearance at rallies to rebut the devastatingly effective but on reflection highly unlikely charge that he was, in actual fact, a 'caged simpleton'.

So there have been peaks and troughs, but we seem to be in a particularly deep trough at the moment. Why? That's a good but also hard question, and in trying to answer it, I know I'm setting myself an impossible task. A complete answer would require a long and detailed history of the social, economic, political and psychological forces that have landed us where we are. That kind of thing is beyond me – and anyway it's not the sort of book I'd want to read, much less write. Some of the larger moments in the explanation of our current malaise, if that's what it is, are themselves fascinating and enough to satisfy my own curiosity. So I won't raise the *Titanic*, but I will dive for pearls.

The topics considered here reflect my own odd path through the tangled history of persuasion. I sometimes used the unimpeachably scientific method of discussing discoveries with friends in the pub, and if an experiment or event or personality got them talking it probably made it into these pages. Someone else with different friends in another pub might have chosen differently. In the end this book contains a mix of history and theory, good stories and large personalities, experimental evidence and ridiculous ideas that somehow managed to catch on. Among many other things, you'll read about contemporary propaganda, new theories influencing the minds of our leaders and policy-makers (and in turn changing our lives too), the manipulative language of political campaigns, the rise of psychological theorising on Madison Avenue in the 1950s and what that did to our culture, and how an understanding of the human brain and the effects of social media might give some people a powerfully persuasive edge. There are also some worrying possibilities to consider, about what it is that modern persuasion does to human freedom, well-being, mental health, social cohesion, morality, the flow of power, and our prospects for living happy lives in a peaceful, interconnected world. The chapters are largely self-contained, so feel free to skip around if you like. I'll try to stand back and leave you free to come to your own conclusions, but often I find I can't help butting in. I will certainly say what I think at the end of chapters and at the end of the book.

A lot of things really must be said, because this shift in persuasion matters more than you might think. As a people, we're unusually quiet about it, and that has to change. I sometimes wish I had a god's-eye view of the causal history of my beliefs, a spider's web of connections I could follow right back to where and when I first came to think what I think. There's a lot I take to be true, about how the world is and how it should be, a conception of religion, thoughts about politics and the value of science, beliefs about corporations, power, money, and what ultimately matters to me and how I think I ought to live my life. I wonder how much of that is owed to clear-headed reflection and rational choice on my part, and how much is actually the result of persuasive pressure from outside. I feel a clear responsibility to try to uncover the difference, figure out what's mine and what's not, otherwise my thoughts aren't really my own, and there's something awful about living like that.

I'm reminded of Bertrand Russell's lines about 'the man who has no tincture of philosophy', the unreflective person who just 'goes through life imprisoned in the prejudices derived from common sense, from the habitual beliefs of his age or his nation, and from convictions which have grown up in his mind without the co-operation or consent of his deliberate reason'.[9]

Russell sees in such a life a kind of horror. Just accepting a view of the world that you've been handed by someone else, without reflection or deliberation, without argument – it's not your view of the world at all. It's not really your life that you're living if the convictions you live by are not your own.

The persuasive pressure on us, to think and feel and choose a way of life, is enormous. It's harder now than it was in Russell's day to make up your mind for yourself, but the stakes are just as high. What we believe shapes us, makes us who we are, and largely determines what we do, who we love, and how we live. So I think we have an obligation, maybe a moral one, to understand what contemporary persuasion does to us. It bothers me, and I hope that now it bothers you too.

The Art of Steering Heads Inside

'The most effective way to restrict democracy is to transfer
decision-making from the public arena to unaccountable
institutions: kings and princes, priestly castes, military
juntas, party dictatorships, or modern corporations.'

NOAM CHOMSKY

In the summer of 1990, the Iraqi Republican Guard over-
whelmed Kuwait's armed forces and took control of the
country. The fighting lasted just two days. Speculation about
the rationale for the invasion has always focused on money and
oil. Iraq accused Kuwait of 'slant drilling' across the border, into
Iraqi reserves. There were complaints by Iraq that high production levels of Kuwaiti oil kept the price too low. Annexing the
country was a clear and efficient way to stop both the sideways
siphoning of oil and the downwards pressure on price.

Whatever Iraq's reasons, Americans were initially indifferent to the invasion. Vietnam had not faded from memory, and
there was no taste for sending American troops abroad, again,
to fight yet more battle-tested soldiers in unfamiliar territory.
When Saddam Hussein appeared on the American public's
radar at all, he was regarded as pleasingly hostile to Iran and
therefore a kind of accidental ally to the United States. Anyway,

most Americans had never even heard of Kuwait. As American military intervention became a live possibility later that year, public opinion was divided, very nearly down the middle. President George H.W. Bush gave Iraqi forces until 15 January to leave Kuwait, and even in the run-up to the deadline, as late as December 1990, a poll indicated that 48 per cent of Americans wanted Bush to wait before taking military action, even if Iraq failed to withdraw in time.[1] There was a real and widespread hope that sanctions and diplomacy could end the conflict peacefully.

Just a few months earlier, in the autumn of 1990, a fifteen-year-old girl appeared before the Congressional Human Rights Caucus and gave evidence of atrocities committed by Iraqi troops during and following the invasion. She was known only as 'Nayirah', apparently afraid to use her real name because doing so would endanger family and friends still trapped back home in Kuwait. You can find her four minutes of testimony online, and it's still riveting – sometimes fighting back tears, sometimes sobbing, but throughout remarkably self-possessed and bold; her eyes up from her notes more often than not, she speaks directly to the caucus' chairmen. She says, early on in her testimony, 'I volunteered at the al-Adan Hospital with twelve other women who wanted to help as well … While I was there I saw the Iraqi soldiers come into the hospital with guns. They took the babies out of the incubators, took the incubators and left the children to die on the cold floor. It was horrifying.'[2]

She said the Iraqis either destroyed or stole everything of value in her country. They took all the food from the super-markets and all the medicine from pharmacies. They ransacked private homes. When she and some friends took a stand and distributed flyers condemning what they saw, they were warned by other Kuwaitis that they were risking their lives. People disappeared. Many were killed or tortured. A friend of hers, 22 but now looking 'like an old man', was beaten and nearly drowned. Iraqi soldiers 'pulled out his fingernails and applied electric shocks to sensitive, private parts of his body'. He was lucky to have survived. In the end she struck a note of calm defiance, startling given her young age: 'I am glad I am fifteen, old enough to remember Kuwait before Saddam Hussein destroyed it, and young enough to rebuild it.'

Those in the room appear spellbound. A woman sitting next to Nayirah wipes away tears. The caucus was chaired by two congressmen, Tom Lantos and John Porter. Following her statement Porter said that in the past eight years, the caucus had held scores of hearings about human rights abuses, but 'we have never heard, in all this time, in all circumstances, a record of inhumanity, and brutality, and sadism as the one that the witnesses have given us today. I don't know how the civilised countries of the world can fail to do everything within their power to remove this scourge from the face of our Earth.' The witnesses who testified before the committee, he said, 'have done a great service to ours and to all countries of the world, who must join together and take whatever action might be necessary to free the people of Kuwait from this aggression and brutality.'

A video of her statement was picked up by US television and broadcast on the evening news by the major networks to millions and millions of Americans. President Bush repeated the story at least ten times in the run-up to the American invasion. He focused on emotions, not reasons: 'We've all heard of atrocities in Kuwait that would make the strongest of us weep', he said. 'It turns your stomach when you listen to the tales of those that have escaped the brutality of Saddam the invader. Mass hangings. Babies pulled from incubators and scattered like firewood across the floor.'[3] Major American newspapers ran stories about it, and there was discussion on talk shows. Amnesty International conducted an investigation, concluding that 'over 300 premature babies were reported to have died after Iraqi soldiers removed them from incubators, which were then looted'.[4]

The UN held an unusual public forum and discussed the theft of incubators and the murder of babies. They heard testimony from Dr Issah Ibrahim, a surgeon working in Kuwait, who said he had supervised the burial of 120 babies, and had himself buried 40 newborns, all taken from their incubators by Iraqis. Days later the Security Council passed a resolution empowering states to use all necessary means to force Iraq out of Kuwait. Reuters passed stories from Kuwaiti women about newborns taken from incubators on to US and British newspapers.

In January, the US House of Representatives passed a resolution for war in Iraq that then went to the Senate. It was a close-run thing. In the end it passed by just five votes, 52 to 47, the narrowest margin authorising military force in a congressional vote since the War of 1812. During the debate, seven senators who backed the resolution mentioned Iraqi soldiers removing babies from incubators. Given how close the final vote was, Nayirah's testimony might well have tipped the balance and put America on course for war.

In a *New York Times* op-ed piece called 'Remember Nayirah,

Witness for Kuwait?' published in early 1992, John MacArthur argued that a little investigation into her testimony 'would have done a great service to the democratic process'.[5] It was originally claimed that she didn't use her real name to protect friends and family back home; but there was a much better reason, he said, for Nayirah to hide her identity. She was actually a member of the Kuwaiti royal family, the daughter of Saud Nasir al-Sabah, who also happened to be the Kuwaiti ambassador to the United States. He sat in the room as she gave evidence. Why didn't anyone, particularly the two Congressmen chairing the caucus, check out her story before allowing her to testify?

'One explanation', MacArthur wrote, 'might lie in how Nayirah came to the Congressmen's attention. Both Congressmen have a close relationship with Hill and Knowlton, the public relations firm hired by Citizens for a Free Kuwait, the Kuwaiti-financed group that lobbied Congress for military intervention. A Hill and Knowlton vice president, Gary Hymel, helped organize the Congressional Human Rights Caucus hearing.'

In six months the Kuwaiti government poured $11.9 million into a front group called Citizens for a Free Kuwait, and almost all of it went to Hill and Knowlton, then the largest public relations firm in the world. Mobilising 119 executives and twelve of the company's offices across the US, they set up press conferences detailing alleged human rights abuses perpetrated by Iraqis, circulated hostage letters, arranged interviews with Kuwaitis for news programmes, organised a National Prayer Day for Kuwait involving churches all over the country, arranged pro-war rallies, and distributed tens of thousands of 'Free Kuwait' T-shirts and bumper stickers on college campuses.

Hill and Knowlton got themselves into the news business, videoing the results of pro-war activities in the US and interviews in the Middle East, as well as useful soundbites gathered from hawkish politicians. They bundled all this up into media kits and press releases for US news networks, which passed on their messages as straight reporting. Hill and Knowlton prepared the video of Nayirah's testimony and ensured it was broadcast as widely as possible.

The New York Times reported that the Congressional Human Rights Foundation, headed by Lantos and Porter, the chairs of the caucus that heard Nayirah's testimony, actually operated out of Hill and Knowlton offices in Georgetown, which they rented at a much reduced rate.[6] Citizens for a Free Kuwait donated $50,000 directly to the Foundation.[7] Hill and Knowlton's political connections went all the way to the top. The man running their Washington office was Craig Fuller, a friend of George H.W. Bush and his chief of staff when he was Vice President. Fuller ran the Kuwait account from the start.[8]

According to John Stauber and Sheldon Rampton, in their exposé on the PR industry, Kuwait quietly funded not just Hill and Knowlton, but as many as twenty public relations, law and lobby firms, all in an effort to tilt US public opinion in favour of war.[9] One group received $100,000 a month for media work, another $50,000 a month for lobbying members of Congress – millions more were spent on advertising, preparing TV spots, and coordinating a stable of as many as 50 speakers who could be dispatched at a moment's notice to rallies and other events to make the case for war.

Hill and Knowlton hired the Wirthlin Group, a research and

consulting firm that specialised in monitoring the effectiveness of sales pitches in advertising. Wirthlin equipped members of 'response groups' with a device enabling them to indicate whether their reaction to an advertisement was favourable or unfavourable, in real time, as they watched it. The results were aggregated and analysed, so the most effective turns of phrase and images could be easily identified.

They could do the same thing with political speeches and other messages sent out by Citizens for a Free Kuwait. The information was used to find messages that 'resonate emotionally with the American people'.[10] If the Kuwaiti ambassador appeared on television and made 30 points, Wirthlin could tell him which three were the most effective, so he could reinforce them in future appearances. As a spokesman for Wirthlin put it, the question was, 'what is it that we can do to emotionally motivate people to support action through the UN to drive [the Iraqi army out]? And the emotional things that would do that were the fact that Saddam Hussein was a madman who had committed atrocities, even against his own people, and had tremendous power to do further damage, and he needed to be stopped.'[11] Focus groups helped Hill and Knowlton find the most effective buttons, and those buttons were then pressed, repeatedly. The hearings in the human rights caucus and in the UN were, as Wirthlin's man put it, 'big events' in the campaign to persuade the American public to go to war.

The Nayirah testimony and the public relations campaign in which it was embedded shifted public opinion without the need for a single persuasive argument. There was no genuine public debate. Americans were not convinced by good reasons to intervene militarily in Kuwait. Something else swayed public opinion, something having to do with money and an understanding of human motivations.

Following MacArthur's revelations about the identity of Nayirah, a number of investigations were launched. Amnesty International retracted its earlier claim and said that it could find no evidence that Iraqis killed premature babies. The Kuwaiti government hired Kroll Associates, a private detective firm, to carry out an 'independent' investigation, and even it found that Nayirah had never volunteered at al-Adan Hospital.[12] When investigators arrived in Kuwait, the story simply evaporated – no one could corroborate it, no evidence could be found. It seems there were no missing incubators.[13]

Following the publication of a report by Middle East Watch, Andrew Whitley, head of its parent group, Human Rights Watch, said: 'While it is true that the Iraqis targeted hospitals, there is no truth to the charge which was central to the war propaganda effort that they stole incubators and callously removed babies allowing them to die on the floor. The stories were manufactured from germs of truth by people outside the country who should have known better.'[14] Middle East Watch suspected that Dr Issah Ibrahim's testimony was also arranged by Hill and Knowlton. His real name was Ibrahim Bahbahani, and he was a dentist, not a surgeon.

*

Citizens for a Free Kuwait is a particularly egregious, well-known and well-researched example of a ubiquitous feature of modern persuasion: a front group managed by a public relations firm on behalf of a hidden interest. What is PR? According to the Public Relations Society of America – 'the world's largest and foremost organization of public relations professionals' – public relations is 'a strategic communication process that builds mutually beneficial relationships between organizations and their publics'.[15] They do this mutually beneficial work, partly, by hiding the real intentions of their clients. Certainly not all public relations firms are engaged in whatever it was that was going on behind the scenes with Citizens for a Free Kuwait – but focusing on the seedier end of the spectrum can sometimes help you see things clearly.

Because the machinations behind PR messages are sometimes intentionally very well hidden, it's impossible to say with much certainty how many front groups are currently operating or how many covert PR messages you hear from day to day. Most of us are unable to name even one or two public relations firms, but the public relations industry is worth an estimated $11 billion a year in the United States alone. It employs nearly 55,000 public relations professionals in more than 8,000 firms.[16] In the United Kingdom, to cast the net a bit more broadly, there are at least 48,000 people working in and around public relations, lobbying, and corporate branding, and the industry is worth more than £6.5 billion each year.[17]

Its influence on the news is enormous. Public relations professionals now outnumber journalists by three to one, and on average they're much better financed than their counterparts in the news business.[18] They place stories, sometimes kill stories, using everything from press releases and stage-managed 'events' to calling in favours and subtle 'leaks' – it's hard to pin down, but by one possibly over-enthusiastic estimate, as much as 80 per cent of the content of the news comes directly from, or is somehow influenced by, lobbyists and public relations firms.[19]

Large corporations have their own, in-house PR teams and employ external agencies for specialist work. The largest PR firms are global, some with offices in more than 100 countries, coordinating international efforts through lobbying, marketing, research, consulting and advertising divisions. It would be difficult to imagine another profession which is as invisible, as unregulated, as unaccountable, and as influential. Given the amount of money involved and the powerful interests in play, the effect of public relations and lobbying firms on what we think and do must be exceptionally large.

There are books devoted to investigations into front groups pushing the interests of tobacco companies, the food and drink industries, Big Pharma, fossil fuel producers, even the Church of Scientology and foreign governments with an interest in international aid hoping to improve their image abroad. The names chosen for such groups can be awe-inspiring. The Animal Welfare Council represents the interests of rodeo and circus operators. America's Wetland Foundation is funded by Shell, BP and other oil companies, and it campaigns for taxpayer assistance for the cost of the coastal restoration work required following the damage BP itself has done, in the wake of the Deepwater Horizon oil spill. The Independent Women's Forum is an anti-feminist organisation sponsored by a collection of conservative foundations. The Non-Smoker Protection Committee attempts to overturn smoking bans in public places that might actually protect non-smokers, with funding from the R.J. Reynolds Tobacco Company. Citizens Against Lawsuit Abuse fights to make it more difficult for citizens to bring lawsuits for injuries and illnesses caused by hazardous products. It is funded by Philip Morris, maker of hazardous products.[20]

Some PR firms specialise in a particular sort of front group method, sometimes called astroturfing, which involves creating the appearance of an upsurge in opinion on a crucial question, perhaps among a representative's constituents, pushing him or her in the direction of a particular policy and a vote that counts in favour of a hidden interest. The representative won't feel lobbied, as it will appear to him or her that a real grass-roots movement is growing back home. PR firms do this by targeting opinion leaders and urging them to spread the word on the ground, sometimes for a fee, or simply emailing local people and inviting them to sign petitions or click on links that make their views known – form letters requiring only a little personalisation can be instantly forwarded to the government in the form of an independent email from a concerned citizen. Other firms focus on creating different sorts of shifts in public opinion, disseminating information via front groups that look like concerned neighbours, swaying voters towards a client's interests in time for anything from a vote to a town hall meeting.

The strategies for sending out positive messages about a client are varied, and they keep pace with changes to technology. Getting a good story into the news is still a viable tactic, but so is making changes to Wikipedia pages. It recently emerged that Bell Pottinger, one of the UK's largest PR firms, operated at least ten fake Wikipedia accounts, some making edits to more than 100 pages each. The accounts were set up under assumed names, and both the clients and the firm itself were carefully hidden from view. A user called Diginerd84, for example, did not describe himself as a Bell Pottinger employee, but as a '50-year-old retired stockbroker in Mayfair with an interest in classic cars – particularly a 1929 Rolls-Royce Phantom II'.[21]

Understanding Google's search engine algorithms and manipulating them is another dark art mastered by some in the PR world. In an investigative sting, *The Independent* recorded Tim Collins, managing director of Bell Pottinger Public Affairs, and David Wilson, chairman, describing the firm's ability to influence information online, in this case burying Uzbekistan's record of human rights violations. Collins said: 'And where we want to get to – and this will take time, this is where David's team are magical – is you get to the point where even if they type in "Uzbek child labour" or "Uzbek human rights violation", some of the first results that come up are sites talking about what you guys are doing to address and improve that, not just the critical voices saying how terrible this all is.'[22]

These examples can be multiplied, and if an online platform could conceivably be useful to someone interested in how a corporation or government is perceived, it is probably being exploited in some way. It's believed that representatives of the Chinese government manage a '50 cent army', paying as many as 300,000 people to post pro-Chinese government comments on message boards and social media sites worldwide. A Russian 'troll army' is thought to coordinate hundreds of accounts that post pro-Putin messages in the comment streams of articles published by *The Guardian* and *The Huffington Post*. Bogus Twitter accounts or just paying someone for helpful tweets or vlogs; planted stories on Reddit, 'click farms' and sites with subtle names like buyamazonreviews.com that employ people to manage multiple accounts and 'like' particular products; sock-puppet commenters hired to criticise rivals and write favourable comments for clients; other commenters paid to fight the opposing corner badly so as to bring it into ill repute; bogus email accounts delivering tips to bloggers who pass messages on as news – a very great deal of what we encounter online is prepared by those in the business of public relations and lobbying. While there has been considerable investigative work on what such firms get up to, there's very little discussion of what, if anything, is wrong with all of this.

*

When people do reflect on the morality of the worst of public relations and lobbying, the discussion is focused on whether or not there's deception involved, and how bad that is. Where lies are straightforward, it's easy to think them through and come to clear conclusions, and we've got a lot of theoretical help at our disposal. Philosophers and other thinkers have taken an interest in lies, from Plato's noble lie through to Harry Frankfurt's agreeable bestseller, *On Bullshit*. There's no shortage of definitions of lying and reasons for thinking about when and why lies are wrong.

One of the most influential recent definitions of lying is owed to Bernard Williams. As he puts it: 'I take a lie to be an assertion, the content of which the speaker believes to be false, which is made with the intention to deceive the hearer with respect to that content.'[23] Not every instance of this kind of thing is wrong, obviously – lying to a drunk about the location of her car keys might be a perfectly ethical thing to do – but philosophers have identified two things that can help us decide when lies are wrong, and in fact how wrong they are. What matters are the intentions of the liar and the consequences of the lie.

Those dubious about PR typically raise objections couched

in these terms. Who is really behind the front group and what do they intend to achieve? Did the PR people involved knowingly lie or were they misinformed? What are the consequences of the lie – did it make any difference or would things have played out the way they did with or without deception?

And PR firms tend to reply in these terms too. In response to revelations about the identity of Nayirah, for example, a representative of Hill and Knowlton said that they never 'collaborated with anyone to produce knowingly deceptive testimony'.[24] They were representing a client, certainly doing nothing illegal. They had no reason to doubt the stories they were hearing, and they were coming from multiple witnesses. When faced with allegations of deception, the caucus' co-chair Tom Lantos neatly combined claims about intentions and consequences in his defence: 'The notion that any of the witnesses brought to the caucus through the Kuwaiti Embassy would not be credible did not cross my mind ... I have no basis for assuming that her story is not true, but the point goes beyond that. If one hypothesizes that the woman's story is fictitious from A to Z, that in no way diminishes the avalanche of human rights violations.'[25]

Reflection on deception is a start on thinking about what's wrong with some public relations work, but the problem is that what front groups do is not always, and not exactly, lying. This results in the kind of dialectic characteristic of the incubators case in particular and public relations more generally – a bit of back and forth about intentions and consequences, and not much more.

This cycle of objections and replies is as old as public relations itself. Ivy Lee and Edward Bernays were probably PR's most influential pioneers – we'll consider them in a little more detail in a moment – and both had views on what might count as ethical public relations practices. Lee argued that a PR firm should always concern itself with the facts and make it clear that it was acting for its client, never hiding behind a front group. His detractors have argued that his concern for the truth was regularly put to one side when it served him. Sticking to the truth where possible might have been merely prudent – getting caught in a lie might damage his and his client's reputations.

For his part, Bernays distinguished between ethical and unethical PR, often in terms of intentions and consequences. In his early days he did not shy away from the term 'propaganda' to describe his work, and in a book actually called *Propaganda* he approvingly quotes these lines from an article in *Scientific American*: 'Propaganda becomes vicious and reprehensive only when its authors consciously and deliberately disseminate what they know to be lies, or when they aim at effects which they know to be prejudicial to the common good.'[26]

In couching the question of the morality of public relations in these terms, there's always wiggle room, always an opportunity for the PR apologist to play down consequences or deny bad intentions. And this way of looking at PR presupposes that there's such a thing as ethical public relations. Like any tool, Bernays argued, PR is in itself neutral, becoming a good or bad thing only when used by someone in one way rather than another. Firms still set out codes of conduct based on this old distinction between bad intentions and consequences on the one hand, and decent public relations practices on the other. But thinking about deception in this way distracts us from seeing where the real moral trouble might well be.

Is anyone lying when a PR firm hires a social-data company

to data-mine Twitter for information on how women in Oklahoma feel about gun control, tweaking messages accordingly, urging those against it to contact their representatives ahead of a crucial vote?* Is anyone lying when a PR firm is paid to set up a Facebook page and plant stories in local papers, inviting like-minded individuals to fight 'intrusive legislation' that might force a county-wide smoking ban in bars and restaurants and 'hurt the local economy'?† Maybe not. Maybe much of what public relations professionals do involves no lies at all – perhaps they are simply building 'mutually beneficial relationships between organisations and their publics'. Even so, there still might be something ethically objectionable going on. Something one might consider morally outrageous.

I think that the real moral trouble with public relations and lobbying has less to do with deception and more to do with justice, fairness, and the subversion of democracy. To see it requires at least a partial grip on the origins of public relations

---

* In 2013, Twitter earned almost $50 million selling data to social-data firms specialising in spotting trends and producing 'sentiment scores', gauging the moods of Twitter users in real time. See Elizabeth Dwoskin, 'Twitter's Data Business Proves Lucrative', *Wall Street Journal*, 7 October 2013.

† Local news in a small West Virginia county reports that 'a group of private sector businesses, organizations, unions and individuals, launched its coalition in opposition to the pending Hancock County comprehensive smoking ban' ('Hancock County Coalition Group – No2theBAN – Launches' (15 April 2014), State News Wire). Mona Lisa Communications are listed as a contact for further information. The link leads to a website offering the services of 'The Agency', a PR firm with offices in Washington, DC and Scottsdale, Arizona.

and the mix of ideas and circumstances in which it was born. Its historical roots can tell us a lot about what it has grown into in the last century or so, and what it is to us now.

*

In the early 1900s, young American women had more kinds of freedom than their mothers and grandmothers ever had, but there were still a number of things that a proper lady just could not do. The taboo against women smoking in public, for example, ran particularly deep. As long ago as the seventeenth century, prostitutes could be identified in paintings just by the cigarettes that they held. The association between smoking and loose morals carried on well into the Victorian era, with cigarettes and women appearing together in erotic photography.[27] Smoking was associated with idleness, sometimes a kind of rebellious delinquency, even among male smokers. A lady just would not smoke in public. It was brazen, shameless.

There was talk of a law against women smoking in Washington, DC, but a woman took her chances with law enforcement even by lighting up in the privacy of a car. In 1904 an ever-vigilant police bicycle patrolman spotted a woman smoking in a car in New York and demanded that she put it out at once. 'You can't do that on Fifth Avenue while I'm patrolling here', a newspaper reported him as saying. As the car pulled away, the woman, a Mrs William P. Orr, gamely exhaled a puff of smoke in the cop's face and flicked ash in his general direction. He gave enthusiastic chase, breathlessly catching the car at the next intersection, where there were 'high words'. In the end the driver was charged with being drunk and disorderly. For her part, Mrs Orr managed to escape prosecution. 'Yes I was smoking a cigarette', she admitted, 'and I don't see that I was doing any harm.' Harm or not, smoking in the streets was not an option for a decent woman in New York City.[28]

It wasn't just out in the streets. The owners of some hotels and restaurants refused to allow women to smoke, whether it was bad for business or not. It was simply a matter of principle. William Merritt, manager of the Martha Washington Hotel, said plainly: 'I really do object to the habit from a moral standpoint. I do not want the type of woman who smokes in public stopping at this hotel … I have always maintained that the old-fashioned type of American woman who does her own cooking and housekeeping is the woman who has made this country. Does she smoke? No.'[29]

So on a bright Easter afternoon in 1929, New Yorkers must have been scandalised by the sight of ten well-dressed, perfectly respectable women, some arm in arm with admiring husbands or boyfriends, defiantly lighting up in the middle of the Easter Parade. The practice of strolling from church to church on Easter morning had been going on for decades, with more and more people turning out to visit churches and view the spring flowers on display in their sanctuaries. It grew into an occasion, a big day on the social calendar, an opportunity for the great and the good to be seen in their finery. It was very nearly the perfect place for a demonstration of this kind. Stylish ladies smoking? Calling their cigarettes 'torches of freedom'? Striking a blow for the liberation of women? You would expect the press to fall over itself.

The New York Times printed photos of the women, looking not militant but chic. A number of papers, from Nebraska to New Mexico, reported the story, and editorials rumbled back and forth, for and against women smoking. It sparked copycat protests in other cities, with follow-up news stories in local papers. An early dispatch from the United Press put it like this: 'Just as Miss Federica Freylinghusen, conspicuous in a tailored outfit of dark grey, pushed her way thru the jam in front of St Patricks, Miss Bertha Hunt and six colleagues struck another blow in behalf of the liberty of women. Down Fifth Avenue they strolled, puffing at cigarettes. Miss Hunt issued the following communiqué from the smoke-clouded battlefield: "I hope that we have started something and that these torches of freedom, with no particular brand favoured, will smash the discriminatory taboo on cigarettes for women and that our sex will go on breaking down all discriminations."'[30]

Miss Hunt told New York's *Evening World* that she 'first got the idea for this campaign when a man with her in the street asked her to extinguish her cigaret [*sic*] as it embarrassed him. "I talked it over with my friends, and we decided it was high time something was done about the situation."'

As you may have already anticipated, things were not quite as they seemed. Bertha Hunt was the secretary of Edward L. Bernays, counsel for public relations for the American Tobacco Company, on a retainer of $25,000 a year. He had been charged with undermining the taboo against women smoking in public by the far-sighted George Washington Hill, head of the company, who saw the financial potential of encouraging the other half of the population to smoke too. 'If I can crack that market I'll get more than my fair share of it', he said to Bernays. 'It will be like opening a new gold mine right in our front yard.'[31]

Bernays planned the campaign meticulously, and he began, extraordinarily, by thinking about the symbolic meaning of smoking in the minds of women. It turns out that Bernays was the double nephew of Sigmund Freud – a fact he mentioned more and more often as Freud's fame grew. Bernays was impressed by Freud's writing and sought to bring his principles to bear on understanding and influencing human beings in the marketplace. He hired America's first practising psychoanalyst, who was also a disciple of Freud, A.A. Brill, to determine what smoking meant to women, what it might symbolise to them.*

There was some unfortunate but no doubt unavoidable talk of phallic symbols and oral titillation, but in the end Brill thought that smoking might be tied in a certain sort of woman's mind to feminism. The emancipation of women meant repressing their natural, feminine desires, or so he thought. This was reflected in their having fewer children and becoming more like men in the jobs they took. Cigarettes might be equated with male freedom in the minds of women – men could smoke freely; why shouldn't women? So smoking in public could be a powerful symbol of their liberation, their taking freedom for themselves – hence Brill's image of cigarettes as 'torches of freedom'. The half-conscious connection to the Statue of Liberty and all that symbolised did no harm either. Bernays hit the ground running.

Using a contact at *Vogue*, another of his clients, Bernays acquired a list of 30 debutantes and sent them telegrams signed not by him, but by his reliable secretary. They said this: 'In the interests of equality of the sexes and to fight another sex taboo

* For a fascinating account of the way Freudian concepts influenced government and corporate persuasion, see Adam Curtis' 2002 BBC documentary *Century of the Self*, particularly Part 1.

I and other young women will light another torch of freedom by smoking cigarettes while strolling on Fifth Avenue on Easter Sunday. We are doing this to combat the silly prejudice that the cigarette is suitable for the home, the restaurant, the taxicab, the theater lobby but never, no, never for the sidewalk.'[32]

Many answered this call. According to an office memo, Bernays thought the women should be 'definitely decided upon' by Monday, and they should appear in his office by appointment on Good Friday to be 'given their final instructions'. Who smokes, where and when, who asks whom for a light, what happens at which church – the whole morning 'must be worked out as if by a theatrical director'.[33]

In 1923 women purchased only 5 per cent of the cigarettes sold. By 1929, the number had more than doubled, with women accounting for 12 per cent of the market.[34] At a stroke, the legend goes, Bernays changed the country's attitude towards cigarettes, and he did so not by convincing anyone with good reasons, but by manipulating the unconscious with powerful symbols, harnessing the crowd's collective mind and steering it exactly where he liked.

That's certainly overstating it. The 'torches of freedom' campaign is now hailed as *the* perfectly stage-managed pseudo-event in the history of public relations, textbook press manipulation, but in fact it was just a single day, a part of a larger campaign to get women smoking, which had a number of fronts. (Bernays himself had been working for years to sell cigarettes to women as an alternative to sweets, pushing a slim figure as an aesthetic ideal in the process.) It's a good story, and it gets embellished in the telling.

It's said that the protest was headline news all over America, but certainly not all the newspaper clippings from the time suggest that he pulled the stunt off exactly as planned. The *Chicago Daily Tribune* noted that 'the customary efforts of advertisers to profit by the Easter parade were very much in evidence', including 'five stunningly dressed girls [who] puffed industriously at a certain brand of cigarette as they giggled their way down the street'.[35] It doesn't sound like a blow for women's liberation, much less a successful covert sell. The *LA Times* had just this to say on the subject: 'Presumably employed by a cigarette-manufacturing concern, a bevy of fashionably dressed women, most of them young, paraded Fifth Avenue today past St Patrick's Cathedral, calmly smoking cigarettes. They attracted but little attention and told reporters they were opposed to the sex taboo on women smoking elsewhere than in the home, in cafes, theatre rest rooms and private vehicles.'[36]

It's hard to shake the feeling, the more you discover about Bernays, that he spun the campaign himself into something larger and more successful than it actually was. The story is so good that it now has a life of its own, and Bernays, who died aged 103 in 1995, is somehow still getting good PR from the inertia of the narrative. As his biographer Larry Tye puts it: 'The parade story in particular became part of his repertoire on the speaking circuit and in scores of interviews he granted up until his death in 1995, and with each retelling the tale got more colourful and his claims more sweeping. In his 1965 memoirs, for instance, he discussed the slow process of breaking down conventions like the taboo against women smoking. But by 1971 he was telling an oral historian at Columbia University that "overnight the taboo was broken by one overt act."'[37]

Bernays could spin spin. Following a long lifetime in the business, it's easy to think that he simply couldn't help himself. The truth of the story no longer matters that much, but what's sunk into the minds of those in the business of persuasion is the possibility of controlling the crowd with powerful images and symbols, with a stage-managed spectacle that grows legs of its own and spreads a message for a high-paying client.

*

At least a part of the tactics behind the torches of freedom 'protest' wasn't entirely new to Bernays. His first use of the front group method, so far as I know the first front group as it now exists in the landscape of contemporary persuasion, simply occurred to him after he got himself into trouble while helping to edit and run two medical magazines. He published a good review of the script for a play called *Damaged Goods*, which frankly discussed such things as sexually transmitted diseases and prostitution, not the sort of thing tolerated in polite company at the time – this was, in itself, a bold step. But Bernays got in touch with an actor he heard was interested in actually producing the play in New York and offered to help. In a fit of enthusiasm, Bernays agreed to underwrite what on reflection was actually a risky production, despite not having the money to do so.

Rather than selling the play on its artistic merits as a contemporary press agent might, Bernays faded into the shadows. The key to promoting the play, he thought, the key to getting it past public censure and into profitability, was to package it as part of a crusade against old-fashioned prudishness and for sex education, and to get prominent, progressive people behind those worthy causes. He set up a front group, the *Medical Review of Reviews* Sociological Fund Committee. Initially, the committee consisted of just him.

Through it he solicited money and endorsements from highly respected, influential public figures keen to support so worthy a cause. John D. Rockefeller Jr., Mrs William K. Vanderbilt, Mr and Mrs Franklin D. Roosevelt and other leading lights signed up and spoke up in favour of sex education and, of course, in favour of the play. *Damaged Goods* not only wasn't raided by the police, it was a smash hit – sold-out performances were attended by the great and good of the day. It was also, as one reviewer put it, 'dull and almost unendurable'.[38]

Encouraged by this triumph, Bernays found work making hits of other plays, using refined versions of the same trick that worked for *Damaged Goods*. He found ways to promote plays by tying their themes to social causes, and searching for groups interested in those causes that might in turn back the play. When he was hired to publicise a tour by the Russian Ballet, Bernays asked around, engaging in proto-opinion research, trying to understand what Americans thought about European culture and how a grip on that might help him promote the ballet. He represented Enrico Caruso and was fascinated by how an impression of the man could be shaped by careful press releases and the placing of stories in magazines and newspapers. People could be made to admire Caruso before they met him or heard his famous voice.

But there's a difference between the slightly sneaky press agency he engaged in then and the kind of manipulation characteristic of the 'torches of freedom' protest and his later work. Early on in his career he did what most press agents and publicists did – he promoted something by telling people about it, planting stories, giving people information, spreading the word to interested parties who might be inclined to offer support. It was persuasion by a kind of factual argumentation. By the time he worked for American Tobacco, he did something very different from disseminating facts. He created images, circumstances, happenings, symbols – all of it intended to affect emotions and result in largely unreflective reactions on the part of the public he intended to influence.

You can see a similar, perhaps more dramatic shift in the work of Ivy Lee, the other man in the running for the title of The Father of Public Relations. At the start of his career, in the early 1900s, Lee saw himself as a 'news engineer' whose job it was to get the facts, or anyway his version of the facts, out there in the world for a reasonable public to reflect and act upon. Tell people the good things your client does, build a case for them, and let people make up their minds, ideally in your client's favour. But by the time Bernays was creating images and aiming to affect emotions, Lee thought of his vocation as something much more than just creating positive publicity. It was the 'art of steering heads inside ... the secret art of all the other arts, the secret religion of all religions', the secret means that might be used to save 'civilization' and build 'a successful and permanent business'.[39]

What explains this extraordinary change in both Lee's and Bernays' thinking? As Bernays explains: 'It was, of course, the astounding success of propaganda during the [First World] war that opened the eyes of the intelligent few in all departments of life to the possibilities of regimenting the public mind ... [T]he manipulators of patriotic opinion made use of the mental clichés and the emotional habits of the public to produce mass reactions against the alleged atrocities, the terror and the tyranny of the enemy. It was only natural, after the war ended, that intelligent persons should ask themselves whether it was not possible to apply a similar technique to the problems of peace.'[40]

As the historian Stuart Ewen writes, this shift in both Lee's and Bernays' thinking 'epitomized a broader change that was taking place in the way public relations specialists thought about their work. If, prior to the war, the idea of publicity was still grounded in a premise of rational argumentation – in the appeal to conscious reason – post-war conceptions of publicity were increasingly being premised on tactics of psychological manipulation, on seductive appeals to the subconscious recesses of mental life.'[41] The last remnants of Enlightenment ideals – the elevation of reason, the belief that individuals should think for themselves, should 'dare to know' as Kant put it – were finally and comprehensively on their way out.

Behind all this, or at least bound up with it, was a kind of anti-democratic or elitist presupposition. The 'intelligent few' were in a position to 'regiment the public mind', lining up the thoughts of the unwashed masses and directing them so as to build 'a permanent business'. Extraordinarily, as the PR men of the day would have it, and as Lee actually put it, this kind of control was necessary if civilisation was to be preserved. Preserved from what, exactly?

*

The Committee on Public Information (CPI) or the Creel Committee, named after its chairman, the journalist George Creel, was set up in 1917 and charged with creating public support for the war effort in America. It did this by disseminating propaganda through every conceivable medium: posters, news stories, radio messages, films, cartoons, rallies, leaflets, and a network of 75,000 influential local leaders, the Four Minute Men, who would rise in cinemas all over America when the reels were changed, giving partly scripted, pro-war speeches.

Bernays worked for the CPI's Foreign Press Bureau. He convinced large American companies to put posters in the windows of their foreign offices. He had propaganda translated into Spanish and Portuguese and placed it in journals bound for Latin America. He planted messages in Germany, intending to sow dissent and weaken morale. He saw the background work that resulted in Woodrow Wilson being welcomed by huge crowds as a liberating hero in Paris. It was an extraordinary training ground, a laboratory, and Bernays must have learned a great deal. When the war ended, he had a plan: 'I was intent on carrying forward what I had learned in my work with *Damaged Goods*, the Russian Ballet, Caruso and the Committee on Public Information. The impact words and pictures made on the minds of men throughout Europe made a deep impression on me. I recognized that they had been powerful factors in helping win the war ... [Europe] had been a training school without instructors, in the study of public opinion and people.'[42]

A generation of journalists and publicists who served as propagandists were now familiar with the practices that enabled them to change hearts and minds, but they were also aware of a number of theories behind wartime persuasion. These ideas were the intellectual foundation of the public relations industry, largely making it what it is today.

Gustave Le Bon's *The Crowd: A Study of the Popular Mind*, which appeared in 1895, was among the most influential early studies of social psychology. Le Bon argued that the 'crowd mind' is something quite different from the minds of the individuals who make it up, and understanding how and why it acts the way it does is the key to controlling and managing groups of human beings. Perfectly reasonable individuals become something else when gathered together. The feeling of personal responsibility slips away, reason departs, and instinct takes over. The individual swept up in a crowd 'descends several rungs in the ladder of civilisation'.[43] Le Bon argued that the crowd itself is a wild thing – impulsive, irritable, and generally incapable of reason or sound judgement. Above all what it does is feel emotion and translate its feelings into quick, usually destructive action.

What was wonderful about this for those interested in persuasion was Le Bon's very satisfactory thoughts on the suggestibility of crowds. Crowds lack a critical faculty and readily yield to simple suggestions, almost like a hypnotised person. 'A chain of logical argumentation is totally incomprehensible to crowds', Le Bon claims, 'and for this reason it is permissible to say that they do not reason or that they reason falsely and are not to be influenced by reasoning.'[44] What works on crowds are images, sounds, and the strong voice of a leader repeating simple messages. 'The powerlessness of crowds to reason aright prevents them displaying any trace of the critical spirit, prevents them, that is, from being capable of discerning truth from error, or of forming a precise judgment on any matter.'[45] Crowds are credulous. This was all very good news to those selling half-truths in the marketplace.

Equally cheering were claims made by the surgeon and social psychologist Wilfred Trotter, who fleshed out a concept of the 'herd instinct', the view of human beings as 'gregarious animals', defined largely by their need to belong to a group. Trotter argued that an ordinary person has strong and settled views on all sorts of topics about which he actually knows almost nothing. Trotter's list of such certainties is inspired: one thinks one knows how the country should be governed, why it's actually going to the dogs under the current idiotic leadership, why some laws or policies are excellent ideas and others terrible, how taxation ought to work, the advisability of military intervention, even how and why the universe came into existence and whether or not we survive death.

But the 'bulk of such opinions must necessarily be without rational basis, since many of them are concerned with problems admitted by the expert to be still unsolved, while as to the rest it is clear that the training and experience of no average man can qualify him to have any opinion on them at all'.[46] If reason were behind our opinions, we'd suspend judgement on most matters, but in fact we do not. Trotter concludes that most of what we believe actually follows from the herd instinct, from our desire to fit in to a group defined by the beliefs its members are supposed to have. We believe what we believe not because of good reasons – the world is too complicated and our time is too limited for that wild hope to be true – but because of an instinctive desire to belong to a group, whether it's a group of liberals or conservatives, theists or atheists, greens or sceptics. Get a grip on group identity, early public relations men reasoned, and you stand a chance of shepherding the crowd where you like.

Running alongside this view of the public as fundamentally irrational, emotional, but thankfully manipulable if you knew what you were doing, was a growing disquiet on the part of the rich and powerful about the possibly alarming consequences of actual democracy. Where once the right to vote was extended only to moneyed property owners and taxpayers, a very large number of Americans had been enfranchised relatively recently. In 1870 African American men were given the vote, followed in 1920 by women. There was the sobering prospect of the now enlarged, perpetually irrational herd voting for what it wanted, and among the things it wanted at the time was a limit to the power of wealthy capitalists, who, a moment ago, were the only ones in charge.

Muckraking journalists writing sensationalist stories about the moral corruption and greed of 'robber barons', the rising clout of labour unions, the Bolshevik Revolution, anti-trust laws, the breaking up of monopolies, calls for regulation and controls placed on markets – all were real signs of growing and entrenched discontent with the rich, and the rich noticed. As Lee warned: 'You suddenly find you are not running a private business but running a business of which the public itself is taking complete supervision. The crowd is in the saddle, the people are on the job, and we must take consideration of that fact, whether we like it or not.'[47] Or, as he later put it, much more succinctly, 'The crowd is enthroned.'[48]

The journalist and author Walter Lippmann set out the thinking behind a possible solution, a solution seized upon by Lee, Bernays and other men at the heart of post-war public relations. Lippmann drew a distinction between the real world out there and 'the pictures in our heads', the simplifications we actually use to navigate a complicated world. 'The real environment is altogether too big, too complex and too fleeting for direct acquaintance', he wrote in 1922. 'We are not equipped to deal with so much subtlety, so much variety, so many permutations and combinations. And although we have to act in that environment, we have to reconstruct it on a simpler model before we can manage it.'[49] The simpler model, the pictures in our heads, is formed of stereotypes, simplifications by which we navigate a world that is genuinely beyond us.

For Lippmann, now that we have learned more about human psychology and as changes in technology have made communication on a massive scale possible, particularly communication with compelling images rather than words, 'democracy has turned a corner. A revolution is taking place, infinitely more significant than any shifting of economic power ... It is no longer possible, for example, to believe in the original dogma of democracy; that the knowledge needed for the management of human affairs comes up spontaneously from the human heart.' We cannot rely on 'intuition, conscience, or the accidents of casual opinion if we are to deal with the world beyond our reach'.[50] What's really in the public interest isn't obvious – it's unlikely to bubble up from the votes of self-interested citizens or trickle down from political leaders who also lack a sure grip on 'the invisible world'.

We might be good democrats and hang everything on the importance of government by the people, giving everyone the opportunity to express his or her will in a vote. Or we could aim for a government that produces 'a certain minimum of health, of decent housing, of material necessities, of education, of freedom, of pleasures, of beauty'.[51] Wouldn't it be better to have experts, whom Lippmann called 'insiders', working out what's really in the public interest, rather than trust it to arise spontaneously from the will of distracted voters, who are really like 'a deaf spectator in the back row' when it comes to political affairs?

Wouldn't lives improve, Lippmann suggested, if experts work out what's best and then 'manufacture consent' using the tools of the propagandist after the fact? The public, he concluded, must 'be put in its place' so that 'each of us may live free of the trampling and the roar of a bewildered crowd'. Looking forward, looking very nearly at us, Lippmann concludes: 'Within the life of the generation now in control of affairs, persuasion has become a self-conscious art and a regular organ of popular government. It is no daring prophecy to say that the knowledge of how to create consent will alter every political calculation and modify every political premise.'[52]

The prospect led Bernays almost to rhapsody – who better than a trained propagandist to practise the art of persuasion and manufacture the consent of the governed for those in power? – but he was at least steady enough to spin Lippmann's anti-democratic conclusion into a slightly wobbly democratic one. Here are the first lines of Bernays' book *Propaganda*: 'The conscious and intelligent manipulation of the organized habits and opinions of the masses is an important element in democratic society. Those who manipulate this unseen mechanism of society constitute an invisible government which is the true ruling power of our country.'[53] Never mind how a democracy could have invisible governors manipulating opinions. He goes on: 'In almost every act of our daily lives, whether in the sphere of politics or business, in our social conduct or our ethical thinking, we are dominated by the relatively small number of persons … who understand the mental processes and social patterns of the masses. It is they who pull the wires which control the public mind, who harness old social forces and contrive new ways to bind and guide the world.'[54]

It was a compelling solution to the problems posed by democracy for the wealthy, and it was taken up in earnest by corporate America. It was also taken up by the Nazis, who were much more open about their doubts about the supposed merits of the democratic process. Lee's work was also much admired by the Germans. He was hired by a German firm in the run-up to the Second World War, and he contracted with a number of foreign governments to represent their interests in America. He met with senior Nazis, including Hitler, briefly, and was eventually accused of being Hitler's publicity agent by the House Un-American Activities Committee. Goebbels was enthusiastic about the prospect of 'crystallizing public opinion', to borrow Bernays' turn of phrase. Bernays' books on propaganda were on Goebbels' shelves.

'Propaganda got to be a bad word because of the Germans', Bernays said, studying his shoes while recalling the unpleasantness many years later in an interview. 'So what I did was try to find some other words. So we found the words Counsel on Public Relations.'[55] The aim was to sound like something in the neighbourhood of a Counsel on Legal Relations, with the professional associations those words bring, rather than the nastiness attached to the word 'propagandist'. But as Bernays knew, and as perhaps we have forgotten, public relations is peacetime propaganda, at its worst, a tool used to protect corporate power against the dangers of democratic interference.

Big business embraced public relations, money poured in, and as Bernays put it, corporations were transformed from ogres to 'friendly giants'. Where once businesses sold products, now trade organisations funded by corporations sold business itself to America – the notion of progress was elevated, free enterprise was linked to other democratic freedoms, like free speech, a free press, and the freedom to practise religion – anything deemed anti-capitalist was smeared as un-American. To give you a partial glimpse of the magnitude of it, just one trade body, the National Association of Manufacturers, embarked on a propaganda campaign at the end of the Second World War, aiming to 'identify the free enterprise system with every cherished value, and identify interventionist governments and strong unions with tyranny, oppression and even subversion'.[56] That group alone produced 1,600 business periodicals and 577 commercial and financial digests, funded 2,500 advertising agencies, paid 500 public relations men, sponsored 4,000 PR firms and produced more than 6,500 in-house magazines, with a circulation of more than 70 million.[57] This is only a cartoonish sketch of a very small part of the enormous, extraordinarily well-funded, ongoing pro-business propaganda campaign characteristic of the last one hundred years. The world has never seen anything remotely like it.

*

As David Miller and William Dinan put it in their discussion of PR and democracy: 'Public relations was created to thwart and subvert democratic decision making. It was a means for "taking the risk" out of democracy. The risk was to the vested interests of those who owned and controlled society before the introduction of voting rights for all adults.'[58] When we try to come to conclusions about the meaning of public relations and lobbying, worries about deception should certainly figure in, but if some social critics are right, the real moral outrage consists in the various ways in which PR subverts and twists the democratic process.

Democracy as we have it in the West might still respond to the will of the people, but that will itself is managed in part on behalf of those with money. A case could certainly be made for the view that anything like a meaningful democracy ended for us just as it was getting started, early in the last century, as new forms of persuasion took hold and diminished the freedom of voters to come to their own conclusions. It is hard to write something like that without sounding like a conspiracy theorist, and you might wonder where that smear itself originates, but if it's too rich for you, join me halfway: democracy is at least compromised by the fact that a great deal of what we think comes about not from sound reflection and careful argument, but from our lifelong exposure to images and messages that serve the interests of those who pay for them.

There is now a class of very well-informed, well-funded, highly organised, professional persuaders. Just as it's more or less impossible for an amateur to unseat a professional politician, so now it's unlikely that amateur persuaders stand a chance of being heard or having much of an impact in the wider world. Something is made of the fact that anyone can have a say on Twitter, set up a blog or speak up in comment streams, but an individual, even a large group of like-minded individuals, is much less able to get messages out compared to the work of a small team of well-connected, experienced professionals who do this sort of thing full-time and for a living. It is now extraordinarily difficult for a genuine grass-roots movement, much less a single voice, to have anything like a persuasive effect compared to the overwhelming power of the pros.

You might say that I've had a swing at the worst of PR, and at least some firms are innocuous, maybe others help people – there are large programmes of corporate social responsibility, which of course improve a company's image but also do some good too. What's wrong with a public relations firm organising and drawing attention to all that?

I think that's almost fair enough, and it would be an over-simplification to conclude that all public relations practices are uniformly awful. I think probably a number of people think of public relations as a kind of marketing or advertising – and when that's all it is, when it's just finding new ways to tell people about a product or service, then the objections I've raised will certainly miss the mark. But public relations has been and is something else too, something in the tradition of Bernays and Lee – realised recently in the work of Citizens for a Free Kuwait and other such groups – and without meaning to demonise those two, it's that idea of the practice that I think does deserve criticism, even condemnation.[59]

Can anything be done about this sort of corporate influence? There are optimists. Perhaps most put their money on education. Stuart Ewen, for example, argues that learning about how images work can help us understand and to some extent see through the persuasive methods used on us. As he puts it, public relations 'is rarely intended to inform the population about the intricacies of an issue and is more often calculated to circumvent critical thinking'.[60] We are exposed to images, not arguments, and often persuaded without even knowing it, but we can regain our critical faculties through an understanding of the methods used by public relations firms. 'For democracy to prevail', he concludes, 'image making as a communicative activity must be understood by ordinary citizens.'[61] Seeing it for what it is might give us some control over it. It's a hope shared by the philosopher Randal Marlin: 'The best goal for propaganda analysis is to develop such an understanding of the phenomenon that it will no longer be profitable for people to engage in it.'[62]

Others put their faith in regulation. William Dinan and David Miller argue that: 'Lobbying-disclosure legislation and the requirement for corporations to disclose which think tanks, front groups and institutes they fund would help improve the ability of citizens to understand and act to hold corporations to account.'[63] But what's really needed, according to them, is making deceptive public relations practices illegal and imposing large penalties on those who practise them. The ultimate aim is 'a massive programme of democratic renewal – we would need to roll back corporate power and specifically remove corporate influence from decision making in governmental bodies and in the public services. This will not be accomplished quickly or easily, but it can be done.'[64]

I confess to feeling a certain sort of queasiness when I think that these are, in fact, the best solutions available to the problem of corporate power and the subversion of democracy. I recall a similar sort of queasiness when I was told that the best I could do, in response to climate change, was turn down the thermostat and buy better light bulbs – those can't be actual solutions to such an enormous problem, I recall thinking. That can't be it, can it?

While I'm all in favour of education and democratic renewal, and I think these and other authors are entirely right to point to both, I worry that education and legislation might never actually manage to thwart an industry worth so many billions of dollars, an industry that's better at 'education' than any university system, and an industry that specialises in ensuring that laws that might harm its clients' interests never see the light of day.

Politicians do sometimes make noises about reforming the system, but it's not easy to take any of it seriously. In a speech in Tallahassee, Florida, ahead of the 2016 US presidential election, Republican candidate Jeb Bush gave a rousing speech condemning the pernicious influence of lobbyists. As one paper reported, Bush 'derided what he called the capital city's "comfortable establishment" that leverages lobbying power to unduly shape public policy. "I was a governor who refused to go along with that establishment," Bush said.'[65] What Bush didn't say was that the event was probably organised by the Florida Chamber of Commerce, a pro-business lobbying group that also made donations to his campaign. Leaked emails seem to show Bush's team coordinating with the Chamber, but his team also denied that the event was hosted by lobbyists. Records show that Bush himself was once registered as a lobbyist, but again his campaign team deny that he ever actually worked as one. Our chances of working out what's really going on in this part of the world of covert persuasion, much less doing something about it, can seem slim.

They can seem slim for other reasons too. A group of systems theorists from the Swiss Federal Institute of Technology in Zurich examined a database of 37 million companies and investors worldwide, focusing on the 43,060 trans-national corporations and share ownerships linking them. Using a computer model to examine the interconnections, they discovered that a dominant core of 147 interconnected firms controlled 40 per cent of the whole world's wealth. Just over 700 corporations control 80 per cent of everything there is.[66] In trying to come to terms with our position in this world and our prospects for finding ways to change it, you can do worse than imagine a comparable task faced ages ago by those stuck somewhere at the bottom of the feudal system. They somehow managed to get themselves out from under aristocratic rule and into a society that at least aspired to democracy. Maybe it's not impossible, but those who would change the balance of power in our world face no less a task.[67]

On Second Thoughts

'The understanding must not therefore be
supplied with wings, but rather hung with
weights, to keep it from leaping and flying.'

FRANCIS BACON

No consideration of contemporary persuasion would be complete without mention of the toilet facilities at Schiphol Airport in Amsterdam. Legend has it that a wise custodian named Jos van Bedoff had the idea of placing an etching of a fly in the basins of airport urinals. Thanks to this simple act, manly marksmanship improved dramatically, and spillage was reduced by as much as 80 per cent. I have no idea how this figure was arrived at, nor do I intend to look into it, but what is clear is that the trick seems to work, and it has caught on. Bedoff has changed the face of urinals from New York to Singapore.

If a modest tweak to the environment can encourage men to urinate in a socially responsible way, you might think that any number of social improvements could be similarly achieved, and you would not be alone. The hope that the social world might be restructured so as to encourage people to choose something collectively desirable or individually beneficial has been seized upon in both London and Washington. David Cameron set up a 'nudge unit' in the Cabinet Office, charging it with using the new discipline of behavioural economics, a combination of novel thinking about decision-making and economic theorising, to push individuals towards better choices in their everyday lives. It is formally called the Behavioural Insights Team, and it is advised by nudge expert Richard Thaler. Cass Sunstein, co-author with Thaler of the book *Nudge: Improving Decisions About Health, Wealth, and Happiness*, took on the role of administrator of the White House Office of Information and Regulatory Affairs in the Obama administration. Thousands of federal regulations, which will have an ongoing impact on the lives of millions of people, were shaped by ideas about nudging on their way through his office.

According to Thaler and Sunstein, 'a nudge, as we will use the term, is any aspect of the choice architecture that alters people's behaviour in a predictable way without forbidding any options or significantly changing their economic incentives'.[1] Since the publication of their book, nudging has gone global. Behavioural economics is informing policy in America, Great Britain, France, Australia, Denmark, Canada and the Netherlands. With unprecedented gusto, governments are embracing the practice of nudging their citizens.

It's a new way of thinking about persuasion, and its roots lie in relatively recent discoveries about how the human mind works, which in turn led to a change in thinking about the choices we make, and how we might be influenced to make better ones. We'll consider some contemporary examples of nudging in the next chapter, but first it's worth taking a moment to understand the theory behind it all. It requires a shift in how we think about the kind of creatures we are. Unless you can see yourself as nudgeable, the meaning of nudging is lost on you.

*

For the past hundred years or so, orthodox economics has operated with a number of assumptions about human nature. It was thought that people are generally rational when it comes to making judgements in the marketplace. They make thoughtful, clear-headed decisions, balancing costs against benefits, finally choosing what's in their interests based on the evidence they have. Why think that people would not act in their own interests? The traditional understanding of supply and demand and the general behaviour of markets depends on these assumptions, but a body of evidence emerging since the 1970s has shown that this picture of human nature is not quite right. It fails to take account of a lot of behaviour, in particular, the less than rational judgements and choices we often make.

Sometimes we are careful thinkers, acting on the evidence, reasonably and with our best interests foremost in mind. But sometimes we sacrifice the benefits of an hour in the gym for an evening in the pub with friends, and end up with an appalling hangover and without improved biceps. If we put our minds to it we know we should save more for retirement, but there's a very real danger that we'll have trouble making ends meet in our dotage because we blew a lot of money, year after year, on the opportunity to lie unconscious on a beach somewhere warm or slide down snowy hillsides on skis.

Psychologists explain some of this by distinguishing between two kinds of thinking: fast, automatic, intuitive thinking; and slow, reflective, rational thinking. You can imagine that these two kinds of mental activities are the work of two parts of your mind, two systems that swing into different kinds of action to accomplish different tasks. The part that's responsible for the first kind of thinking is called System 1 or the Automatic System, and the part that engages in slower, more careful thought is called System 2 or the Reflective System.

System 1 operates quickly and automatically. This feels instinctive and intuitive, and it requires no effort on your part. System 1 is in charge when you orient yourself to a sudden sound, wince involuntarily when you see something that disgusts you, read anger in the lines on someone's face, and recognise written words in your native tongue – it all just clicks fluently and automatically, without you thinking about it at all.

The work of System 2, the Reflective System, takes effort, an act of deliberate concentration on your part. Your deliberative efforts are limited and cannot be sustained for very long without degradation, a phenomenon called ego depletion. System 2's work is voluntary, slower than your gut reactions, and associated with the experience of choice and agency. When you scan a crowd for a friend, tell someone your email address, fill out a complicated form or consider the validity of a complex argument, System 2 is engaged. System 1 is active when you see a big spider on the ceiling and your eyes instantly widen, you freeze and feel nervous. But if you're asked to figure out what 45×57 is, you'll slow down, make a conscious effort, get a pen and paper, and rely on System 2.[2]

The two systems interact with each other in a number of surprising ways. System 1 typically engages in a kind of constant monitoring, throwing up a series of impressions and feelings that System 2 might endorse, ignore, check, focus on, act upon, or simply go along with. Much of the time System 2 is in a low-power state, aroused only when the Automatic System encounters something it can't handle.

Through careful training, some of the high-effort activities undertaken by the Reflective System can fall under the automatic purview of System 1. This happens when you learn to drive, or when you train yourself to perform any complicated task intuitively – once you can touch type or play the guitar, it just flows, and by then System 2 will only get in the way. When you know how to drive you can carry on a conversation while speeding down the road, but everyone stops talking to you when you check for oncoming traffic and accelerate to pass another car – they know you need to focus on driving, and you probably wouldn't hear them if they said something to you at that moment anyway. You turn the radio off when you have to drive and search for an address at the same time. When your reflective System 2 is engaged, it's too busy to talk or listen to music and concentrate on the task at hand all at once.

Our mental resources are therefore limited. It is an effort to bring System 2 into play, and it can be overloaded by trying to do too much. So evolution has taught us a number of shortcuts, rules of thumb or heuristics, which conserve our mental energies and serve us very well most of the time. The upshot is that although we have the feeling of being in control, in fact the automatic mechanisms of our mind fling thoughts and conclusions forward, and most of the time the reflective part of us just goes with it. But it also means that we go wrong in systematic, predictable ways – we are constitutionally susceptible to cognitive biases and, in turn, we can be nudged.

Some examples will make this clear to you. It will help if you try to think of an answer to these questions fairly quickly.

A bat and a ball cost £1.10. The bat costs one pound more than the ball. How much does the ball cost?

If it takes 5 machines 5 minutes to make 5 widgets, how long would it take 100 machines to make 100 widgets?

In a lake there is a patch of lily pads. Every day the patch doubles in size. If it takes 48 days for the patch to cover the entire lake, how long would it take for the patch to cover half of the lake?

System 1 probably flung some numbers at you – numbers that felt right, and if you didn't take the time to think about it you might have just gone along with it. It feels right to think that if the ball and the bat cost £1.10 and the bat cost one pound more than the ball, then the ball must have cost 10 pence. But if you take a moment to work it out, recruit System 2 to the task, you'll realise the ball has to cost 5 pence – if the ball cost 10 pence, then the bat must cost £1.10, which would bring the total to £1.20, not £1.10. Now System 2 is on the job, you'll also see it would take 100 machines not 100 minutes, but 5 minutes to make 100 widgets. If the patch doubles in size each day, and it takes 48 days to cover the whole lake, it won't take 24 days to cover half of it – the answer has to be 47 days.[3]

Thoughts about mental shortcuts and biases were first explored by Daniel Kahneman and the late Amos Tversky, in a 1974 paper called 'Judgment under Uncertainty: Heuristics and Biases'. Kahneman went on to win the Nobel Prize in

Economics in 2002 for his work on how human beings make decisions and the shortcuts they use to do so.

In that early paper, Tversky and Kahneman argue that the way we assess probabilities is very much like the way we assess distance – we cut through complexity by relying on rules of thumb. Our perceptual system determines how far away an object is based partly on how clearly we see it. The rule of thumb is: 'The more sharply it's seen, the closer it is.' That automatic heuristic works fine most of the time, because usually distant objects are not seen as clearly as nearby ones, but it can get us into trouble too. When visibility is poor, sailors sometimes over-estimate distance, because even nearby objects appear blurred. Polar explorers routinely under-estimate how far away objects are, partly because visibility is so good that even distant objects are seen quite sharply.

We use shortcuts to arrive at judgements too, and we encounter certain biases and errors in this domain as well. Tversky and Kahneman identified three heuristics in that early paper, and it's well worth knowing about them. If you understand how they work, you'll see how powerful a nudge can be. A grip on all this is worth having. It's a large part of the theoretical framework behind contemporary persuasion, and it's already shaping our world and changing our lives.

*

Consider this description of Steve.

'Steve is very shy and withdrawn, invariably helpful, but with little interest in people, or in the world of reality. A meek and tidy soul, he has a need for order and structure, and a passion for detail.'[4]

What do you think Steve does for a living? Is he more likely to be a farmer, salesman, airline pilot, librarian or physician? Once you have an answer to that question, ask yourself what job he is least likely to have. How would you go about ranking the possibilities, from most likely to least likely?

Very many people, including me when I first read that description, conclude that Steve is most likely a librarian – how could a shy guy like that possibly be a salesman? – and in coming to this conclusion we make use of what Kahneman and Tversky call the representativeness heuristic. We let our automatic faculties rip and take a shortcut to an answer. If one slows down and thinks about it, though, there are a lot more farmers than librarians in the world. That's extremely pertinent information if you're trying to guess which job on a list is most likely for anybody, including Steve, and it should lead us to conclude that it's most likely that Steve is a farmer, maybe a shy and withdrawn farmer, but still a farmer. The probability that Steve is a librarian is instead assessed by the extent to which the description of Steve matches up with or is representative of the stereotype of a librarian that we have in our heads.

When asked how likely it is that A belongs in category B, our Automatic System answers with a shortcut, by determining how similar A is to a stereotype of B, how representative A is of B. When asked how likely it is that Steve is a librarian, System 1 answered that it's very likely, because Steve fits the librarian stereotype – even though there aren't many librarians in the world, making the chance that Steve is a librarian actually pretty slim.

We do this entirely automatically, and it has an effect on a host of judgements – how likely we think politicians are to be good leaders, how likely a new business is to succeed, and how likely our doctor is to be competent. If the man has a good square jaw, if he fits the politician stereotype, you might support him, thinking it's likely he's a good leader. If the new business' premises look well appointed, you might be confident that it will succeed and consider investing in it. If the doctor's office has some reassuring diplomas on the wall and staff in white coats, if she looks like a doctor is supposed to look, you might think she's likely to be a source of sound medical advice. If whatever we're evaluating matches the relevant stereotype, we conclude that things are likely to go in one way rather than another, but we might do better by thinking of probabilities.

The square jaw actually helps when it comes to securing votes, thanks to another bias we have, but many other things ought to go in to clear-headed reflection on a candidate's qualifications for leadership. Maybe the rate of success for new start-ups like the one you're thinking of investing in is actually pretty low – the relevant fact might be that only one in three such businesses are still standing in two years. Your chances of getting good medical treatment might be better estimated by facts about your doctor's age, training, and experience with whatever it is that ails you, rather than the look of her and her office. Relying on the representativeness heuristic can get us into a lot of trouble. People who understand persuasion will take care to fit the right stereotype and make it easier for us to come to conclusions about them automatically.[5]

A second set of biases results from what Kahneman and Tversky call the availability heuristic.[6] When we think about how likely some event is, we're affected by how readily examples come to mind. Do politicians have a lot of affairs – more than dentists? If you go swimming in the sea, should you worry about sharks? What are the chances of a disaster at a nuclear power plant? We are likely to over-estimate the number of wayward politicians, shark attacks and meltdowns at nuclear plants because we can probably easily recall instances of such things. The problem is that how easily we can recall something has less to do with how likely or common or worrying an occurrence is and more to do with what we happen to have heard about in the news recently and how striking that news was to us. The news you choose to watch therefore has a lot of power over you. The stories it repeats reinforce your susceptibility to the availability effect.

To prove the influence of availability to yourself, imagine that you close your eyes and put your finger on a word at random on this page. You don't know what the word is, but you're told that it has the letter K in it. Is it more likely that the word begins with the letter K or that K is the third letter in the word? Do more words begin with K or have K as the third letter? If you're like most people, you'll find recalling words that begin with K is much easier than recalling words with K as the third letter – words beginning with K are more available to you in memory – so you might conclude that words beginning with K are more likely. In fact there are about twice as many words with K as the third letter as with K as the first letter.[7]

How easily you remember something depends on several things. Some events are just more salient, they simply stand out – Hollywood sex scandals are striking, and we tend to remember them easily and perhaps over-estimate their frequency as a result. Dramatic events like plane crashes or child abductions are easily remembered too, and for a time after a widely reported airline disaster or missing child case, people wrongly inflate the risk they associate with flying or children being taken from them. Our own experiences, as opposed to what we read or hear about, stand out to us and affect us much more deeply, and this can also skew our perception of the world. If you know someone who lost a job, your pessimism about unemployment rates might well be exaggerated. If you just lost your job, your pessimism will most likely deepen. And if you get into an argument with your partner about who does more household chores, who compromises more often, or who remains reasonable longest when heated words are exchanged, bear in mind that your contributions to the relationship will be much more available to you, and you are likely to over-estimate them.[8]

Following a natural disaster, people are more likely to take precautions, like buying home insurance and stocking up on food and water, but as the memory fades they take fewer steps to protect themselves, even though the risk associated with such things as wildfires, earthquakes and hurricanes has not changed at all. We over-react at first, then under-react as time goes on. Something as memorable as the financial crisis of 2007 and 2008 can be expected to have a substantial availability effect too. When investors were asked to rate the stock market's performance in 2009, 2010 and 2011, about half characterised it as flat or down, even though the S&P 500 saw double-digit gains in 2009 and 2010, and modest gains in 2011.[9] People under the influence of availability almost certainly kept money out of the market and missed opportunities during those years.

Following 9/11, terrorism has seemed like a large risk to us, much larger than the more mundane, less available, but far more common dangers we face each day. According to the US Department of State, seventeen private American citizens, individuals who were not working for the government, were killed by terrorism, worldwide, in 2011.[10] In the same year, nearly 600,000 people died as a result of heart disease in the United States. Cancer killed another 575,000.[11] Because of its salience, we think homicide is more common than suicide, but it isn't. In fact, Americans are more likely to take their own lives than be murdered or die in a car crash, but because murder and car accidents are more newsworthy, dramatic and available than suicide, we concern ourselves more with home alarm systems and airbags than the signs of depression. The availability heuristic leads us into error on everything from risk-taking in stock markets to the amount of money spent combatting terrorism rather than heart disease and cancer. It partly explains your uncle's fear of flying, and it's among the reasons why you shouldn't care when a friend tells you his grandfather smoked and lived to be 93.

A final kind of bias identified by Kahneman and Tversky, perhaps the most interesting and difficult to accept of the three, is called the anchoring effect. When people first think about a number and try to estimate an unknown quantity, the initial number affects their guess, anchors it – the estimate they make tends to stay nearby. Again, the rule of thumb in play isn't too bad a guide, and we use it all the time. What's the population of Pittsburgh? If you don't know, but you do know that Philadelphia is the largest city in Pennsylvania, and it has about 1.5 million people in it, you might feel able to guess about Pittsburgh. It's certainly smaller than Philadelphia – maybe it's no bigger than half the size, so perhaps Pittsburgh has a population of fewer than 750,000. Maybe 600,000?

There are two very weird facts about this familiar process of guessing a quantity. First, we tend to undercook the adjustments we make from the original guess. Once we have a number and begin adjusting in the direction we think is right, we tend to stay too close to the anchor, possibly because once we find ourselves in uncertainty, we can't think of a good reason to carry on, so we play it safe and stop too soon. Pittsburgh is smaller than Philadelphia, so we adjust downwards, but how far downwards? In fact in this example we stayed much too close to the anchor, as we usually do. Just 300,000 people live in Pittsburgh.

Second, it doesn't matter where the first figure comes from, it will still anchor our estimates, even if it has nothing at all to do with the domain in question. According to at least one understanding of what's going on in such cases, sometimes System 2 is in charge, finding what it hopes is a reasonable anchor and adjusting off it to estimate an unknown quantity. But sometimes System 1 gets hooked on an anchor and freely associates, without our conscious control, and this cascade of associations ends up affecting our later estimate, whether it's reasonable or not.

Tversky and Kahneman illustrated this second kind of anchoring with a rigged roulette wheel – it showed numbers from 0 to 100 but it actually stopped on either 10 or 65. They spun the wheel and asked a group of students to write the number down, and then answer two questions.

Is the percentage of African nations among UN members larger or smaller than the number you just wrote?

What is your best guess of the percentage of African nations in the UN?

The average guess of those who saw the number 10 was 25 per cent. The average guess of those who saw the number 65 was 45 per cent. A roulette wheel is not a particularly informative thing if you're trying to work out how many African nations are members of the UN, but still, those who saw the high number guessed higher than those who saw the low number. Even ludicrous anchors have an effect on us.

Ludicrous or not, it's a remarkably robust effect, demonstrated again and again in a wide range of studies.[12] Kahneman and Tversky found that students given a few seconds to guess the product of $1 \times 2 \times 3 \times 4 \times 5 \times 6 \times 7 \times 8$ come up with substantially lower numbers than those asked to guess the product of $8 \times 7 \times 6 \times 5 \times 4 \times 3 \times 2 \times 1$ – presumably because they anchor on the first few numbers they see. The median estimate given by those who saw the first sequence is 512, but those who saw the sequence starting with larger numbers guessed much higher: their median was 2,250. It's somehow reassuring that both groups were way off anyway. The correct answer is 40,320.

Anchors work on us even when we are aware of them and deliberately try to put them to one side. This happens most obviously in contexts involving money. (Given the way anchors work, the first person to speak in any financial negotiation has a lot of influence on how things will go – you should obviously avoid the expression 'make me an offer'.) The asking price of a house is of course a potent anchor. A study on the behaviour of property agents, using houses that were actually on the market, showed an anchoring effect even on professionals trying to avoid its influence. Half the agents saw an 'asking price' much higher than the listed one, and the other half saw a price that was much lower. The agents gave an estimate on the value of the house and were asked to list the factors that figured into their opinions – all claimed to have studiously ignored the asking price. But the anchoring effect worked on both groups equally, pulling down or pushing up their estimates depending on whether they saw the high or low anchor. The effect was only slightly larger on students with no experience at all in estimating the value of houses.[13]

The anchoring effect still has us in its grip even when we are explicitly warned about it. In a study that can leave you gently thumping your head on a table, students were set up with a high anchor and asked to estimate the number of physicians in the local phone book. But first they were told all about the anchoring effect. They were warned that 'large numbers in people's heads can cause them to increase their estimate of answers to subsequent questions'. They were given hypothetical examples of anchoring. Some were very specifically informed that, in just a moment, they would be asked to write down an ID number the experimenters had given them, and that that number might influence the answers they were about to give. They were unambiguously cautioned: 'When you answer the questions on the following pages, please be careful not to have this contamination effect happen to you. We would like the most accurate estimates that you can come up with.' The results were the same – whether the students were warned or not, their answers were equally anchored by their ID numbers.[14]

*

In the decades since these odd features of human cognition were discovered, researchers have found a whole host of biases and principles that affect the judgements and choices we make.

Many of them are well known to those who wish to persuade us, and we will encounter several more in this book. But the point now is just that our understanding of how the mind works has expanded dramatically in recent years, and this fact is a large part of the explanation of the changes that have taken place in the practice of persuasion. Whether or not new discoveries actually lead to new and effective kinds of persuasion is another question – the fact is that many people are now pursuing the possibility.

The obvious question to ask is nevertheless a good one: What can we do about all of this in our own lives? Can we learn to take control of the heuristics we think by, particularly when we know they can lead us astray? Facts just scouted about anchoring should make you sceptical, and it turns out that the ironic part of the answer is that some biases we have actually get in the way of our efforts to think past others.

The social psychologist Robert Levine undertook a study to map the contours of what he calls the better-than-average-effect, a tendency we have to think optimistically about our capacities and prospects. We typically believe we are less likely than other people to suffer from disease – from everything from tooth decay to dementia. Most people think they have a better chance of living past 80 than others do. In a survey of those registering for marriage licences, all knew that about half of all marriages end in divorce, but when asked about the chances of their own marriage ending up that way, the median estimate was 0 per cent.[15]

We also think we are much less vulnerable to manipulation than we actually are. Levine found that 70 per cent of those questioned said they were more aware than average of how manipulation works. 61 per cent said they knew more about deception than their peers. 66 per cent believed that they have above-average critical thinking skills.[16] It's worth dwelling on these numbers when thinking about the persuasive forces that act on us. We are very likely to over-estimate our ability to resist them, and this feature of our psychology actually makes us more vulnerable. It's not a bad idea to remember this when you encounter a persuasive tactic in this book and are tempted to shrug it off, thinking it wouldn't work on you. This effect probably also gets in the way of our seeing our own biased thoughts for what they are. We are wildly over-confident creatures.

The other half of the answer is that it's a mixed bag. Some cognitive illusions are like optical illusions. When you see the Muller–Lyre illusion – one of those drawings with two lines of the same length, bookended by arrows going in different directions, which makes you see one line as longer than the other – just knowing that it is an illusion does not make it go away. It gets its hooks into us, and conscious thought can't shake it. Some biases are like this too. Knowing about anchoring is clearly not much protection from it. Some biases we can think around, and some we can't.

At some point in my life I read about the bystander effect – the greater the number of people present, the less likely an individual is to take certain sorts of helpful action. A few years ago I saw a fire in a bin in an Underground station, and there were perhaps twenty people standing around, apparently oblivious to the growing cloud of smoke and flames pouring out of it. A little old lady from central casting was sitting too close to it and might actually have been in some danger. I thought, 'Christ, it's the bystander effect!' grabbed a fire extinguisher and put the fire out. Knowing about that cognitive quirk might have helped me think past it. Even so, I know I get anchored on prices in shops all the time, and there's nothing I can do about it.

For his part, Kahneman thinks there's not much we can do about biases either. 'Except for some effects that I attribute mostly to my age', he writes, 'my intuitive thinking is just as prone to overconfidence [and] extreme predictions ... as it was before I made a study of these issues.' But we can get a little better at spotting when we are in situations where error is likely. You can try to 'recognize the signs that you are in a cognitive minefield, slow down, and ask for reinforcement from System 2'.[17]

We can expect to fall into error when we're rushed and facing an unfamiliar choice, when we don't have much to go on and have to act. Oddly, we're likely to make mistakes when we're in a good mood and all seems to be going well – System 2 just lazily leaves it to System 1. But when we're in the moment, facing a choice and happy to have an easy answer flung at us, we're unlikely to spot the minefield. What we can do, though, is look out for each other. It's much easier to see someone else in cognitive trouble than think ourselves out of it.

This, maybe, is the white-hatted rationale behind nudging. Given that human beings are not the perfectly rational actors of traditional economics, given that we are subject to biases that can get in the way of making good choices, what can we do to help people avoid errors and make better decisions? As Thaler and Sunstein put it: 'By properly deploying both incentives and nudges, we can improve our ability to improve people's lives, and help solve many of society's major problems. And we can do so while still insisting on everyone's freedom to choose.'[18] There's a lot of tension in those good-natured sentences, as we'll see.

When Push Comes to Shove

'The only purpose for which power can be rightfully
exercised over any member of a civilized community,
against his will, is to prevent harm to others. His own
good, either physical or moral, is not sufficient warrant.'

JOHN STUART MILL

In a TED Talk in the winter of 2010, against the backdrop of a
huge screen displaying a giant brain and images of Sunstein,
Thaler, Kahneman and other gurus glittering high above and
very nearly in the firmament, David Cameron, soon to be
Prime Minister, promised a revolution in government. 'Now,
if you combine this very simple, very conservative thought –
go with the grain of human nature – with all the advances in
behavioural economics', he said, looking hopefully at the reassuring images of the boffins above, 'I think we can achieve a
real increase in well-being, in happiness, in a stronger society
without necessarily having to spend a whole lot more money.'[1]
When Cameron took office, the revolution began in earnest
with the establishment of the Behavioural Insights Team (BIT),
right inside Number 10 Downing Street. It quickly got to work
on that perennial barrier to human happiness and a stronger
society: our collective failure, as a people, to insulate our lofts.

Given carbon emissions targets, the government had been trying to persuade people to save energy for years, partly by pushing for the installation of better loft insulation. Heat rises, and insulation is a very simple and obvious way to save money and energy – in nearly all cases, the cost of insulating or improving insulation is recouped in savings on heating bills within two or three years. It pays for itself, and it permanently lowers fuel bills – saving hundreds of pounds per year for an average household. But almost no one was interested. Even financial incentives were largely ignored.

The government's BIT swooped into action. According to their website, a four-part methodology was applied to the problem: 'define the outcome; understand the context; build your behavioural insights; test, learn and adapt.'[2]

How do you achieve the outcome of enticing more people to buy insulation? Understand the context; in other words, find out why they're not doing it. A survey revealed that many people have cluttered lofts, and it's easy to think of other things to do on a Sunday afternoon than sort that dusty mess out. In the language of behavioural economics, human beings have a troubling tendency to 'discount the future'. We prefer gratification now rather than later, even if it means what we get now is worth less than what we get in the future.

We are even less inclined to put an effort in now for a return we won't see for some time. Most people would rather have £100 now than £110 in a year, even if 10 per cent is an otherwise attractive return on an investment. Still more people would take the £100 now rather than work a bit to get £110 next year. This fact about us, our short-sightedness, explains a lot about our failure to rein in credit card use, avoid sweets, stop smoking, remain faithful in relationships, and a whole range of so-called 'control problems' we seem to have – it's also a reason to walk away if anyone offers you the opportunity to buy now and pay later.

BIT then ran a number of randomised controlled trials. Such trials have been used for years by pharmaceutical companies to determine which drugs are effective – naturally, businesses have adopted similar techniques to determine which sales pitches work – but this might be the first time policymakers gathered information in so level-headed a fashion. The trials use control groups to test the efficacy of a proposed intervention. If you want to see how effective a financial incentive is when it comes to getting people to insulate their lofts, try suggesting insulation and an incentive to one group, and suggesting only insulation to the control group. When you compare uptake of insulation between the groups, you have a measure of the effectiveness of the incentive.[3]

So a control group heard the usual messages about insulation, but another group was given this plus the enticing opportunity to avoid a month's council tax. This proposition was behaviourally beefed up by invoking the so-called scarcity heuristic or, as BIT put it: 'This offer will be time limited, which we hope will tap into people's aversion to anticipated regret.'[4] Human beings tend to place more value on something if there's not much of it, or if there's a chance it might be lost to competitors. It's a reasonable rule of thumb for a hunter gatherer who's not in a land of plenty, but it means we tend to over-value limited time offers, blue light specials, the stock in closing down sales, limited editions, and rare coins and baseball cards.

Another group was promised vouchers for products from

Homebase and Argos. But what seems to have done the trick was offering to subsidise loft clearance, with unwanted items going to charity, on the promise that the cleared loft would then be insulated. This option actually cost consumers more than the original offer of subsidised insulation, but eliminating the hassle of clearing out the loft was worth it to them: the uptake rate tripled. If home-owners were offered subsidised insulation and subsidised loft clearance as well, the rate increased five times.[5]

*

Perhaps more impressive is BIT's work on organ donation.[6] Each year, about one million people in the UK sign up to the Donor Register, but there remains a certain divergence between intention and action. Nine out of ten people think that organ donation is a good idea, but only one in three people actually sign up for it – a clear opportunity to nudge people towards choices they say they want to make but somehow fail to follow through on. The team trialled eight different messages on a prominent government web page, a different one appearing just after a user paid car tax or registered for a driving licence. The first was a control prompt, simply saying, 'Thank you. Please join the NHS Donor Register.' Seven other messages were tested, each based on a principle of behavioural psychology.

The second said, 'Every day, thousands of people who see this message decide to register.' As innocuous as it looks, this way of putting it makes use of a powerful mechanism of social influence: the principle of social proof. We often determine what the correct course of action is based on what we see others doing. Like many rules of thumb, this is a fine idea most of the time. It seems to work in two ways. Sometimes the behaviour of others results from information they have and you don't, so going along with the crowd is a way of tapping into what they already know. When people have to choose a restaurant in an unfamiliar city, they walk around until they see one with a crowd in it – probably the locals know where to find a decent meal. But social proof also works on us in the form of peer pressure, and we naturally feel compelled to go along with what others do. Maybe it just makes good evolutionary sense to hardwire a strategy that leads us to make more friends than enemies.[7]

You can find examples of social proof used as a mechanism of non-rational persuasion almost anywhere you look. Coins are left in tip jars or in a busker's open guitar case rather than quickly pocketed. Some nightclubs wisely keep the line to get in long. Movie posters quote favourable reviews. Laugh tracks accompany sitcoms. Book covers tell you that they're bestsellers. Campaign strategists carefully manage both the composition of the crowd behind the candidate and the numbers of those cheering at political rallies. Amazon reviews and Facebook likes, as well as websites telling you what people who bought what you just bought also bought – it's all geared to put social pressure on you. In no case does anyone tell you that the service, nightclub, film, series, book, candidate or product is in any way good – you are shown only what other people are doing or what other people think. That is often enough.

What's surprising is the strength of the hold social proof has on us, and like many such mechanisms it can operate without our awareness of it. In the 1950s the psychologist Solomon Asch tested the power of conformity by placing a person in a group with six confederates, individuals who were in on the experiment but were presented to the actual test subject as other volunteers. The task was extraordinarily easy – a line was displayed and the participants were asked to pick a line of matching length from three choices on a card. The confederates gave their answers first, aloud, followed by the actual participant. In the first few rounds, they all chose correctly, but then the six confederates chose the same, incorrect answer, one after the other. The social pressure on the volunteers was large enough to drag them away from what their own eyes told them and into the wrong answer one third of the time. In a series of twelve rounds, three-quarters of those taking part went along with the group, wrongly, at least once.[8]

Social proof has effects not just on how we see the world, but on our sense of who we are, even the values we think we hold. In a series of experiments, the psychologist Richard Crutchfield placed volunteers into booths and told them that the panel of lights in front of them indicated the responses of the four other participants – in fact the lights were controlled by the experimenter. It was set up so the participants always gave their answers last. In a study of army officers, all said they would make fine leaders when asked privately. In the booth and under the weight of social proof, 37 per cent agreed with the bogus majority statement that in fact they would not make good leaders. University students were asked, privately and individually, whether they agreed with the statement: 'Free speech being a privilege rather than a right, it is proper for a society to suspend free speech when it feels itself threatened.'[9] Only 19 per cent agreed. When others seemed to endorse it first, the number leaped to 58 per cent.

When the BIT tried the social proof variant in the organ donor trial, they knew they were on to a good nudge. A study in Minnesota showed that telling people how much electricity their neighbours were using could reduce energy consumption – if they saw that they were high energy users, compared to their peers, a significant percentage lowered their energy use. A bit like laugh tracks, even obviously artificial social feedback can have an effect. High energy users who learned about their more frugal peers consumed even less when also confronted with a frowning emoticon.[10]

It's so powerful that BIT tried two more variations on the social proof message. Both contained the same words, but one showed a health service logo while the other presented an image of a number of people of different races, ages and genders, arm in arm, smiling. In a report on the trial, they said their aim was 'to see whether we could increase the salience of the messages using visual clues alongside written text'.[11]

Another message was couched in terms of loss: 'Three people die every day because there are not enough organ donors.' The hope here was to tap into another psychological fact about us, our tendency towards what's called 'loss aversion'. As Tversky and Kahneman put it, 'losses loom larger than corresponding gains'.[12] The pain we feel when giving something up is much greater than the pleasure we feel when getting the same thing. You can prove this to yourself by thinking about this question: 'What is the smallest gain I need to balance out an equal chance to lose £100?' A coin will be tossed, and if it's heads you lose £100. What does the win on tails have to be before you're willing to play? Most people say £200 or thereabouts. The gain has to be twice the loss. The unpleasantness associated with losing £100 is so bad that we'll consider it only for the chance of gaining double the amount.[13]

The fear of loss is itself a powerful mechanism of persuasion. Anyone who offers you the opportunity to try before you buy, to test drive a car, rent to own an appliance, try on a suit, sample some wine, walk around a house that's for sale and think about where you'd put your furniture or how you might repaint the bedroom – all are attempts to give you a feeling of ownership, making use of the so-called 'endowment effect'. People ascribe more value to things if they own them or feel as though they do. Just the act of imagining something in your possession is enough to make you more likely to buy it and willing to pay more than you otherwise would for it.

While they were at it, BIT tried pitching the message positively too. It turns out that messages involving a loss that we do not feel directly might not be enough to activate loss aversion – talk of 'other people dying' might not do it. So they tried a message promoting the positive effects of organ donation and the gains that might go along with it: 'You could save or transform up to 9 lives as an organ donor.'

The seventh variation said: 'If you needed an organ transplant, would you have one? If so, please help others.' It's not as punchy as the other messages, it's actually a bit clunky, but it appeals to another psychological principle: the rule of reciprocity.

When someone does something for us, we feel an in-built, strong obligation to repay them.[14] The feeling is extraordinarily deep-rooted in human nature. The sociologist Alvin Gouldner claimed that the norm of reciprocity is both universal and general – all societies have it, and almost no one in any society is exempt from it.[15] Anything so pervasive in culture might well be required for culture itself, and some have argued that a network of obligations makes possible such things as trade, the division of labour, social stability, and coordinated activity generally. When someone gives us something – very nearly no matter who they are, and very nearly no matter what it is – we feel obliged to return the favour.

You are a lot more likely to make a charitable donation if you are given a 'free gift' in the post, and you are much more likely to hand over spare change to a member of the Hare Krishna movement once he offers you a flower you don't want. Taking a free sample is sometimes inadvisable. A slice of free cheese in a market, a bit of ham on a stick in a store – it might be enough to cloud your judgement. You feel you really should buy something from someone, probably sooner rather than later.

A classic study conducted in the 1970s shows how naturally returning a favour comes to us – and how easily reciprocity might be exploited.[16] Subjects thought they were taking part in an art appreciation study, rating the aesthetic quality of works of art along with another participant, but in fact it was a study of reciprocity, and the other person was in on the experiment. During a short break, the confederate excused herself and left the room. In the control group, she came back empty-handed, but in other trials she returned with an unsolicited gift for the participant, saying, 'I asked the experimenter if I could get myself a Coke, and he said it was OK, so I bought one for you too.' After the evaluation of the works of art finished, the confederate asked the subject if he would do her a favour. She was selling raffle tickets and whoever sold the most won a prize. The people who received the Coke bought twice as many tickets as those who didn't.

The final version in the organ donor trial attempted to motivate people by urging them to line their beliefs up to their choices: 'If you support organ donation please turn your support into action.' The thinking here apparently relies on cognitive dissonance theory, first sketched by the social psychologist Leon Festinger in the 1950s – Festinger famously infiltrated a cult to study the reactions of members when the apocalypse they predicted unfortunately failed to materialise.[17] Remarkably, many cult members found ways to keep their religious beliefs, even though the end was not actually nigh.

When we are forced to confront conflicting attitudes and beliefs about the way the world is – when you expect the world will end in a deluge on New Year's Eve and it doesn't, or, perhaps less dramatically, when you're about to light up a cigarette and see the warning on the pack – the result is psychologically uncomfortable. Festinger argued that this motivates us to find a way to reduce the dissonance. We sometimes do this irrationally, by downplaying or ignoring the inconvenient evidence against our beliefs. Sometimes we simply avoid whatever experiences cause conflict. But on occasion we're forced to change our choices or beliefs and bring them in line with the facts. The nudge unit hoped this would be the case with attitudes towards organ donation.

The team found that the best-performing messages drew on reciprocity and loss, followed quickly by social proof. All of the variations did better than the control, except one, the social proof message coupled with the image of smiling, happy people. According to BIT's account, 'One hypothesis is that the use of a stock photo discouraged individuals, who saw it as a marketing gimmick.' When people feel nudged, they nudge back.

If the top-performing message were used over the course of a year, as many as 96,000 more people would register as organ donors, compared to the control message. The nudge would save many lives. The National Health Service clearly paid attention. Its current website has a lot of familiar language on it.

'96% of us rely on the other 4% to give blood. Please don't leave it to someone else.'

'More than 19 million people have already joined the NHS Organ Donor Register. It's a magnificent number. But we know that millions more support organ donation yet haven't got round to signing up. If they did sign up, then many more lives could be saved.'

'Did you know? You are more likely to need a transplant than become a donor.'

The front page is also largely devoted to a banner with buttons enabling you to 'share your organ donation decision' via social media, and put the weight of social proof on your Facebook friends.[18]

There have been other successes – automatically enrolling people in pension schemes has significantly increased saving rates, and just telling people who haven't paid tax that others have paid up did wonders for government revenue – but it hasn't been entirely smooth sailing for the Behavioural Insights Team.

*

Recent visitors to a Job Centre north-east of London, hoping to sign up for financial help while looking for work, experienced unusually focused treatment. Instead of filling in as many as nine forms, tediously giving the same information over and over again and then waiting weeks for an interview to explain to a real person why they haven't found work yet, jobseekers met an advisor on day one. They were given help with checklists and worksheets that enabled them to form a plan and break down the task of finding a job into manageable chunks. If they were still out of work after eight weeks, their 'psychological resilience and wellbeing' were improved with 'techniques such as "expressive writing" and "strengths identification".[19]

Some were told their strengths would be identified by completing an online personality test. 'Failure to comply with this direction', they were warned, darkly, 'may result in loss of benefit.'[20] The test consisted of 48 statements, such as 'I never go out of my way to visit museums', 'When the topic calls for it, I can be a highly rational thinker', 'I can rarely stay on a diet', 'Pain and disappointment often get the better of me', 'I have taken frequent stands in the face of strong opposition', 'I have not created anything of beauty in the last year', and 'I do not have a calling in life'. Each statement was followed by a range of possible responses – 'very much like me', 'like me', 'neutral', 'unlike me', and 'very much unlike me'. On completion, test-takers were greeted with their results and cheerily urged to 'Think about how you can use these strengths in your job search and in your life in general. Try to find a new way to use them every day.'

The test is still online, and, what the hell, I just took it.[21] It turns out that, despite being entirely unreligious and accepting from my early teens that we are nothing more than insignificant but sometimes happy specks in a vast, cold and indifferent universe, *spirituality* is the first of my many strengths: 'You have strong and coherent beliefs about the higher purpose and meaning of the universe.' That's unexpected, because if anything I think one can only have extremely incoherent beliefs about meaning in the universe – I don't think that the notion that the universe has a meaning or a higher purpose makes any sense at all.

Perhaps my initial suspicion about the whole spirituality thing is explained by another of my excellent strengths, 'Critical thinking: Thinking things through and examining them from all sides are important aspects of who you are. You do not jump to conclusions, and you rely only on solid evidence to make your decisions.' That's reassuring, and perhaps it means the test is accurate after all. Quite possibly I'm now willing to give it the benefit of the doubt because I have just learned that fairness is one of my 'abiding principles'. I am also in possession of considerable social intelligence. 'You are aware of the motives and feelings of other people. You know what to do to fit in to different social situations, and you know what to do to put others at ease.' Not to put too fine a point on it, but I think it's very safe to say that this might miss the mark, a bit more than fractionally, too.

The test appears to be completely bogus. A blogger who broke the story discovered that no matter how you answer, you get a very similar set of strengths. In a letter sent to job-seekers, the Department of Work and Pensions claimed that the test was 'scientifically shown to find people's strengths', but it seems to have been cribbed from a much larger 'character strengths survey' devised by a non-profit called the Values in Action Institute on Character, based in Ohio. Kelly Aluise, the Institute's Director, said she was approached by someone from the UK's nudge unit about borrowing the survey but told them not to use it. It was, as she put it, a 'non-validated version', that is to say, *not* scientifically shown to find people's strengths. 'We tested it a while back and it failed', she admitted.[22] When pressed, a spokesperson from the Department of Work and Pensions nevertheless maintained that the test was 'intended to help jobseekers identify their strengths, and we have had extremely positive feedback from both jobseekers and their advisers – it is right that we use every tool we have to help jobseekers who want to work find a job'.[23]

That's just asking for it. The Department of Work and Pensions certainly didn't have positive feedback from an unemployed single mother of two, threatened with losing £71 per week if she didn't take the fake test. She told reporters, 'It's a waste of time … I felt really disappointed. I thought, you've made me do this and there's a chance I might lose my benefits if I didn't do it.'[24] Is it really right for a government to 'use every tool we have', including lying to its citizens, threatening them with losing the money they need to feed their children if they don't jump through a ridiculous hoop? It's also worth noting that those involved didn't consent to the trial – they didn't know it was a trial – and that in itself raises ethical concerns. Either way, deception and coercion are not the kind of tools most of us think a government ought to use when trying to get people back to work. Even if the hope was to bolster people who were having trouble finding a job, giving someone an inaccurate picture of their strengths can't do them much good. If nothing else it's just patronising to think that jobseekers wouldn't see through it. I did.

There has been something of a backlash against nudging in the United Kingdom, partly as a result of the fake test. The press has resorted to 'creepy', 'sinister', 'controversial' and 'shadowy' in some descriptions of the nudge unit, and its earlier successes have been reconsidered. Their work on organ donation got a lot of press – headlines said there would be 100,000 new donors each year as a result of their efforts – but some argue that the jump in numbers had a lot to do with the fact that they chose to put the appeal in a new, high-profile place, a government website that gets a lot of views because so many people use it to pay tax and apply for driving licences.

All the variations on the message increased registrations over the control message, but by very small and very nearly identical amounts, and it might well be that just saying something enticing, almost anything more alluring than 'Please join the NHS Donor Register' will improve the response a little. Critics argue that you can do that with or without the behavioural buzzers and bells, and anyway, some say, these so-called biases are 'stuff my grandmother knew' dressed up in a lab coat. Certainly human beings have long been aware that a lot of our choices are less than rational – Pascal noticed that 'the heart has reasons that reason doesn't know' long before Freud got in on the act. Do you really need a psychologist to tell you that peer pressure has a strong effect on us?

The least appealing 'positive intervention' increased registration by just over 2 per cent, and the best by just over 3 per cent – so there's really not much in it at all. Reciprocity, loss aversion and social proof clearly do have effects on us, and they can serve as powerful persuasive tools, but it might be difficult to tap into these facts about us with a few words on a website. Did behavioural insights really swing it? Can discoveries about human decision-making really be translated so easily into public policy?

Some have begun to think that BIT's nudges are just common sense or at most the application of better design, jazzed up with some trendy talk of biases and heuristics.[25]

The story of nudging has gone very differently in the United States. Instead of a small team charged with bringing insights from psychology to government policy-making, America got something nearer a nudger-in-chief.

*

From 2009 to 2012, Cass Sunstein was administrator of the White House Office of Information and Regulatory Affairs (OIRA) – it's been called the most powerful government department you've never heard of, 'the cockpit of the regulatory state', as Sunstein puts it.

OIRA was established in 1980, originally as part of a move to reduce the burden of paperwork placed by the government on businesses and individuals. It was provided with teeth the following year, when Ronald Reagan gave it oversight of federal regulation more generally. As Sunstein describes it in his account of his time at the White House: 'I helped to oversee the issuance of nearly two thousand rules from federal agencies … I argued in favor of the use of "nudges" – simple, low-cost, freedom-preserving approaches, drawing directly from behavioural economics, that promise to save money, to improve people's health, and to lengthen their lives.'[26] OIRA oversees almost everything, from regulations involving the environment and energy to healthcare and national security. 'As a general rule', Sunstein writes, 'no significant rule can be issued by any of the nation's Cabinet Departments – including the Department of Transportation, the Department of Treasury, the Department of State, and the Environmental Protection Agency – unless OIRA says so.'[27]

The nudges Sunstein built into the nation's regulatory framework are mostly more subtle, gentler than clearing out lofts or pushing people into psychometric testing, but a lot of people were spooked by his appointment, particularly Americans jumpy about anything that might curtail freedom of choice. In some suspicious corners of American television and radio, he was regarded as 'the most dangerous, the most evil man in America', in favour of sterilisation, making hunting illegal, using the military against citizens, and 'controlling the internet'. There were, it was claimed, 'frightening similarities between Sunstein and Joseph Goebbels'.[28]

Sunstein sees himself in considerably less worrying terms. By his account, he was just doing regulatory *Moneyball*. In the book and eventually the film of that name, about the success of the Oakland Athletics baseball team, hard data – not hunches, intuitions or the 'wisdom' of old baseball insiders – were used to assemble a top-tier team on the cheap. Sunstein tried to do a similar thing with regulation. What matters are costs and benefits and the results of empirical tests, not what the polls say or what special interest groups might think. The overriding question is, 'What does the most good and the least harm?' It didn't win him universal acclaim. To take just one set of examples, Sunstein backed higher fuel efficiency standards for cars and placed restrictions on emissions from power plants, but he also delayed the implementation of rules about ozone pollution and coal ash disposal. Environmentalists were confused. So were business leaders, consumer advocates and other special interest groups.

Sunstein is drawn to nudges that convey information simply. The thought is that people will be able to make better decisions in unfamiliar situations if the information they need is
presented in a way that's clear and easy to understand. The
less that gets in the way of System 2 the better. For example,
Americans were once subjected to an image called 'The Food
Pyramid', which was meant to convey advice about food groups
and recommended portions, but its meaning is not at all clear.
There's a triangle with images of piles of food at the base and
portion sizes somehow conveyed by lines of varying thickness
converging at the apex, all entirely unaided by a stylised figure
sprinting up a flight of stairs sticking out of the side of the
thing. The US Department of Agriculture adopted a new image
– a plate divided clearly into sections of varying sizes, labelled
fruits, vegetables, protein, grains and dairy. Just looking at it
will tell you how much of what kind of food makes for a healthy
meal. Similar work was done with fuel economy labels on cars,
efficiency labels for refrigerators, calorie information in fast
food restaurants. Sunstein also produced regulations intended
to clarify hidden costs in plane tickets and credit card fees.

The use of defaults is another nudge favoured by Sunstein:
'ensure that if people do nothing at all, things will go well for
them.'[29] Human beings tend to stick with their current situation – this has a name, the status quo bias.[30] It's easily exploited
by companies that automatically renew your subscription or
require you to tick a box to opt out of the less than enticing
opportunity to receive special offers by email. Advertisers know
they have a powerful moment of intervention when you first
make choices about the products you will probably end up
using for the rest of your life – the same shampoo, the same

toothpaste, the same coffee, the same bank. It's also why the current settings on almost anything we own – from phones to televisions to web browsers – are probably still mostly set to the factory defaults. And if you have played around with those settings, you probably did it just once, and then left it as is.

Automatically enrolling people in various programmes and plans – from pensions to healthcare – will therefore have large and lasting effects. If the nudge unit really wanted to ramp up organ donation in the UK, they might have made donor registration opt-out, rather than opt-in. In Germany, where you have to take steps to register to donate organs, the uptake rate is 12 per cent. Next door in Austria, where the default is organ donation, the consent rate is 99.9 per cent.[31] The effects of automatic enrolment in things like savings plans are more complicated. Obviously people who wouldn't have signed up at all are better off, but there's reason to believe that at least some people end up saving less over time under default enrolment than they would had they signed up voluntarily. As is sometimes the case with defaults, more people are better off following a change to a better default option for all, but there's a chance that some members of the group are actually made worse off too. There are ongoing arguments about this with regard to Obamacare in the States – some people might end up paying more for coverage they don't want – and the jury is still partly out. For his part, Sunstein advocates a variety of kinds of defaults and choices, in an effort to do something about this effect.[32]

Increasing salience, making what matters more visible to us, is another kind of nudge favoured by Sunstein. System 1 might skip over the slightly wishy-washy 'Smoking can be hazardous to your health' warning on a pack of cigarettes. But very recently considerably more salient messages were required by the US government, for example, 'Smoking can kill you', 'Cigarettes cause cancer', 'Tobacco smoke can harm your children', and 'Cigarettes cause fatal lung disease'. The impact was enhanced by rubbing System 1's nose in disturbing images of damaged teeth and lungs, dead bodies, crying babies and loved ones, and a particularly grim image of a man exhaling smoke through a tracheotomy hole. The US Food and Drug Administration estimated that, in a few years, the new warnings would push 213,000 smokers away from smoking.[33]

Sunstein is of course also aware of the power of social pressure. The US Department of Transportation became concerned about the dangers of texting while driving. Instead of pushing for a law to make it illegal, President Obama signed a very public executive order that bans federal employees from texting while driving. It got a lot of attention and seems to have served as a powerful social nudge. People began discussing the problem – some states and even the United Nations followed suit with similar directives for their employees. 'Distracted driving' became *Webster's Dictionary*'s term of the year.* Businesses were helped to find ways to discourage their employees from texting and driving. Sunstein is in favour of similar social nudges that might have effects on such things as childhood obesity and healthy eating generally.[34]

But it hasn't been smooth sailing for Sunstein either,

* 'Distracted driving' was actually *Webster's Dictionary*'s *word* of the year, not term of the year, despite being two words. Runners-up were 'cloud computing' and 'wallet biopsy'.

particularly with regard to default rules and healthcare reform. Many of those in the land of the free have taken great exception to being nudged.

*

At least some of the language used by proponents of nudging hasn't helped, and detractors can easily find turns of phrase that seem to confirm their worst fears. Thaler described nudging as an attempt to make the world easier and safer for the Homer Simpsons among us, and that line has come back to haunt him.[35] Some people just find the very idea of being nudged insulting, alongside the implication that we're too stupid to find our way through the world without help from the nanny state. But it is hard to argue with so many studies and so much evidence that points to, if not our irrationality, then at least the fact that we can go wrong in predictable ways.[36] What's the right thing to do about it? Nudges are one kind of answer, but if you want to think your way through them, you need a bead on exactly what nudges are. Some definitions can help.

Thaler and Sunstein call their position 'libertarian paternalism'. The policies they advocate are libertarian because, unlike a law or a fine, they are liberty-preserving – as they put it, 'people should be free to do what they like – and to opt out of undesirable arrangements if they want to'.[37] Their view is a kind of paternalism because it 'tries to influence choices in a way that will make choosers better off, *as judged by themselves*'.[38] Better off in what sense? They say that 'it is legitimate for choice architects to try to influence people's behaviour in order to make their lives longer, healthier, and better'.[39] You might have qualms about the ambiguity of 'better' in that sentence – better according to whom? – but presumably people would want to have longer, healthier lives.

Writing on his own, Sunstein puts it a bit more controversially: when a government acts paternalistically, it does not believe that people's choices actually promote their own welfare, and it takes '*steps to influence or alter people's choices for their own good*'.[40] Maybe in John Stuart Mill's day a government was expected to curtail a person's actions only to prevent harm to others, not to themselves, but it's clear that governments now interfere in this way all the time – think about seatbelt laws and mandatory helmets for motorcyclists. The difference with a nudge, at least, is that you are merely influenced, not commanded or coerced by the threat of possible sanctions. Your choice is preserved in a sense. You might normally be inclined to choose delicious cake for dessert, but if a choice architect puts fresh fruit at eye level and the cake somewhere behind it, maybe you're more likely to choose the fruit and be a little healthier as a result. You can still have the cake if that's what you want, but you have to reach over the fruit to get it.

There are two useful distinctions in this neighbourhood.[41] One is between paternalism about ends as opposed to paternalism about means. The nearly well-worn example is a GPS system. A GPS gives you the means to go where you like – the end or destination is up to you, and if you wish you are free to ignore what the GPS says and go your own way. Similarly, *means paternalists* steer people towards information (or away from System 1 errors) so that they're helped to achieve whatever goals they might set for themselves. However, *ends paternalists* direct people towards particular ends instead – people should be healthy or wealthy or wise, the ends paternalist decides, and they are then pushed towards one of those goals, regardless of what the people in question say they want.

A second distinction is between hard and soft paternalism. Some paternalistic acts on the state's part are hard; they impose material costs on people. Others are soft insofar as they affect choices but impose no real costs. Jail terms and hefty fines are forms of hard paternalism. Requiring cigarette packs to carry graphic images is a kind of soft paternalism.

Putting variations on these two distinctions together can help you distinguish between potentially problematic and unproblematic kinds of paternalism. As Sunstein puts it: 'Nudgers are focused on means paternalism; they are reluctant to question people's ends.'[42] And nudges themselves are a kind of soft paternalism, 'because they do not impose material costs on people's choices'.[43] By these lights, messages about organ donation and requiring the publication of the hidden costs of flying are mere nudges, but perhaps BIT's work with jobseekers was something else. You can imagine a spectrum, with less questionable, soft, means paternalistic nudges at one end, and dubious, perhaps morally suspect, hard shoves towards ends on the other. It's shoving that raises the most questions, and the closer we get to that side of the spectrum, the more objectionable the practices appear to be. The questions cluster around well-being and freedom.[44]

You might think that individuals are authorities about what they want. They know what makes them happy, what makes their lives go well, and at the very least they know better than some distant, desiccated technocrat.

Sunstein's response to worries such as these is simply to point at all the empirical data that counts against the claim that people's choices always promote their own well-being.

Maybe you think you know what you want, but if all this Nobel Prize-winning research is on the mark, actually in certain cases you don't, and that's where nudges might be legitimately applied. If your happiness really matters to you and if you take account of the evidence, you'll agree that you need a nudge now and then. 'If welfare is our guide', Sunstein concludes, 'soft paternalism might be required, not forbidden.'[45]

Other concerns have to do with the idea that nudges violate our freedom in some sense. Sunstein identifies a thin and a thick version of these worries. According to the thin version, freedom to choose is something people want and enjoy, and when the government forces people to do something like save money, it ends up making people less happy. Against this, Sunstein argues that 'The welfare gain of the paternalist action may outweigh the welfare loss.'[46] In other words it's a matter to be empirically investigated and decided case by case. Maybe the pain we experience in being told to save is outweighed by the pleasure we have when the pension cheques finally appear. In fact, he argues, sometimes people would rather not be lumped with the burden of choice – wading through deeply boring literature on savings plans and trying to decide what's best might be more painful for someone who would rather just accept a default and get on with his life.

The thick version takes freedom as an end in itself: 'By what right can government interfere with the choices of free adults?'[47] If people are to be treated with respect, with dignity, a government cannot override their choices, even if this means they're worse off as a result. Sunstein has a lot to say in response, but consider just these two points. First, he claims that, in most cases of nudging – providing clear information, giving people the option to go their own way if they wish – freedom of choice is preserved. 'Are warnings and default rules out of bounds? We should be able to agree that insofar as choice architects are maintaining freedom of choice, the grounds for reasonable objection are greatly weakened.'[48]

Second, and you have to admire him for this, Sunstein suggests that what really matters is well-being, and perhaps calls for the preservation of freedom are a kind of malfunctioning moral heuristic – a mental shortcut, like anchoring and stereotyping, that usually works well enough when we're thinking about the right thing to do, but sometimes leads us astray. System 1 is in favour of freedom, but on reflection System 2 can see that sometimes making people better off is more important than preserving their freedom to choose. He admits this is a reckless suggestion, but it might nevertheless be true.[49]

I wonder if what's needed here is more careful reflection on what freedom is. In at least some of the nudge literature, 'free' seems to mean 'not coerced or forced', but something more fine-grained might be useful. If I'm defaulted into an organ donor programme, I'm of course free to opt out insofar as no one is forcing me to stay in. But the fact that 99.9 per cent of Austrians don't opt out is suggestive. They're not coerced, but if the choice architecture works 99.9 per cent of the time, it's not quite right to say they're free either.

The philosopher Isaiah Berlin makes a distinction between merely having a choice and the full-blooded experience of autonomous action. When I act autonomously, he writes, I am 'conscious of myself as a thinking, willing, active being, bearing responsibility for my choices and able to explain them by references to my own ideas and purposes'.[50] When we're nudged it certainly does not feel like coercion – that's part of the wonder of it – but what's missing is that feeling of autonomous action, being able to explain our choices by reference to our own ideas and purposes, not the purposes of the government, purposes we might not even know. Maybe that's what's really wrong with nudging, but we'd need a richer conception of freedom to see it clearly.

There are, of course, other worries. You might simply not be in favour of nudging because the last thing we need is a government that's really good at covert persuasion. As the economist Edward L. Glaeser puts it: 'Soft paternalism requires a government bureaucracy that is skilled in manipulating beliefs. A persuasive government bureaucracy is inherently dangerous because the apparatus can be used in contexts far away from the initial paternalistic domain. Political leaders have a number of goals, only some of which relate to improving individual well-being. Investing in the tools of persuasion enables the government to change perceptions of many things, not only the behaviour in question. There is great potential for abuse.'[51] It's hard to think that Glaeser is wrong about that.

While the motivations of politicians are on the table, you can also worry that nudges enable them to avoid difficult, unpopular, but possibly necessary decisions. Maybe what's really needed to cut greenhouse gas emissions is a large tax on fossil fuels. If you're thinking about re-election, would you opt for the tax or a less effective nudge in the form of clear fuel efficiency labels? At least you're doing something, you might say to yourself. There is the real worry that nudges are a kind of political cop out, a way a leader might avoid the costs of real leadership while still appearing to take action.

Persuading us to act in certain ways with nudges, rather than arguments and reasons, has another kind of dubious effect. If you're nudged into something, you're not doing it for your own good reasons, and that's going to have a knock-on effect on your behaviour. If, instead of defaulting people into savings plans, they were given good reasons to save, perhaps convinced of the importance of saving, they might not only save, but save more because they see how important it is – they might pay attention to their contributions and maximise them in line with increases to salary. Persuasion through reasons, it might be said, can change a person through and through and have a large number of desirable effects, certainly in comparison to the mere surface changes to behaviour brought about by a nudge. But persuasion of this kind is difficult, and nudges are easier and much more reliable. You'll get the organs of 99.9 per cent of us with a default nudge, but how many people could you convince to donate organs, just by giving them good reasons? How difficult a task would that be in comparison to a nudge?

The nearly knock-down response to all this, on the part of the paternalist, is that choice architecture is in a sense inevitable. As Sunstein rightly says, it's 'the social environment against which we make our decisions. It is not possible to dispense with a social environment, and hence choice architecture is an inevitable (though often invisible) part of our lives.'[52] Given that governments have to set up choices somehow, why not at least try to set them up in a way that's known to be helpful to those who have to make the choices?

It would seem that we are stuck with nudges, and if anything their influence on us is likely to grow. According to a recent survey as many as 41 countries – from Botswana to Finland to

Swaziland – now have centrally orchestrated state policy initiatives clearly influenced by nudge theory. Another 128 countries are undertaking public initiatives in some way influenced by behavioural economics, if not fully-fledged, state-sponsored policies.[53]

For its part, the British nudge unit has left government for the business world – it's now part-owned by the charity Nesta, the British government, and its staff. It's branching out, advising not just the UK government, but other governments, businesses and independent concerns. When asked about the move, the team's director said the main motivation for setting up the new company was 'staff retention'. According to the BBC, 'staff will not be bound by civil service pay grades and will be able to earn bonuses'.[54] Those best able to affect the choice architecture that scaffolds the social world in which we all live are following the money. I can't help wondering how paternalistic those who are hired to nudge us will be.

Lost for Words

> 'He who wants to persuade should put his trust not in
> the right argument, but in the right word. The power of
> sound has always been greater than the power of sense.'
>
> JOSEPH CONRAD

When John Kerry lost to George W. Bush in the 2004 US presidential election, at least some Democrats, maybe very many Democrats, had no clear understanding of how it could possibly have happened. Bush's invasion of Iraq was increasingly looking like an extremely bad idea. No weapons of mass destruction were ever found, and more and more people began openly to question the point of the war, particularly as the death toll continued to rise. Although the world rallied around America immediately after 9/11, its reputation abroad was at an extraordinary low – thanks to what some former allies were calling 'The New American Imperialism'. Bush's approval rating fell more or less steadily from a peak following the attack on the World Trade Center. Kerry, a war veteran, seemed able to capitalise on all this and was generally able to make his case clearly and sometimes even presidentially. No doubt it's hard to unseat a wartime president, and certainly Kerry wasn't the perfect candidate, but he had a lot going for him, and Bush had a lot going against him. Why didn't Kerry win? Some analysts and commentators were genuinely dumbfounded.

The reaction to Bush's re-election was unrestrained in left-leaning papers abroad. *The Independent* was traumatised, sighing, 'Four More Years', alongside grim images of hooded prisoners in Guantánamo and torture at Abu Ghraib. *The Guardian*'s G2 covered its front page entirely in black, with two small words at the centre: 'Oh, God.' Even the *Daily Mirror* ran a cover with an image of a smiling Bush and the headline, 'How can 59,054,087 people be so DUMB?' It was, in many quarters, an unexpected result.

In the US, *The New York Times* saw the Kerry campaign as an unexplained plane crash: 'Democrats were like aviation investigators sifting through twisted metal in a cornfield, struggling to posit theories about the disaster all around them.'[1] Did Kerry lack a clear message? Did a video of Bin Laden taunting Bush give the president a welcome, patriotic boost just before the election? Was it the Swift Boat Veterans for Truth who came forward, casting doubt on Kerry's service record? (If you've now got an ear for this kind of thing, you might wonder whether this was a front group, and some allege that the PR firm Arthur J. Finkelstein and Associates were behind it, funded by wealthy Texan Republicans and at least one billionaire.*)

---

* See 'Swift Boat Veterans for Truth' at www.sourcewatch.org. Various papers published investigations into funding that seemed to come from Texan Republicans and at least one pro-Bush billionaire. For parallels to a possible campaign against Barack Obama and special operations soldiers who objected to his presidency, see Paul Harris

A diagnostic clue, for some, was found in polling data. Most polls showed that Kerry trounced Bush in the televised debates. Never one for rousing oratory anyway, in their meetings Bush was hesitant, occasionally stammering and scowling – he seemed to have particular trouble defending the war. Rumours swirled about a suspicious-looking bulge in his jacket that may or may not have been a receiver beaming in help with his answers – at one point he seemed to say 'let me finish' to an unseen interlocutor. An ambitious image analyst from NASA concluded that Bush was obviously concealing something under his jacket in the debates, while others thought it was probably just a bullet-proof vest. Something of Bush's standing in the court of popular opinion might be discerned from the fact that many believed he needed help, was probably getting help, and doing badly anyway. All the while Kerry was generally able to explain his views and answer questions with complete sentences. It wasn't spellbinding, but he certainly spoke comparatively carefully and reasonably.

A poll undertaken by *Newsweek* reflected what many other polls and pundits were saying: 61 per cent of respondents thought Kerry won the debates, with a mere 19 per cent handing victory to Bush.[2] Despite this, Kerry enjoyed almost no post-debate bounce, and Bush maintained his lead. A tentative explanation, suggested by some, was that the Democrats might be able to win debates, but they failed in a different, much deeper way. They were unable to control the political language in which the debates took place.

(16 August 2012), 'How the Swift boat veterans stack up against 2012's special ops group', *The Guardian*.

Democratic strategists now found themselves fascinated by insights from cognitive science and linguistics. There were animated conversations in back rooms about the power of metaphor and the value of narrative structure when it comes to persuasion. Not arguments, but the careful use of resonating turns of phrase was the key – words that evoked or fit into established worldviews were better heard and more strongly believed. As *The New York Times* put it: 'Even before the election, a new political word had begun to take hold of the party, beginning on the West Coast and spreading like a virus all the way to the inner offices of the Capitol. That word was "framing".'[3] The Democrats could win as many debates as they liked, but if you want to persuade voters, just having good arguments won't do it. You have to frame the debate, the context, the language in which the arguments, and our very thoughts, are enmeshed and understood.

The example at the time was 'tax relief', a phrase that seems to have emerged from the White House soon after Bush took office.[4] Talk of tax relief conjures up a conception of tax as an illness, an affliction, a source of anxiety from which one seeks respite. In a financial context it might harmonise with the notion of 'famine relief', emergency aid given to unfortunates unable to secure the basic necessities of life, no doubt through no fault of their own. The conservative with a plan to offer tax relief is therefore doing us all a great favour, like a doctor relieving us of pain or an aid worker saving our lives. Anyone who tries to block this relief, a liberal pushing for raising taxes, is therefore framed as the villain, the one getting in the way of much-needed help.

This way of framing taxation appeared first in White House press releases, and then it was picked up and used unreflectively by the mainstream media reporting on 'the president's tax relief plan'. Democrats who tried to take issue with tax relief only ended up reinforcing the image in voters' minds. Finally and catastrophically, Democrats themselves offered their own doomed plans for tax relief. Once this happens, once a debate is framed in a way favourable to one party and not another, the deck is seriously stacked. Maybe a Democrat can score points in a debate about tax relief, but only by playing along and using the words they've already lost – in answering the question, 'What's your tax relief plan?', you've been drawn into a worldview, a framework that favours a particular, and particularly negative way of thinking about taxation.

Philosophers have a name for something like this, 'the complex question fallacy'. Answer yes or no to the following question: 'Have you stopped pistol-whipping your tailor?' If you don't have a tailor or do have one but don't rough him up, you are nevertheless stuck if you go along with the terms of the question. You can answer no, which suggests that you still do pistol-whip your tailor, or you can answer yes, which implies that you once did but have recently got a grip on yourself. The question is a set-up, and if you try to answer it on its terms, you're trapped. Framing can sometimes operate in a similar way.

So those in the know began to believe that whoever controls the language of politics places limits on the spaces in which a debate can move, forestalling support for one kind of policy and enhancing support for another. Across a large population, where the margins of a debate can swing the whole thing, the careful phrasing of a sentence here and there might have extraordinary effects. Perhaps something like this happened to the Kerry campaign. Conservatives framed the language of the election, and framed Kerry himself as a flip-flopper, unable to make up his mind at a time when America needed a leader who at least took decisive action. Against all that, liberal strategists reasoned, a good argument put forward by Kerry didn't stand a chance.

*

People with an interest in persuasion have always known that how you put your point, the words you choose, can make a difference to who's convinced, but the first full-blown empirical study of framing effects took place relatively recently, in the early 1980s. Framing is still only partly understood, but again the work of Kahneman and Tversky is central if you want to understand it. Their early studies focus on risk-averse and risk-taking behaviour, and they discovered that the wording of questions presented to test subjects could result in completely opposite answers. Ask a question one way, and we're risk-averse. Put exactly the same choice slightly differently, and suddenly we're gamblers.

The best example of this effect is called the Asian Disease Problem.[5] Suppose that the Centre for Disease Control is planning for the possible outbreak of a new disease currently spreading in Asia. It is expected to kill 600 people. Two possible responses are on the table:

If programme A is adopted, 200 people will be saved.

If programme B is adopted, there is a one-third probability that 600 people will be saved and a two-thirds probability that no one will be saved.

When presented with this wording of the problem, most people prefer the certainty of saving 200 people and choose programme A, the risk-averse option. Now consider a second framing of the outcomes:

If programme A′ is adopted, 400 people will die.

If programme B′ is adopted, there is a one-third probability that nobody will die and a two-thirds probability that 600 people will die.

With the question worded in this way, a majority of people now choose the more risky gamble, programme B′. The consequences of programme A and programme A′ are just the same. The same numbers live and the same numbers die, no matter that it's described in one case as '200 out of 600 will live' and '400 out of 600 will die' in another – it's the same either way. But the way the problem is framed leads us to express contradictory preferences: playing it safe or taking a risk. As Kahneman puts it, 'Preferences between the same objective outcomes reverse with different formulations.'[6] It was a startling result.

An enormous number of studies have been undertaken since, and there seem to be two general kinds of framing effects at work. There are equivalency framing effects, where two logically equivalent options are framed differently, resulting in different choices. This is what's going on in the Asian Disease Problem. It's the second sort of framing that has become increasingly interesting to researchers and political strategists: emphasis framing, where the language used emphasises or highlights certain elements of the question or topic, eliciting different responses depending on what features are highlighted. Compare your response to the words 'gay marriage' as opposed to 'same-sex marriage' or even 'homosexual marriage'. How do you feel about 'undocumented immigrants', rather than 'illegal immigrants'? What about 'migrants' as opposed to 'refugees'? Would you rather buy a 'used car' or one that was 'pre-owned'? Are 'layoffs' worse than 'downsizing'? Are 'enhanced interrogation techniques' acceptable when a country is engaged in 'a military action'? Would you think differently about 'torture' and 'war'?

Somewhere in the middle are other sorts of framing effects. Simply ordering the questions asked in one way rather than another can make a substantial difference to the responses we give.* In the 1950s, as the Cold War was heating up, test subjects were asked a series of questions, including these two:

'Do you think the United States should let Communist reporters from other countries come in here and send back to the papers news as they see it?'

'Do you think a Communist country like Russia should let American newspaper reporters come in and send back to America the news as they see it?'[7]

When Americans were asked about American reporters first, of course they thought Americans should be allowed to enter a Communist country and freely report back. But then they

---

* This might actually be a kind of priming effect, but the waters are muddy enough without going into that possibility.

might have thought, fair's fair, Communist reporters should also be free to send back news. When they were asked about Communist reporters first, most thought they should be carefully restricted and not be allowed to enter the country and report however they liked – but then respondents were less likely to expect Russia to allow American reporters to report freely. So it's not just beliefs about probabilities and risk-taking, as in the Asian Disease Problem. Our thoughts about what most of us take to be fairly fundamental values, like the importance of a free press, can be manipulated with something as simple as the ordering of questions.

These facts are extremely important to those behind political messaging, but they're also not lost on the people who write and decipher polls. This is of course something quite different from the clumsy but effective tactic of push polling, which is worth knowing about but should detain us only for a moment.

Push polls are attempts to persuade by asking loaded questions under the guise of a poll. The 'pollsters' are not gathering data, and they don't much care what answers are given; the point is to get as many people as possible to hear the loaded questions. Just ahead of the 2000 US Republican primaries, for example, South Carolinian voters heard this question in an otherwise innocuous poll: 'Would you be more likely or less likely to vote for John McCain for president if you knew he had fathered an illegitimate black child?' McCain sometimes appeared on the campaign trail with his adopted daughter Bridget, who was originally from Bangladesh.[8] Just hearing about the possibility of an illegitimate black child and sometimes seeing McCain with his daughter might well have had an effect on the vote. McCain, fresh from a victory in New

Hampshire, lost the early momentum of the campaign, as well as South Carolina, to Bush. This is persuasion by means of rumour-mongering, but actual polls can be worded in much more subtle ways, and this in itself has predictable effects on the people who take them and by extension the results of polls themselves.

According to its website, the US General Social Survey has been collecting data on 'a standard "core" of demographic, behavioral, and attitudinal questions, plus topics of special interest' for the past four decades.[9] While its core questions have never changed, in the 1980s researchers conducted an experiment to see what effects altering the wording of the surveys might have on responses. Part of the survey asks people to evaluate spending in particular policy areas – are we spending 'too much, too little, or about the right amount' on various programmes? – but in some cases how those areas are presented, how the questions are phrased, was found to make a large difference to the support people were willing to give to them.

The changes were minor – in some cases researchers simply added verbs. They found greater support for 'protecting social security' than 'social security'. There was more support for 'solving the problem of big cities' than for 'assistance to big cities'. Respondents were more in favour of 'improving conditions for blacks' than 'assistance to blacks'. They offered more support to 'halting the rising crime rate' than 'law enforcement'. The biggest shift was surprisingly large. Just 20–24 per cent thought that too little was spent on 'welfare', but a majority of 63–65 per cent thought too little was being spent on 'assistance to the poor'.[10]

Changing the words, researchers reasoned, brings to mind different associations, emphasises different things – in this case adding verbs to the descriptions might have created more active associations that suggest actually doing something and therefore getting more for your money. What's remarkable is that while the language might point to the same policy matter – welfare and assistance to the poor amount to much the same thing – the thoughts evoked by slight variations in phrasing could be quite different. Certain words can encourage particular interpretations. As one researcher remarked, '[W]hen a respondent thinks about halting crime he or she may bring to mind a set of uniformly positive beliefs and feelings associated with the personal and social benefits of a lowered crime rate. Conversely, the reference to law enforcement may call up a host of both positive and negative beliefs and feelings, such as those associated with crime prevention, law and order, traffic and parking tickets, corruption, and police brutality, leading to a lowered overall level of support.'[11]

It's not a stretch to think that if the responses to polls can be altered dramatically by re-wording them, then the responses the public might have to different political messages about exactly the same policies might be manipulated by carefully managing language too. You can see this most clearly in the results of referendums.

In 1997 a number of US states contemplated putting affirmative action to a public vote. At issue was whether or not a state's hiring policies should favour people from groups that have suffered discrimination in the past. In the wake of a Californian referendum that scuppered affirmative action policies, the people of Houston, Texas unexpectedly voted to maintain them. Many believed that the framing of the referendum had everything to do with both results. As *The New York*

Times reported, 'Rather than being asked whether they wanted to ban discrimination and "preferential treatment," to which voters said a clear "yes" in California last year and to which polls showed Houston voters would also say "yes," residents were asked whether they wished specifically to ban affirmative action in city contracting and hiring. The legal effect was the same under either wording, but to this revised question they answered "no" by 55 per cent to 45 per cent.'[12]

Notice that the conclusions voters reached in both cases were swayed not by sound argument and reasoned debate, but by the careful choice of a few well-researched words.

The wording of a referendum is therefore hotly contested by those who know what they're doing. In the UK a substantial part of the debate about Scottish independence focused not on the case for independence itself but the wording of the referendum about it. The Scottish National Party proposed: 'Do you agree that Scotland should be an independent country?' The Electoral Commission rejected that formulation, suggesting what came to be the version accepted by all parties: 'Should Scotland be an independent country?' By asking whether or not the voter agrees, some argued, the proposition was framed in a positive light, encouraging agreement and playing down the possibility of disagreeing. Pollsters try to squelch this effect by asking, 'Do you agree or disagree?' instead. Whoever suggested the original version probably had all this in mind.

Some say that the accepted wording still slants opinion in favour of a 'yes' vote by not mentioning an end to the Union, which would call up much more negative associations. All of the versions contemplated, anyway, have the virtue of simplicity. When the question of setting up a devolved Scottish

Assembly arose in 1979, voters were asked, 'Do you want the provisions of the Scotland Act 1978 to be put into effect?' The Act itself was a complicated thing, much debated in Parliament, and quite possibly – and possibly deliberately – beyond the understanding of many voters without the time or inclination to undertake the necessary research.

Tweaking the language in a referendum is comparatively small fry. Those with an understanding of words hope to get a linguistic handle on the minds of voters, and not just win elections, but if all goes well, shape the political futures of entire countries – perhaps for generations.

*

In the summer of 1971, Lewis F. Powell, Jr., then a corporate lawyer with a connection to the Virginia Board of Education, was asked to draft a confidential memo to the US Chamber of Commerce. There were concerns about attacks on the 'American Free Enterprise System' on college campuses and beyond, and as Powell was well-placed to understand what was going on – given his seats on many corporate boards, his legal background, and his interest in education – the Chamber sought his analysis and advice.

'There have always been some who opposed the American system, and preferred socialism, or some form of … communism or fascism', he began, rousingly.[13] He had in mind not just crackpot extremists and dubious revolutionaries, but 'perfectly respectable elements of society' – professors, reformers, priests, the left-leaning media generally, and those who publish and read literary and academic journals. Thousands of bright young things were graduating from the best colleges each year, and many were taught to 'despise the American political and economic system'.[14] Something had to be done about this.

As Powell saw it, American intellectuals were shaping the minds of future generations in a way that was largely hostile to big business and the free market. He singled out Ralph Nader as the personification of this disturbing new evil: 'The passion that rules in him – and he is a passionate man – is aimed at smashing utterly the target of his hatred, which is corporate power. He thinks, and says quite bluntly, that a great many corporate executives belong in prison ... he is not talking just about "fly-by-night hucksters" but the top management of blue chip businesses'.[15] To Powell's associates in the Chamber, it was chilling stuff. 'The ultimate issue may be *survival*', he warned, 'survival of what we call the free enterprise system, and all that this means for the strength and prosperity of America and the freedom of our people'.[16] Nothing less than a large and comprehensive response equal to the defence of America itself would do.

Powell maintained that something had to be done first and foremost to counter the subversion taking place on college campuses. Academic freedom must be respected, of course, but perhaps the Chamber ought to fund a staff of highly respected scholars who actually do believe in the system. They should be set to work not only critiquing the existing efforts of those who might challenge free enterprise and the notion of limited government, but also on producing papers that would restore the balance and perhaps tip it in a direction a bit more favourable to the business world. They should write books, paperbacks and pamphlets and take every opportunity to 'inform and enlighten the American people'.[17]

A speakers' bureau should also be established, mobilis-
ing 'attractive, articulate and well-informed speakers',[18] some
taken from the highest posts in the business world, who would
serve as advocates for corporate America wherever and whenever required. The Chamber should find ways of getting such
speakers invited to campuses to give talks, but they must also
make use of radio and television, using paid advertisements if
necessary.

Education would take time, and by Powell's lights it wasn't
enough on its own to cope with the present crisis. Other tactics
should be used immediately: 'Political power must be assidu-
ously cultivated', Powell insisted, and 'when necessary, it must
be used aggressively and with determination – without embar-
rassment and without reluctance.'[19] The Chamber would have
to become vigorously active in the political arena, by supporting candidates, lobby groups, and policy experts amenable
to business, but also by attacking those who might challenge
conservative causes. A team of extremely competent lawyers,
people of national standing, should also be considered. They
might be tasked with finding opportunities to help the cause
in courts of law.

It wouldn't be cheap. The Chamber would be funding speakers, academics, lawyers, lobbyists and others, and salaries would
have to be at levels expected by successful business executives,
tenured professors and top-notch attorneys. 'It would require
far more generous financial support from American corporations than the Chamber has ever received in the past.'[20] The
Chamber of Commerce, it would seem, took Powell's memo
entirely to heart.

No doubt there were other causes, but Powell's suggestion

seems to have been a large part of the thinking behind the establishment of a number of think tanks and pro-business institutions that emerged in the late 1970s and have proliferated since, all attempting to shape the thinking of politicians, students and the broader public. It could have been the inspiration for bodies like the Manhattan Institute, the Cato Institute, and the Heritage Foundation. To give you a feel for how such institutions understand their mission, here's how the Heritage Foundation describes itself – lines that sound as though they could have been lifted from Powell's memo:

> The Heritage Foundation is a research and educational institution – a think tank – whose mission is to formulate and promote conservative public policies based on the principles of free enterprise, limited government, individual freedom, traditional American values, and a strong national defense … Heritage's staff pursues this mission by performing timely, accurate research on key policy issues and effectively marketing these findings to our primary audiences: members of Congress, key congressional staff members, policymakers in the executive branch, the nation's news media, and the academic and policy communities.[21]

The Heritage Foundation employs a large stable of academics and business leaders in an eight-storey building on Massachusetts Avenue in Washington, DC. It's organised into three institutes that preside over a number of smaller centres, covering everything from economic policy and trade to national security and legal studies. There is a 250-seat auditorium, teleconferencing facilities, and accommodation for an army of interns. Staff members are regulars on talk radio and television, serving as an extraordinarily high-powered version of the speakers' bureau envisioned by Powell. Heritage alone has total assets in excess of $230 million. It spent almost $80 million in 2013, 'advancing conservative principles'.[22] This kind of money spent by a number of foundations over decades almost certainly has had a considerable impact on how Americans think and act.

But conservatives did not just spend their time and money talking to America. They did a lot of careful listening too – years of polling and convening focus groups, getting to know how Americans think and what matters to them. The very incarnation of this work is the pollster, adviser and political and corporate communications expert Frank Luntz. He cut his teeth working for right-wing politicians like Pat Buchanan and Newt Gingrich, and he had much to do with the polling work and final wording of the Republican Party's 'Contract with America', which, it's thought, was a substantial part of the reason why conservatives took the House of Representatives in 1994, for the first time in 40 years.

Luntz found a kind of sideways fame in the UK when he ran one of his enlarged and lively focus groups on *Newsnight* in 2005. The group picked David Cameron as the front-runner for leadership of the Tory Party. Some papers suggested that a 'celebrity pollster created Cameron'. That's certainly overstating it, but Luntz's performance on the night didn't hurt Cameron's cause.[23] He did similar work in Ireland and Australia.

As Luntz puts it on his website, he's 'counseled everyone from Presidents to Prime Ministers, Fortune 100 CEOs to nonprofit organizations, even professional sports franchises'. He explains: 'Our creative team is made up of expert wordsmiths that know market research as well as they know language. And here's what matters most for you: as a result, you get language that is tailored specifically to shift support towards your issue, your business or your goals … word by word, phrase by phrase. Tested, researched and perfected, using innovative polling, comprehensive market research, and instant response dial sessions – we make sure you know exactly what your audience wants, and needs, to hear.'[24]

What matters when it comes to word choice, according to Luntz, is emotion, not the giving of good reasons. As he put it in an interview, '80 per cent of our life is emotion, and only 20 per cent is intellect. I am much more interested in how you feel than how you think.'[25] Strong emotions are sometimes what animate us, what get people to go out and vote, and that is what Luntz tries to elicit in both focus groups and their end product, words that pull heartstrings and push people towards particular policies and candidates.

Depending on which side of the table you're sitting on, the most famous (or infamous) result of his polling work is the publication of various memos prepared for Republican politicians, outlining the words they should avoid or use when addressing particularly contentious issues.

When discussing financial reforms put forward by Democrats following the financial crisis, for example, Luntz said that 'You must put proponents of the legislation on the defense, forcing them to attempt to justify the "lobbyist loopholes" and exemptions placed in the bill … Highlight the exemptions. Broadcast them.'[26] When discussing healthcare legislation, Luntz found that people were most afraid that 'The gov't will decide what treatment I can or can't have', and urged Republicans to play on that fear where possible.[27] He's known in environmentalist circles for advising the Bush administration to maintain various pro-business policies by couching discussions of climate change in terms of a lack of scientific certainty. As he put it in a leaked memo, 'The scientific debate is closing [against us] but not yet closed. There is still a window of opportunity to challenge the science … Voters believe that there is no consensus about global warming within the scientific community. Should the public come to believe that the scientific issues are settled, their views about global warming will change accordingly. Therefore, you need to continue to make the lack of scientific certainty a primary issue in the debate.'[28] Despite unequivocal agreement in the scientific community on the fact of warming and the human hand in it, this tactic is still being used in America to great, or perhaps tragic, effect.

In his various memos, Luntz starts with short bullet points – a page of urgent advice – followed by polling results and very specific recommendations on precisely what words to use, which symbols to invoke, how to empathise and connect emotionally with voters, and examples of 'words that work' from speeches made, sometimes from both sides of a debate. He called one large handbook 'The New American Lexicon' – horrified liberals, smearing Republicans as Republican Thugs or 'Rethugs', dubbed it 'The Frank Luntz Rethug Playbook'.[29] It offers page after page of very detailed advice on language, intended to help Republicans win mid-term elections. The advice in it, coming from polling results, is amazingly specific, and the language Luntz recommends can still be heard in US political rhetoric.

Luntz advocates the use of American symbols by those running for election – the flag, the bald eagle, the Statue of Liberty. Which is best? 'When asked, 64% of Americans chose the Statue of Liberty as one of the greatest symbols of America and American patriotism.'[30] So aspiring politicians are advised to make judicious use of it.

Obviously they'll need more than symbols to secure election victory, and Luntz points out that the careful deployment of 'core fundamental American principles' is just as important as the use of symbols. But which ones should candidates mention? 'At the top of the list in the American mindset are Democracy (52%) and Justice (40%). These principles above all others should be essential components of the communications agenda.' Candidates might bring up equality, opportunity, security and fairness, which also polled quite highly. Talking about fairness and opportunity together works very well too. Still not sure how to proceed? Luntz presented Americans with three definitions of fairness, and the highest rated one was: 'Fairness means that every American has the chance to succeed even if the ultimate outcome may vary.'[31]

Luntz places a premium on the power of 9/11 in the American mind, particularly when it comes to defending the seat of incumbents presiding over tough financial times for their constituents: 'September 11th changed everything. So start with 9/11. This is the context that explains and justifies why we have $500 billion dollar deficits, why the stock market tanked, why unemployment climbed to 6% and why we are still in a rebuilding mode. Much of the public anger can be immediately pacified if they are reminded that we would not be in this situation today if 9/11 had not happened, and that it is unfair to blame the current political leadership or corporate America for the consequences of that day.'[32]

Traditional Republican supporters are alarmed by the very idea of financial irresponsibility, and 'without the context of 9/11, you will be blamed for the deficit ... The trick then is to contextualize the deficit inside of 9/11 and the war in Iraq.' As the emotional reaction to 9/11 fades among voters and becomes less useful, Luntz suggests that candidates begin to 'link the war on terror to the economy' instead.[33]

When it comes to discussing fiscal policy, 'Bring a copy of the federal budget to use as a prop' to indicate its enormous size, make it a thing that looks out of hand and in need of control. Polls indicate that above all voters want politicians capable of 'putting our national priorities in order', so Luntz advises the use of the words 'accountability', 'responsibility', and 'discipline' – 'three words. That's what Americans want to hear: these three words. And when you put the word "budget" before them, their impact soars.'[34]

Following similar work on trade, tax, energy, social security and law reform, Luntz concludes with an appendix entitled '14 Words Never To Use ... because effectively communicating requires you to STOP saying words and phrases that undermine your ability to educate the American people.'[35] Americans might appreciate their local government, so always use the word 'Washington', not 'government', when making a critical point. 'Personalizing' is much better than 'privatizing', particularly when it comes to social security. Americans worry that 'tax reform' might result in their paying more tax, but almost everyone is in favour of 'tax simplification', so couch your points in those terms. A narrow majority would repeal 'inheritance tax' or 'estate tax', but an overwhelming majority would vote against a 'death tax'. Do not advocate 'drilling for oil' when 'exploring for energy' paints much better pictures in people's heads. Americans are split when it comes to 'school choice', but everyone is in favour of 'giving parents the right to choose the schools that are right for their children'. Never refer to 'undocumented workers' when you can say 'illegal aliens', and do not address 'immigration reform', which polarises Americans, when you could instead use the words 'border security', which is something almost everyone supports.

It's a tour de force in the careful use of persuasive political language. As Luntz puts it: 'Frame the issue right and you get the support you need.' It's a thought shared on the other side of the political spectrum by the father of framing, a cognitive linguist from Berkeley called George Lakoff. It's also possibly the only thought shared by the two.

Famous enough in his corner of the academic world but not a household name outside it, when Washington began to take an interest in language, Lakoff was suddenly a hot property, invited to strategy meetings, Democratic caucuses, and dinner parties hosted by political insiders, eventually selling out auditoriums on the speakers' circuit on both sides of the Atlantic. His slim book *Don't Think of an Elephant: Know Your Values and Frame the Debate* – originally conceived as a handbook for campaigners and published by the only small press that would take it – was now shifting hundreds of thousands of copies. In it he argues that the problem for Democrats boils down to an insufficient appreciation of the nature and power of language.

*

Aristotle was the first to try to understand metaphorical language, discussing it in two works: *Poetics*, his treatment of poetry and tragedy, and *Rhetoric*, his account of persuasive speech. You can tell just by the titles of those works that Aristotle thought that metaphor was a special and fairly unusual way to make a point – the preserve of poets and public speakers, perhaps, but not a natural part of everyday language. To borrow one of Aristotle's examples, we might refer to old age metaphorically as 'the evening of life' – the idea is that old age is to a life as evening is to a day. Metaphor can enable us to think of things in a new way, as Aristotle puts it, by 'the application of a strange term' to a new context. In this case talk of day and night is pulled into the description of a life, enhancing or enlarging our thoughts about living as a result.

Lakoff argues that this traditional way of thinking of metaphor is much, much too narrow. In a book co-authored with the philosopher Mark Johnson, called *The Metaphors We Live By*, he argues that 'metaphor is pervasive in everyday life, not just in language but in thought and action. Our ordinary conceptual system, in terms of which we both think and act, is fundamentally metaphorical in nature.'[36] According to Johnson and Lakoff, our metaphorical concepts shape our perceptual experience, structure how we think about the world, figure into how we act and how we interpret the words and actions of others.

The book is packed with examples of everyday metaphors, and the first one, fitting given our subject, is 'argument is war':

> Your claims are *indefensible*.
> He *attacked every weak point* in my argument.
> His criticisms were *right on target*.

I *demolished* his argument.

I've never *won* an argument with him.

You disagree? Okay *shoot*!

If you use that *strategy*, he'll *wipe you out*.

He *shot down* all of my arguments.

The point is that we do not simply talk about argument in terms of war, we really *attack* our opponent and *defend* our own position. What we actually do, and what we think we are doing when we argue, is structured by the 'argument is war' metaphor. 'The metaphor is not merely in the words we use', they claim, 'it is in our very concept of an argument. The language of argument is not poetic, fanciful or rhetorical; it is literal. We talk about arguments that way because we conceive of them that way – and we act according to the way we conceive of things.'[37]

This way of thinking about argument is what Lakoff calls a frame. The argument-is-war frame not only shapes what we do when we argue, it shapes how we think about arguments, and how we understand what an argument itself is. If someone understands argument differently, with a different frame – Lakoff's example is 'argument is dance' – we might have trouble understanding what they're doing when they argue. We might not see it as argument if it doesn't fit the frame that we've got.

Lakoff claims that if we are going to understand ourselves and the way our minds work, we need to rethink the nature of rationality. This is part of a large trend across several disciplines that focuses on the fact that cognition is in a way embodied, that is to say, our thoughts are constrained and structured by our bodies and brains. There's an old dualist picture, owed to Descartes, that sees the self as a disembodied, abstract, thinking thing – something spiritual and not of this world. Physical bodies are entirely different, merely lumps, existing in space and disassociated from the process of thought. It follows that reason is in a way universal – it is what it is independently of the physical world. All human beings are capable of the same sort of logical reflection on the facts, no matter who we are and no matter where we are. If we're careful, assenting only to our clear and distinct perceptions, we'll all discover the truth together.

But Lakoff and other theorists argue that the old view is giving way to a picture of ourselves as embodied and imperfect reasoners. Our thinking can be properly understood only in relation to our bodily nature. Mind and body are not two different kinds of things. They're in constant interaction, and they shape and constrain one another. Among other things, this means that we think in terms of different frames and metaphors, and some of these are dependent on physical facts about the way we move around in space. Furthermore, different people apply different frames to the same questions and come to different conclusions as a result. So if you want to get a political message across, just giving people the facts or presenting them with an argument won't do it unless the discussion is framed in ways that make sense to them. We talk right past one another when we approach the same subject matter through different frames.

Metaphors can be very deeply embedded, and in some cases the process of creating them can kick in at an extraordinarily young age. What's more, Lakoff argues that frames are hardwired, physically realised in the neural circuitry of our brains. To use one of Lakoff's examples, when we're babies and our parents pick us up to cuddle us, we begin to connect the feeling of warmth with good attitudes towards another person, and a vast array of metaphors begins to take hold. We warmly welcome someone, have the hots for another, and give someone we don't like the cold shoulder. Neurons that fire together, wire together, and once the neurons associated with warmth hook up with those associated with positive attitudes, the frame has sunk in, and it's almost impossible to think our way clear of it or make sense of claims that operate outside of it or in tension with it.

It's important to notice that much of our metaphorical think- ing goes on without our awareness of it. In a recent study, stu- dents read a report about crime and were then asked what to do about it.[38] Half read a version of the report describing crime as a 'wild beast preying on the city' and 'lurking in neighbourhoods'. Of that group, 75 per cent then suggested solutions involving enforcement or punishment – such as building jails or calling in the military. Just 25 per cent advocated social reform, such as improving education and boosting the local economy.

The others read a version of the report describing crime as a 'virus infecting the city' and 'plaguing communities'. After reading this description, only 56 per cent of them thought pun- ishment would help, and the number in favour of social reform jumped to 44 per cent. The frames, the authors conclude, invite 'structurally-consistent inferences' – if you think of crime as a beast you'll be led to certain ways of dealing with the problem, like hunting it down and putting it in a cage. But what's extra- ordinary is that when asked to identify the parts of the story that influenced their decision, most cited crime statistics, which were the same in both versions of the report. Just 3 per cent spotted the fact that metaphors had something to do with their conclusions.

Lakoff argues that many of our most elementary metaphors are spatial – they organise whole networks of other concepts. The thought is that, as embodied creatures, spatial awareness is fundamental to our thinking and acting, and in order to understand something complex, we sometimes express it in the more familiar terms of physical action. The most basic sorts of metaphors at the root of many of our thoughts depend on simple orientation. For example, we associate happiness, health and goodness with 'up', and sadness, illness and badness with 'down'. We say 'I'm in high spirits' or 'I've sunk into a depression'. 'I'm at the peak of health' or 'He's about to drop dead'. 'Things are looking up' or 'He's gone downhill'. 'Most of our fundamental concepts', Lakoff and Johnson conclude, 'are organized in terms of one or more spatialization metaphors.'[39]

So it's not a surprise that a great deal of political messaging, particularly during elections, attempts to connect to us on this fundamental level. We understand the words used so easily and effortlessly that the messages stand a chance of flying in under our critical radar. One of the most prominent messages in Obama's 2012 re-election campaign was the idea of 'moving forward'.[40] A long video central to the campaign begins with references to the Bush years and a jagged red line falling downwards on a graph, listing various catastrophes blamed on Republican leadership – a 'drop in sales', the 'Dow plunged', there was a 'decline in consumer spending'. But the camera angle is often looking upwards or moving upwards when Obama's policies are mentioned, and in the end an itemised list of his accomplishments travels up the screen, one by one. The words appear at the bottom, accelerate upwards and then stop in the middle of the screen. While watching it online I found myself involuntarily nodding 'yes' as I tracked the words.

Several studies into the nature of embodied cognition have shown that adopting positive or negative postures – sitting back with your fingers interlocked behind your head as opposed to sitting tightly cross-legged, for example – can have an effect on what we think. So can simply shaking one's head yes or no. In one test, students were told that they were evaluating the sound quality of new headphones, particularly when they were jostled around. Half were told to shake their heads up and down and the other from side to side, all the while listening to a carefully prepared radio programme with an editorial making a case for the introduction of student ID cards. Those nodding their heads yes were more likely to agree with the arguments they heard than those shaking their heads no.

There's reason to believe that people positioned behind candidates while they make a speech, carefully nodding and sometimes clapping in agreement to points made, have a similar influence on us.[41] This has not gone unnoticed by some with an entrepreneurial streak. A company called Crowds on Demand provides crowds for campaign rallies, protests and corporate marketing 'events'.[42] According to their website, the illusion of support can work wonders: 'A foreign government hired Crowds on Demand to help generate a positive reception for its newly elected leader during the UN General Assembly … The crowds that we deployed drew in more supporters creating a strong presence for this leader at the UN and an improved perception of him by the American public.'[43]

In interviews the company is coy about its clients, but a reporter called Ian Cioffi telephoned them, pretending to be an employee of a politician looking for the illusion of support that Crowds on Demand might conjure up for a fee. When asked if they'd had success not just in the UN, but in US politics, the company founder replied: 'We have worked with dozens of candidates in the US, primarily but not exclusively Republican … The candidates have been primarily congressional/senate candidates. We've only worked with one (serious) presidential candidate thus far. I have found our approach has led to increased poll numbers and in many cases made the margin of victory.'[44]

There are crowds in Obama's campaign video too. It ends with him telling an approving crowd that 'America is on the way up'. The camera cuts to close-ups of smiling individuals in the audience, all looking up at him, full of hope. The individuals in these shots were almost certainly chosen very carefully, to resonate with certain viewers in desirable ways. His opponent Mitt Romney also made motion metaphors central to his campaign – getting back on track, returning America to greatness, turning things around, and so on. Republican challenger Paul Ryan promised to 'put the nation back on the path to renewed prosperity for all'.[45]

While spatial and motion metaphors are a large part of it, Lakoff argues that people understand politics in terms of two fundamental metaphorical frames.[46] The overarching conception containing both frames is of the nation as a family. America has 'Founding Fathers' and 'Daughters of the American Revolution'. France's national motto includes the notion of *fraternité* or brotherhood. There is sometimes talk of the Commonwealth Family in the United Kingdom, and many countries make use of the words 'fatherland' and 'motherland'. Perhaps we all 'send our sons to war'. It's easy and perhaps natural to try to make sense of something as large as a country in terms of a smaller, more familiar social unit that is understood much better. According to Lakoff, the trouble is that there are two competing frames at play here – the strict father model, which informs the conservative worldview, and the nurturing parent model, which is the foundation of the progressive or liberal outlook. These metaphors are not exactly conscious, but Lakoff argues that they shape conscious thoughts on both the left and the right.

The strict father model assumes that the world is a dangerous, Hobbesian place, full of people competing against each other, trying to get ahead in an uncertain world. Life is not easy. Children are born bad insofar as they naturally want only what feels good to them. If they are to survive they must be taught moral goodness by the father, the authority who knows best, sometimes by means of corporal punishment to push the child past merely immature desires. Through strict discipline, the child becomes self-disciplined and self-reliant – these two qualities are the bedrock of the strict father model's moral outlook. People who take care of themselves and pursue their own self-interest are therefore good, and they're the ones who will prosper in a difficult world. Well-being is understood mostly monetarily: good, hard-working people do well financially and are economically independent. Those who lack the discipline to do well – who do not become good, decent and self-reliant people – are dependent on others, and that's morally wrong. Taking handouts and not working hard just isn't right. Such people therefore deserve the bad lives they get.

Lakoff argues that people with the strict father frame in their head are likely to be all in favour of free-market capitalism.

'The link is the morality of self-interest, which is a version of Adam Smith's view of capitalism ... if everyone pursues their own profit, the profit of all will be maximized by the invisible hand.'[47] Conservatives are also likely to take a dim view of social programmes. It's just wrong to give people something they have not earned – dependency is a kind of immorality. From this point of view, it also makes sense to reward people who have worked hard and done well for themselves. Tax cuts for the wealthy are entirely reasonable, even morally right. The thought is that by pursuing their own self-interest the rich have made things better for everyone by creating wealth and greater opportunity. Why shouldn't they keep more of their own, well-earned money?

The nurturing parent model, on the other hand, takes it that both parents are responsible for bringing up children, not just a single, strict disciplinarian. The world might be difficult, but it can be made better with cooperative effort, by looking after ourselves and each other. Children are generally good, but with care they can grow up to be even better people, people able to contribute to society as a whole. Mere self-interest, looking out for number one, is on this view a moral mistake. What does nurturing mean? 'It means two things', Lakoff explains, 'empathy and responsibility. If you have a child, you have to know what every cry means ... And you have a responsibility – you have to take care of this child.'[48] Ultimately, you want your child and yourself to live fulfilling lives, to be happy, and this is understood in terms of well-being as opposed to being financially independent and well off. Lakoff argues that seeking happiness and fulfilment for ourselves and wanting to help others to be happy is the bedrock of progressive morality.

A nurturing parent is highly protective, and this translates into liberal political policies. Democrats want a government that protects its people – from such things as smoking, dangerous driving, and harmful additives in foods. They want the poor to have healthcare, the protection of union power for workers, and laws that protect the natural environment. Some people need help to get out of bad lives, help in the form of welfare – perhaps paid for by taxes levied on those who are already well provided for. It's the decent thing to do.

If Lakoff is correct, there are a number of implications for political messages and the possibility of finding compromise or agreement in political matters. We are not all pure enquirers, capable of looking at the facts, listening to well-made points, and coming to the same reasoned conclusions. As he puts it, 'People think in frames. The strict father and nurturing parent frames each force a certain logic. To be accepted, the truth must fit people's frames. If the facts do not fit a frame, the frame stays and the facts bounce off.'[49] Lakoff explains this by reminding us that the concepts we have are 'instantiated in the synapses of our brains'.[50] We can't make sense of facts without an interpretive conceptual framework, and if the one you have regards self-interest as the wrong basis for morality, you'll be unable to understand why conservatives think voting for tax cuts for the rich is a reasonable thing to do. It will just seem crazy to you, as crazy as your views about universal healthcare seem to someone with different interpretive frames. If the frameworks are physically realised in our brains, Lakoff thinks that this means we can't help but see the world as we do. Sometimes each of us, conservative and liberal, simply puts the facts that don't fit to one side.

Lakoff concludes that progressives have two options. Everybody has a mixture of models in their heads, applying the strict father model to some parts of their lives and the nurturing parent to others. By his lights, about 35 to 40 per cent of the voting public has a strict father model governing their politics, and another 35 to 40 per cent has a nurturing model governing theirs, leaving some percentage in the middle. His advice to progressives is therefore straightforward: 'The goal is to activate *your* model in the people in the "middle". The people who are in the middle have *both* models, used regularly in different parts of their lives. What you want to do is to get them to use your model for politics – to activate your worldview and moral system in their political decisions. You do that by talking to people using frames based on your worldview.'[51]

By doing a lot of this, a second, long-term strategy becomes possible. Following decades of conservative think tanks creating dominant conservative frames, what's needed is consistent reframing in terms of liberal values. This might well take many years, Lakoff admits, but the hope is eventually to rewire America's brains for the better. His example is taxation. If political advertising, policy papers and Democrats speaking on talk shows managed to reframe tax as a wise investment in the future, or perhaps as membership fees paid for enjoying the benefits of being a member of the country, over time taxation might not be the kind of thing we think we'd need 'relief' from.

While this analysis of liberal and conservative thinking has been influential, particularly among Democratic activists, not everyone buys it. The stuff about frames being physically realised in brains can rankle. No doubt all thoughts are physically realised in some sense, but spelling out that sense is tricky.

Making a case for the notion that frames are hard to shift *because* they're neurally realised is even trickier.

Lakoff's general views about the left and the right are certainly easy to caricature too. As one reviewer put it, 'Couldn't be simpler, then: redneck, chain-smoking, baby-slapping Christers [are] desperately in need of some gender-free nurturing and political counselling by organic-gardening enthusiasts from Berkeley.'[52] That's harsh, but it might only just fall short of fair. A number of critics, even heavy-hitting ones like the experimental psychologist Steven Pinker, argue that Lakoff's own liberal views distort his account of political ideology. His 'cartoonish depiction of progressives as saintly sophisticates and conservatives as evil morons', as Pinker puts it, makes Lakoff's recommendations impossible to take seriously. Pinker writes: 'Lakoff tells progressives not to engage conservatives on their own terms, not to present facts or appeal to the truth ... Instead they should try to pound new frames and metaphors into voters' brains. Don't worry that this is just spin or propaganda, he writes: it is part of the "higher rationality" that cognitive science is substituting for the old-fashioned kind based on universal disembodied reason. But Lakoff's advice doesn't pass the giggle test.'[53]

*

Framing is of course just a part of the thinking behind modern political messaging. There's much more to understanding what's going on when we hear a politician speak. But even with this limited grip on political language, I now find myself turned off by political speeches. I don't want to hear and be affected by them. Sometimes I look away and hum to myself when a politician appears on television to respond to the news of the day. I know that I can't keep this head-in-the-sand solution going for very long, and I know it's slightly batty, but it's less painful than the alternative, which is listening to the sound-bites and playing political buzzword bingo. The words now leap out at me, and I can't hear anything other than a communications specialist stressing the repetition of the words 'freedom', 'forward', 'opportunity', 'transparency', 'dialogue', 'innovation', 'a balanced, responsible approach' or whatever it is that the word merchants say will do the trick. I can discern almost no actual argument in political discourse. I hear only tactical phrasing.

But bracket the worries we might share about the very real possibility that political language is almost entirely an attempt on the part of elites to manipulate us in some way or other. There is something that's possibly much worse to worry about when it comes to reflection on framing.

Remind yourself of the Asian Disease Problem. A disease is expected to kill 600 people. Given one framing of the problem most of us go for the certainty of saving 200 people, and given another framing we gamble rather than accept 400 deaths. Now that you can see that those choices are inconsistent – you pick one under one description of the problem and the opposite under another – how do you decide which one to choose? Should you opt for the certainty or the gamble? Kahneman and Tversky asked a lot of people that strangely disturbing question, and 'the answer is usually embarrassed silence'.[54]

Kahneman hypothesises that the intuitions that push us towards different choices under each frame come from our automatic System 1. Saving lives is good, and death is bad. But when we see the inconsistency for what it is – when we see that the two sets of choices are the same, just worded slightly differently – and we bring System 2 to bear, we find that we have no moral intuitions left to guide us. As Kahneman explains: 'Your moral feelings are attached to frames, to descriptions of reality rather than to reality itself. The message about the nature of framing is stark: framing should not be viewed as an intervention that masks or distorts an underlying preference. At least in this instance ... there is no underlying preference that is masked or distorted by the frame. Our preferences are about framed problems, and our moral intuitions are about descriptions, not about substance.'[55]

This raises the possibility that we have attitudes and opinions, but they're fundamentally dependent on context. Ask about spending on welfare, and we say we spend too much. Ask about spending on assistance to the poor, and we say we are spending too little. Once we know about all this, how should we decide, as a people, how to spend our money? What policies should we adopt in an effort to prevent crime, once we know that our answers depend on the metaphors we have in mind when we encounter the question? Frame crime as a beast on the loose, and we think more policing is a good idea. Framed as a disease, better community services are the answer. But which is it, really? Which answer is right? What should we choose, knowing as we do that the context of the question shapes our answers? Embarrassed silence again.

It calls into question the very idea of democratic decision-making. As the political scientist Larry M. Bartels writes, 'The problem for democratic theory is that the fluidity and contingency of attitudes make it impossible to discern meaningful public preferences on issues of public policy, because seemingly arbitrary variations in choice format or context may produce contradictory expressions of popular will.'[56] What can we do about it? Bartels suggests further theoretical and empirical work on framing political issues. We might try to find reasons for thinking one context or frame is superior to another, but whatever those reasons are, they had better not aspire to reflecting our preferences. The disheartening alternative, Bartels suggests, might be the opportunity for random popular vetoes on the manoeuvrings of our politicians – a sudden and unannounced public vote would at least have the virtue of sometimes curtailing political power, without giving anyone time to manipulate our attitudes.

Meanwhile we're subjected to constant political messaging. In 2011, half the teachers in the UK and a good chunk of the civil service and National Health Service were on strike. The Labour leader Ed Miliband responded to the growing crisis in an interview: 'The strikes are wrong at a time when negotiations are still underway. The government has acted in a reckless and provocative manner, but it is time for both sides to set aside the rhetoric and get around the negotiating table and stop this from happening again.'[57] He said this, or a slight variation on it, six times, in response to six completely different questions in the course of a two-and-a-half-minute interview.

The words 'wrong while negotiations are underway', 'reckless and provocative', 'put aside the rhetoric' and 'get around the negotiating table' appear in every answer he gives. He looks earnest, his eyes full of purpose, as he says the same thing again and again. The bewildered interviewer, Damon Green, asked about the strikes, about how his role as leader of the Labour

Party could be reconciled with his opposition to the strikes, about whether or not he believed those striking were acting in good faith. By the fourth question, having heard the same answer three times, Green started to wobble. As he recalled shortly afterwards, 'I'm not sure what I asked next. Frankly I was in danger of losing it. On my own, with the eyes of Ed Miliband and his three handlers boring into me but apparently oblivious of my presence, I was getting twinges of what I can only describe as existential doubt. So I said some words. And Ed told me that the strikes were wrong, and the rhetoric was out of hand, and both sides needed to sit down …'[58]

Green was on the business end of what's now called 'message discipline'. Communications advisors, perhaps basing their conclusions on careful polling, determine that certain turns of phrase are most likely to have the desired effect, and then all steps are taken to ensure the relevant soundbites make it through the media and do not end up on the cutting room floor. They do this by repetition.

There are reasons to think that repetition alone is a powerful persuasive device – witness jingles and slogans endlessly repeated in advertising. Mere exposure to repeated words and phrases is enough to make us more inclined to go along with what we hear. The so-called 'illusion of truth' effect has been demonstrated over and over again, and it appears that human beings simply find messages they've encountered before more credible than new ones.[59] It's easier for us to process information we've already heard once or twice, and sometimes we mistake that ease for truth. Familiarity breeds not contempt, but credence. Message carpet-bombing, as it's sometimes called, is a viable political strategy.

Some governments have gone so far as to get the phrases out by distributing laminated cards to foot-soldiers, using pagers and now text messages to broadcast useful turns of phrase at a moment's notice to everyone on the campaign trail. Many teams get together each morning and as a matter of course convey instructions to 'on message' politicians who fan out and say the same thing, in the same words, to different media outlets. It's persuasion by echo, by reiteration, not by the giving of reasons.

All this wordplay has vastly undermined whatever trust we might have had in politicians, and they do what they can about this during elections. In the 2015 UK campaign, David Cameron attempted to reassure voters that he would not renege on his promises by backing them up with laws he actually could not break. Ed Miliband's doomed campaign unveiled an eight-foot limestone monolith, The Edstone, carved with six campaign pledges. Miliband said that, if elected, he would install it in the garden at Downing Street – presumably in the hope that it would remind him to do what he said he would do. These are two variations on a single sentence: 'No really, trust me this time.' Good reasons are now so rare in our political conversation that our leaders scarcely bother with them. Erecting a monolith with some slogans on it appears to be a better tactic than actually trying to convince us to offer our support.

No doubt there are rare exceptions, but in general, political speeches and debates should not be mistaken for opportunities to find out what a politician actually thinks. An interview does not give a journalist the chance to hold a public figure accountable in any meaningful sense. Instead, these are just opportunities for our leaders to persuade us by repeating words that are likely to push the right buttons in our heads. George W. Bush put the point succinctly in a sublimely unguarded moment: 'See, in my line of work you got to keep repeating things over and over and over again for the truth to sink in, to kind of catapult the propaganda.'[60]

Retail Therapy

'To act as a physician, the priest must make one sick.'
FRIEDRICH NIETZSCHE

The father of the sixteenth-century French philosopher Michel de Montaigne had what must have seemed like an excellent idea – and as is often the case with excellent ideas, there was absolutely no way it was ever going to work. The elder Montaigne noticed that people with something to sell would very much like to make as many potential buyers aware of their offerings as possible, and people interested in making purchases would like to know exactly what's out there in the marketplace so that they can make intelligent, informed decisions. Many opportunities are missed just because buyers and sellers don't know about one another. Wouldn't it be wonderful, he reasoned, if a disinterested third party published an honest list of what's for sale and what's sought after?

Montaigne wrote of his father's hopes: 'There might be in every city a certain place assigned [where anyone who] stood in need of anything might repair, and have their business entered by an officer appointed for that purpose. As for example: I want a chapman to buy my pearls; I want one that has pearls to sell; such a one wants company to go to Paris; such a one seeks a servant of such a quality; such a one a master … And doubtless, these mutual advertisements would be of no contemptible advantage to the public correspondence and intelligence: for there are evermore conditions that hunt after one another, and for want of knowing one another's occasions leave men in very great necessity.'[1] No exaggerated claims, no false promises, fair prices, and no lost sales – just clear information provided by both sides of the potential transaction. Everyone wins.

The younger Montaigne's essays were read widely, and the idea soon reached England. It was put into practice when Sir Arthur Gorges and Sir Walter Cope took out a patent for the publication of *The Publicke Register of Generall Commerce*. They hoped it would serve as a 'good, trusty and ready measure of intelligence and intercourse between our said Subjects'.[2] The *Publicke Register* was of course abandoned within a year. No one wanted to read long, uninspiring lists of goods and services, no matter how much better off everyone might be as a result. What did take off, what actually caught the buying public's eye, was not facts and figures, but commercial advertising – engaging pitches made on behalf of the sellers themselves. Had the stars lined up, had it somehow gone the other way, with the mutually beneficial register surviving and taking the place of advertising as we now know it, the world would have been an entirely different, quite possibly more reasonable place.

This is not to say that advertising was a new thing in the world when Montaigne raised the possibility of the public register. Accounts of the history of advertising will tell you either that it's always been with us or that it has very recently transformed itself into something entirely new and remarkable. Perhaps some mixture of these two claims is true.

Cast the net widely enough and advertising is probably as old as buying and selling. Certainly the first people who hung the tools of their trade over their doors were engaged in a kind of advertising, as were those who simply painted pictures of their tools, the first shop signs, and put those up instead. There's evidence that such signs hung over the heads of ancient Mesopotamian and Egyptian artisans and tradesmen many thousands of years ago. Roman streets were cluttered with something approaching posters and billboards, alerting citizens to the line-up at the next gladiatorial match. As the nineteenth-century historian of advertising Henry Sampson observed, 'Rome must have often looked like a modern country town when the advent of a circus or other travelling company is first made known.'³ The disaster at Pompeii preserved what appear to be the alluring adverts of pimps and prostitutes: 'If anyone is looking for some tender love in this town, keep in mind that here all the girls are very friendly.' Painted frescoes left potential clients in no doubt of the possibilities on offer. Athenians heard advertisements sung by town criers, who interrupted their public announcements with sponsored messages. As they were sometimes accompanied by musicians, it might well have sounded like modern jingles.

While it has always been around in some form or other, it's also true that advertising has undergone a number of transformations. Think just about how it has rolled with the arrival of otherwise extraordinarily disruptive technologies. William Caxton introduced not just the first printing press to England in 1476, he also produced the country's first printed advertisement. It was for the 'Pyes of Salisburi', which unfortunately were not actual pies but printed collections of rules for how a priest should deal with the changing order of services and duties around Easter and various Saints' days. Easter is a moveable feast, so a priest who wishes to stay on top of things requires clear instructions concerning which offices to undertake in which order. If anyone wants a copy printed 'wel and truly correct', the little posters promised, let him come to Caxton's place in Westminster, and 'he shal have them good chepe'.[4]

As literacy and printing spread, printed advertising followed and grew. Similar transformations accompanied the appearance of cinema, radio, television and now the internet, social media, and our evolving mobile devices. But there's a much more intriguing revolution in advertising, over and above its adaptation to new technologies, which took place a little more than a century ago. It had to do not with the various new ways advertising might be placed before us, but with what advertising itself is and how it might be understood by the people who created it.

Until then advertisements were almost always in the style of Caxton's original printed version: they soberly reported what was for sale and where you could get it. The word 'advertisement' comes from the Latin *advertere*, meaning 'to turn towards', and that's generally all advertisements were, signs pointing buyers in the right direction. Sometimes an ad went a bit further, as Caxton's did, by offering a prospective buyer some good reasons for making the purchase – perhaps promising that whatever was for sale was good quality ('wel and truly correct') and reasonably priced ('good chepe'). Occasionally advertisements exaggerated their claims or, perhaps less charitably, made things up, but it mostly went on like this until the start of the twentieth century, when a genuine shift in the nature of advertising took place.

As Bob Fennis, professor of consumer behaviour, and Wolfgang Stroebe, professor of social psychology, put it in their account of the recent history of advertising, '[Until] the early twentieth century virtually all print ads used what we would nowadays term an information or argument-based appeal. They straightforwardly informed consumers what was for sale, at what price and where one could buy it. The approach became known as the "tell approach", a more subtle variant on the more pressing "hard sell" approach of "salesmanship in print" which aligned a set of persuasive arguments to convince prospective buyers and thus became known as the "reason-why" approach ... [A] more subtle "soft-sell" approach was developed in the early 1900s which sometimes used an emotional or affect-based appeal, aiming to influence the consumer's feelings and emotions rather than his thoughts.'[5]

A number of ideas about the irrationality of the herd were in the air at the time, as we saw with the rise of public relations work, but what really seems to have changed the nature of advertising was a new understanding of the way we think. It moved persuasive messaging in advertising away from arguments and towards something else entirely.

*

Philosophers have been trying to explain what the mind is and how and why thoughts arise for a very long time. Plato had a recognisable theory of mind 2,000 years ago, and every heavy-hitter since has had something to say on the subject. All this changed when a handful of philosophers levered themselves out of their armchairs and took to scientific experimentation. When Wilhelm Wundt established the first psychological laboratory in Leipzig in 1879, psychology had branched off from philosophy and become a new thing in the world, a distinct discipline. Psychological theories of mind, unlike philosophical reflections, were subject to empirical test. Their results carried a new kind of weight in our understanding of what thinking is and how it works.

It was not long before those with an interest in influence and persuasion took notice. As early as 1895, an editorial in *Printers' Ink*, the national trade magazine for the American advertising industry, sounded prescient: 'Probably when we are a little more enlightened, the advertising writer, like the teacher, will study psychology. For, however diverse their occupation may at first sight appear, the advertising writer and the teacher have one great object in common – to influence the human mind ... [T]he advertising writer is really also a psychologist. Human nature is a great factor in advertising success, and he who writes advertisements without reference to it is apt to find that he has reckoned without his host.'[6] No one agreed more than Walter Dill Scott, one of Wundt's students and among the first to apply the discoveries of experimental psychology to advertising.

Scott argued that some decent 'doctoring' might have been done in the old days, when people picked up medical knowledge of necessity, simply learning by doing, but by the turn of the century there was just no way a person would be permitted to practise medicine without a serious grounding in theory. Doctors need an understanding of anatomy, chemistry and physiology, among much else. So too with architecture and the law. As Scott observed: 'In this day and generation we are not afraid of theories, systems, ideals, and imagination. What we do avoid is chance, luck, haphazard undertakings ... We may be willing to decide on unimportant things by instinct or by the flipping of a coin, but when it comes to the serious things of life we want to know that we are trusting to something more than mere chance.[7]

And what could be more serious than business?

A lot of money was wasted on advertising that did no good at all. Advertising men had simply tried out turns of phrase and images in their campaigns, based on nothing more than their own experience and creative instincts. Sometimes it worked, but often it fell flat. Scott promised that psychological theory could take the guesswork out of advertising, ground it in the same way legal theory grounds the practice of law and the study of physiology guides the surgeon's hand. Scott believed that experimental work on 'habit, self, conception, discrimination, association, memory, imagination, perception, reason, emotion, instinct, and will' would enable copywriters and artists to 'know the customer' in a profound new way.[8] Some elements of the advertising world took to this with gusto, and Scott's influential books ran through many editions.

In his early work, he simply applied insights from experimental psychology concerning some feature of the mind to a relevant aspect of buying and selling. Advertisers clearly want to create memorable ads, for example, so he produced an analysis of the nature of memory, identifying four features of an experience which make it hard to forget: repetition, intensity, association and ingenuity. He then showed how each might be used by a well-informed advertiser.

Repetition might now seem like an obvious advertising technique, but at the time Scott took pains to explain what sort of repetition works and what sort is merely annoying – using the same image with changing copy was recommended, and you can see here the beginnings of modern branding and logos. Creating the intensity of attention required for memorable copy takes more effort, Scott admitted, but he could point to experiments indicating that certain colours are more memorable than others, as well as studies showing that black type on white paper is more memorable than white type on black paper. The position of advertising copy in a magazine was also found to make a difference to the intensity of the experience – what appears on the first and last pages is most easily remembered. Association comes into play when a copywriter presents his pitch 'in such a form that it will naturally and easily be associated by the reader with his own former experience' – in other words, couch the language of the ad in terms that will be familiar and resonate with your target audience.[9] Finally, a writer might use words or phrases that are so ingenious they're impossible to forget. Scott's example is the Uneeda Biscuit – the name 'pleases by its very ingenuity' and is therefore easily recalled.[10]

Things in the advertising world have perhaps moved on from ingeniously named biscuits, but each of these 'principles of memory' as Scott calls them can still be seen at work in advertising today. Repetition is the most obvious tactic that's stuck, but as we'll see in the next chapter, now a great deal of time and money is spent studying the intensity of colours, fonts, shapes, sounds, even smells and what this does to the minds of shoppers. Association, finding ways of tailoring ads to the lives of individuals, has reached a new kind of height as very specific messages are directed to us via our mobile devices. As for ingenuity, clever ads are now so clever that we share them with one another through social media. 'The four principles enunciated above for impressing advertisements on the minds of possible customers are capable of unlimited application, and will not disappoint any', Scott declared, 'for they are the laws which have been found to govern the minds of all persons as far as their memories are concerned.'[11]

Scott made similar claims about psychological discoveries concerning the emotions, habit, sympathy, instinct and the will, but his greatest influence on the thinking behind persuasion has to do with his work on suggestion, and the various senses in which it supplants appeals to reason. Suggestion is, for Scott, a mental process wherein an idea is brought to mind by another person or object, and this new thought comes about quickly, without deliberation of any kind. Once we have an idea in mind, Scott claimed that it will lead to action unless some new thought or a change in circumstances prevents it from doing so. It was suggestion, he argued, not reason, that's behind almost all of our conclusions, including our purchasing decisions. 'We have been taught by tradition that man is inherently logical', Scott writes, 'that he weighs evidence, formulates it into a syllogism and then reaches a conclusion on which he bases his action. The more modern conception of man is that he is a creature who reasons rarely at all.'[12] As he puts it elsewhere, 'Today we are finding that suggestion is of universal application to all persons, while reason is a process which is exceptional, even among the wisest. We reason rarely, but act under suggestion constantly.'[13]

Perhaps most importantly, when we act on the basis of suggestion we do not realise that's what we're doing. In an echo of Gustave Le Bon's take on the psychology of crowds, Scott argues that someone under the influence of advertising is like a person who is simply swept along. He goes with the mood of the multitude, but his actions seem to him like the result of his own deliberate choices. 'In the same way', Scott writes, 'we think that we are performing a deliberate act when we purchase an advertised commodity, while in fact we may never have deliberated upon the subject at all. The idea is suggested by the advertisement, and the impulsiveness of human nature enforces the suggested idea, hence the desired result follows in a way unknown to the purchaser.'[14] We might not recall seeing the ad – maybe it was a pop-up banner we quickly clicked off the screen – but if Scott's right, it has done its work whether we notice it consciously or not.

Scott advised copywriters to try 'the direct command' approach.[15] Instead of making a case for a purchase, simply tell consumers to buy or try or use the advertised product – plant that suggestion. We are inherently suggestible, Scott believed, but it's a fine line. We follow orders so long as it's not clear to us that that's what we're doing, so care is needed in the wording of commands. 'Buy Ivory Soap' might be effective, but it's not as good as 'Let Ivory Soap Do The Work For You'. Scott suspected that we are in a highly suggestible, semi-hypnotic state when half paying attention to ads when flipping through a magazine or driving by a billboard on autopilot. Modern advertisers do sometimes sound as though they are making hypnotic suggestions. Compare McDonald's' 'I'm lovin' it' to something they might have gone with, 'You're lovin' it'. The former does look a bit like autosuggestion, a less intrusive command that you make to yourself whenever you hear it.

But if this is standard fare now, it was revelatory to advertisers who had only to put suggestions on paper again and again to see sales improve. Scott advised placing an image of an authority figure – a doctor or master painter or domestic goddess – next to the product's name and some words indicating that the product is excellent. He predicted that the consumer would make the unconscious inference that the product was endorsed by someone who knows more than they do, and when it came to making a purchase, the thought, 'I've heard that's good' would simply come to mind. Given the way suggestions work, it's unlikely the person who has that thought will remember that it came from an advertisement. We might think that the recommendation came from a friend or that we just heard about it somewhere, Scott claims, but most of the time we don't think about where the suggestion came from at all. It simply does its work on us.

In any case no reasons need to be given – Scott did not rule out persuasion by argument, he just thought the tactic was almost always less effective than suggestion, because human beings reason rarely. People buy without carefully thinking about it, because most of the time we don't carefully think about anything. In this way, advertising began to shift away from the thing it had been since Caxton's day. Advertisers began to experiment with new methods and theories of persuasion that operated outside the space of reasons.

It was the start of a long connection between careful efforts to understand the minds of consumers and the business of selling things to them, but that connection did not take hold all at once everywhere, nor was it entirely uniform where it did catch on. The 1920s for example saw the rise of behaviourist thinking and its elevation of observable behaviour over and above the hidden mental events going on inside our skulls. What matters, behaviourists maintained, was what you could see and hear and test in a laboratory, and the one thing no one could really see were the thoughts of a test subject. So thought really wasn't the proper object of a truly scientific study.

By examining the observable relationship between stimulus and response, on the other hand, behaviour might be understood well enough to be manipulated. In some board rooms it was hoped that a skilled behavioural psychologist might procure purchasing behaviour with the application of the right sort of positive reinforcement. Just as Pavlov could make a dog drool by ringing a bell whenever a meal appeared, perhaps the behaviourist could stimulate purchasing in response to some advertised signal. The approach was not without impressive results. The psychologist John Broadus Watson – recently fired from Johns Hopkins University following an affair with a young graduate student and now much more gainfully employed by The Maxwell House Coffee Company – managed to make millions of us want a coffee at lunchtime by establishing the enduring tradition of the lunchtime coffee break.

*

By the 1950s, two-thirds of the largest 100 advertising firms in America were making use of what was then called 'motivation research' or 'the depth approach'.[16] The mind was thought to have three levels: a conscious level of which we are aware; a subconscious level we have a vague grip on, containing our half-hidden prejudices, fears and desires; and finally a deeply buried level of attitudes and feelings that has an impact on our behaviour but is entirely hidden away from our everyday, conscious awareness. Firms now employed teams of 'whiskers':

academics specialising in sociology, psychology, psychoanalysis and cultural anthropology, as well as experts in the understanding of symbols, colour perception and body language. The hope was to gain access to the hidden layers of the mind, the parts containing facts about us we're either unlikely to divulge or simply not aware of ourselves.

In 1957 the journalist Vance Packard exposed what was then the largely unknown world of advertising and marketing in his book *The Hidden Persuaders*. The book was, he wrote, 'about the large-scale efforts being made, often with impressive success, to channel our unthinking habits, our purchasing decisions, and our thought processes by the use of insights gleaned from psychiatry and the social sciences'.[17] His many examples of the manipulative tactics used by the industry scandalised readers at the time. We'll come to some of this in a moment, but what is perhaps equally interesting is his explanation of how and why the advertising world turned to this new sort of persuasion in the first place. Packard thought that it had a lot to do with a shift in the assumptions those in the business world made about the rationality of human beings, alongside fears for the growth of the American economy.

First of all, advertisers discovered that people might not actually know what they want. This realisation undermined the faith many had in polling and straightforward interviewing as sources of reliable information, and it led some enterprising companies to look for new ways to determine what consumers actually desire. Businesses altered packaging or product lines because that's what people said they wanted, but in fact the changes sometimes resulted in lost sales. Beer drinkers, to take just one example from the time, said that what they really wanted was a nice dry beer, but when asked how a beer could be dry, what a dry beer was, many had absolutely no idea. Those who thought they knew what dry beer was gave conflicting answers.[18]

Another problem was that even when people do know what they want, they might not tell the truth when you ask them about it. They are more likely to give answers 'that will protect the informants in their steadfast endeavour to appear to the world as really sensible, intelligent, rational beings'.[19] People said they preferred to read classy magazines when questioned, but in fact gossipy rags outsold the more tasteful publications by twenty to one. Those who enjoyed a beer after work said that they preferred the more refined flavours of specially brewed beer over ordinary, regular beer, but brewers were in fact producing and selling nine times as much of the ordinary stuff. When asked why they weren't buying the humble kippered herring, interviewees said they preferred the finer things in life and certainly didn't like the rough and ready, fishy taste of the things. On further examination it was discovered that 40 per cent of those who said that they did not like the flavour of kippers had never actually eaten one.

Beyond uncertainty and fabrication, there was another problem for those trying to work out what to sell and how to sell it. As Packard remarks, beating behavioural economics to it by several decades, 'it was dangerous to assume that people can be trusted to behave in a rational way'.[20] His examples include presenting women with three boxes of what's actually the same detergent, dressed up in different packaging, and then recording their reports of non-existent differences in their washing. In one case a woman using detergent in a brilliant yellow box found it so strong that she claimed it damaged her clothing. The same stuff in a blue box was so weak that it left the washing dirty. But when placed in a box prepared by experts on the effects of colour and visual perception, the detergent resulted in wonderfully clean clothes. In another case of consumer irrationality, a store discovered that sales of a slow-moving product priced at 14 cents could be dramatically increased by changing the price to two for 29 cents. The examples, while bewildering, also suggested that something other than clear-headed deliberation was behind many of our choices.

New kinds of economic pressure also pushed the business world towards the depth approach. People were, as Packard reports, 'too easily satisfied with what they already have', and this was a kind of disaster for manufacturers.[21] Following the Second World War, the American economy enjoyed remarkable and steady growth. In the twenty years or so before the publication of Packard's book, the gross national product had increased by more than 400 per cent, and the average American's disposable income had itself increased five times.[22] The trouble was that no one was spending enough. A man had a decent suit, a nice hat, a good pair of shoes and a reliable car – why buy more when you're happy with what you have? It did not help that American products were well-made and irritatingly long-lasting. There was a real danger of over-production, crashing prices, and an end to America's economic rise. People had to be persuaded to consume much, much more – but how?

Half of the solution was to create the idea that perfectly good products were somehow no longer desirable and needed replacing. As Packard put it, 'One big and intimidating obstacle confronting the stimulators was the fact that most Americans already possessed perfectly usable stoves, cars, TV sets, clothes, etc. Waiting for those products to wear out or become physically obsolete before urging replacements upon the owner was intolerable. More and more, ad men began talking of the desirability of creating "psychological obsolescence".[23]

It's hard to imagine it now when we think a phone is no longer serviceable after a few months of use, but the very idea of fashion had to be created in the minds of many people in the middle of the twentieth century, particularly men. 'Being trendy' itself was a concept that had to be built up and managed in a country where many people were taught to work hard and not waste what they had. Puritan values still had a kind of hold. Things were worse in many parts of Europe, where the Depression and then wartime scarcity wove frugality deep into the social fabric. But by deploying, as Packard put it, 'the double-barrelled strategy of 1) making the public style-conscious, and then 2) switching styles',[24] new products could be created and sold much more quickly to people who already had enough of everything they actually needed. This move worked just as well with blenders and washing machines as it did with hats and blazers. Everything could be given new features or a new look each year, ideally making people dissatisfied with the 'old-fashioned' items they already had.

The other half of the solution was the creation of new psychological needs or the careful exploitation of old, buried ones. The famous example that combines both is the marketing of Listerine mouthwash. Originally sold as a surgical antiseptic, then a floor wash, and finally an unlikely treatment for gonorrhoea, it made serious money only when promoted as a cure for 'chronic halitosis', a term and a condition introduced to the wider world by the makers of Listerine themselves. Before their marketing campaign, hopeful suitors had no idea they were grossing out the ladies with their appalling breath. The ladies had no idea either. 'Don't fool yourself', an advert warned, the words hovering above the image of a woman staring suicidally at the floor next to a happy, dancing couple, patently and cheerfully breathing in one another's faces, 'Halitosis makes you unpopular'. What's more, 'you'll be the last person to notice'. Sales skyrocketed.

The trick of creating a sense of inadequacy still works spectacularly well – think of the many advertising messages that suggest you are lacking in some way, that you are too wrinkled, your clothes are not good enough, your hair isn't right, your skin is too oily or too dry – or worse, you have 'combination skin', a soul-destroying mixture of dry skin *and* oily skin. It's part of a larger strategy in which mere wants are transformed into desires that feel much more like needs. The distinction between wants and needs is nearly lost on us in the Western world of plenty, but it's clear that many of the 'must have' items shoppers sometimes literally fight over in the aisles are things that no one actually needs at all. The feeling of needing has been transferred to objects we actually only want. As Jim Pooler, professor of urban and population geography, has it: 'It can be argued that in our modern economy virtually all purchases, even those that appear to be excessive, reflect real needs on the part of shoppers, and that nothing less will satisfy them. A teenager just doesn't want the latest fashion trend. Rather in his mind it is absolutely essential that you have clothes or accessories that are in style … This is the essence of shopping in the modern economy, where virtually everything, no matter how superfluous, is perceived not as a want, but as a need.'[25]

According to Packard, the final factor that forced marketing people to take up new sorts of persuasive tactics was the fact that the goods on offer in an increasingly crowded marketplace were all more or less the same, all more or less equally good. Just about everything had reached a respectable level of quality thanks to standardisation and automation. One can of soup was just as good as another. Packard asks: 'How can you make a logical sales talk to a prospect to persuade him to swear by your brand when in truth the brands are essentially alike in physical characteristics?'[26] The solution, then as now, was to appeal to something other than logic and reason. Advertisers found ways to add what they called 'psychological value' to the more or less identical products lining the shelves. Once some hidden desire 'was identified and certified to be compelling', Packard explains, 'they began building the promise of its fulfilment into their sales presentations of such unlikely products as air conditioners, cake mixes, and motorboats.'[27] How exactly?

If all air conditioners are equally capable of cooling a house and nothing really makes one stand out over another, researchers suggested that manufacturers might consider playing on a potential customer's hidden need for emotional security and personal safety. The Weiss and Geller advertising agency's analysts discovered that some individuals have a strong if unconscious desire to return to the security of the womb, and this manifests itself in a need to feel enclosed and protected. Such people would rather not leave their windows open at night while they sleep, so either they miss out on the cooling night-time breeze or have a restless, nervous night next to an opened window. They are, however, an excellent market for air conditioners, and playing on their fears is a good way to improve sales.

For what it's worth, an entirely unscientific online search reveals that this psychological insight is still selling, whether or not it's in every case a deliberate attempt to play on the desire to return to the womb. Here are 'air conditioning and electrical installation specialists' Climatize UK making the pitch: 'The ability to keep doors and windows closed in the summer also improves the **security** of your home, especially at night time. With air conditioning installed, those sleeping in bedrooms at ground level can enjoy a safe and secure night's sleep!'[28]

Cake mixes are trickier because cakes themselves are apparently loaded with psychological symbolism. A market researcher found that 'baking a cake traditionally is acting out the birth of a child'.[29] Consciously or not, researchers revealed, the woman of the 1950s felt as though she was presenting her family with a new baby when she appeared with a freshly baked cake. This is why baking a cake is so delightful to her. The makers of instant cake mixes, which contained powdered eggs and milk, carried the instruction, 'Just Add Water', and this seemed to meet with unexpected resistance. The story goes that women encountered a psychological barrier because making a cake by just adding water was too easy. And if cake-making itself had symbolic attachments to pregnancy and childbirth, making a cake painlessly and effortlessly created feelings of guilt. Analysts suggested that women should be asked to add an egg to the mix, symbolising their own fertility, to restore the feeling of feminine creativity to cake-baking.[30]

Motorboat sales might be enhanced by selling not just boats, but the feeling of enhanced power the right boat might convey to the buyer. Car sales had for years been improved by marketing horsepower, bringing out new and slightly more powerful cars each year. According to one researcher, the major appeal of buying a new car for a man is that 'it gives him a renewed sense of power and reassures him of his own masculinity, an emotional need which his old car fails to deliver'.[31] The same thing was even truer on the water, where 'you can show that you are all man and let her rip – without having the fear you are bound to have on the road'.[32]

Other hidden needs were used to peddle more or less everything. Luggage-makers were told that they were actually selling a sense of self-worth to businessmen. Steam shovel manufacturers found ways to sell the experience of ego-gratification by downplaying the fact that the shovels did all the work and putting the operator's visual perspective into their advertisements. Life insurance salespeople could cater to our hidden desire for immortality by assuring potential policy-holders that their payments now would guarantee their continued control over their families' lives long after they themselves are dead. Even the promoters of Liberace were advised to employ Oedipus symbolism in order to sell his image to women 'beyond child-bearing age'.[33] Freudian thinking was all the rage, and whether or not you believe there's anything actually true in Freud's theories, his views about what makes us tick, particularly our hidden sexual urges, had wide-ranging effects on those exposed to this new wave of advertising.

But how were all of these hidden needs identified? Because they were thought to be deeply buried, concealed even from the person who has them, the methods used to uncover what people really want and think were of necessity mildly devious. Indirect probing elicited answers, and it was up to the analyst to interpret their true significance. As Lawrence R. Samuel puts it in *Freud on Madison Avenue*, 'The tools at these researchers' disposal were indeed impressive, ranging from sentence completion, word association, narrative projection, picture frustrations (illogical illustrations) and adaptations, free association to symbols, story association tests, description of others, thematic apperception test adaptations, shopping lists, error choice, and the Rorschach test. After analysing the "data" uncovered in hundreds of interviews using these tools came the tricky part – interpreting the results and drawing out the business implications.'[34]

People were shown cartoon images featuring a product and asked to make up a story about what they saw. Sentence completion tests – 'I like the feel of these socks because …' – were also helpful. Subjects were asked to put themselves in the place of the product and say whatever might occur to them. Researchers asked others to say the words that popped into their heads when they heard phrases or words that might figure into possible sales pitches. This alone could be revealing. Procter & Gamble decided to drop the word 'concentrated' from its soap packaging when word association tests revealed that 40 per cent of women thought it meant 'blessed by the pope'.[35]

Researchers also had recourse to the wonder that is the Szondi test. Subjects were shown photographs of a number of faces and asked who they would most like to sit next to on a long train journey. What they didn't know was that all the people in the photos suffered quite seriously from a particular mental illness. The thought at the time was that everyone was at least a little neurotic, and interviewees would pick the photo of the person whose madness they shared.[36] You could then sort your consumers into personality types and pitch your messages accordingly. Maybe the depressives get messages tilted towards the relief of their troubles. Different copy might be prepared to entice the phobics.

But the in-depth interview was the most important source of detailed information for many motivation researchers. The consumer was as good as reclining on the couch, and a careful analysis could finally begin.

*

The first person to use a 'psychological interview' to understand consumer behaviour was Paul Lazarsfeld, then a psychology lecturer at the University of Vienna. In 1930 a local laundry asked him if he could somehow help increase their trade. He conducted interviews and discovered that women didn't like sending out their laundry because it made them feel they weren't doing their job as housewives. It seemed like a cheat. Conversations with those who did use the service revealed that they were initially reluctant too, but some household emergency forced them to try it – the sudden arrival of unexpected guests, for example, made it impossible to do the job themselves. Once they discovered the convenience of having their laundry done for them, they usually stuck with it and became loyal customers. It was getting past that initial reluctance that was the problem.

Armed with these insights, Lazarsfeld recommended that the laundry dispatch a letter outlining their services to the families of people who had recently died, anticipating that this sort of emergency might be just the thing that would lead an otherwise proud housewife to try out the service. Business picked up quickly. Just five years later, Lazarsfeld was advising clients in New York and writing papers and book chapters explaining how 'consumer motivation' might be examined in an entirely new way. As Samuel puts it: 'Lazarsfeld's introduction of psychology-based, in-depth market research made a giant splash in a field in which counting bodies was the height of sophistication.'[37] But the undisputed master of the technique, and very much the manipulative villain of Packard's book, was Lazarsfeld's student Ernest Dichter.

Fleeing the rise of German nationalism, Dichter arrived in New York City and found work by writing to a dozen large firms, saying simply, 'I am a young psychologist from Vienna and I have some interesting new ideas which can help you be more successful, effective, sell more and communicate better with your potential clients.'[38] It landed him his first consulting job with *Esquire*, where he uncovered the perhaps unsurprising fact that men were very attracted to the magazine's nude photographs. What was surprising was his advice: rather than shying away from the nude images, he suggested that they be turned into a selling point by telling potential advertisers that gentlemen readers tend to spend a bit more time on these particular pages, so they should pay more to advertise on them.

But it was his open-ended psychological interviews and the unexpected, often sexually-charged discoveries that resulted from them that earned him the most attention. Eighteen months after his arrival with no clear job prospects and just $100 in his pocket, Dichter's unusual advice had shaken Madison Avenue sufficiently to earn him a write-up in *Time* magazine: 'It's futile to argue in advertising. So believes Dr Ernest Dichter, 32-year-old, Vienna-born psychologist … Psychology is of course no new thing in advertising, but Dr Dichter claims that practically all of it is hit-or-miss stuff, and that he is the first to apply to advertising really scientific psychology. That includes psycho-analysis – probing into the subconscious. Dr Dichter scoffs at advertising which tries to reason with potential customers, to scare them or lecture them on their shortcomings. He believes in tapping hidden desires and urges.'[39]

From the beginning Dichter understood that what a product was used for and how it looked were of course important in a way, but it was the *gestalt* or 'personality' of objects, the 'soul of the product' as he put it, that really mattered when it comes to our hidden motivations. He was the first to talk about a product's image – building this idea up from the psychological concept 'imago', the idealised image one person might have of another, say a child's image of her mother. The idea that a product had a personality in the minds of consumers, that interacting with something as simple as a lighter or bar of soap could have hidden, often sexualised meaning, was extraordinarily radical. It gave Dichter a unique position, a platform from which to offer a new kind of advice to the business world, and the business world listened.

How useful his advice was to the writer of advertising copy is another question. He reported that smoking was actually about satisfying 'oral erotic needs'. He discovered that while some men feared flying because of crashing, they also harboured a deeper fear of 'sexual relationships with strange women'. People who take Bufferin for their headaches have more hostility towards 'life and living' than the users of Anacin. Fibrous cereals 'make people feel like losers'.[40] It's not at all obvious how one might go about translating these insights into nifty slogans – 'Smoke Marlboro, *They'll* Satisfy Your Oral Erotic Needs!' – but it didn't matter much. Dichter was in demand.

Once hired, Dichter conducted hundreds of 'depth interviews' (his words) – inventing the 'focus group' (also his words) in the process. He examined the responses he was given for concealed clues about the hidden meanings of objects. He pored over the history of various ordinary things as they appear in art and literature, teasing out their psychological and cultural significance. He created a 'living laboratory' at his headquarters, a 26-room mansion he called 'The Institute for Motivational Research', filming and observing families in mock household settings, watching for clues to their true thoughts and desires. At one point he had as many as 70 people on his staff, a third of them social scientists, working with up to 2,000 part-time interviewers all over the country, conducting many thousands of focus group sessions with people from every conceivable walk of life on almost every product and service imaginable. He opened offices in Paris, Rome, London, Zurich and Frankfurt. His reports were incredibly detailed, some running to several hundred pages and even multiple volumes.

You can get something of a feel for the depth and breadth of his work by consulting his *Handbook of Consumer Motivations*. It's an extraordinary document, the product of twenty years of research and 2,500 studies undertaken in the United States, Europe, Canada, Latin America, Africa and Australia – all of it an attempt to understand the deeper meaning that ordinary objects have for the average person. It's clear that Dichter thinks that the things all around us, and our attitudes towards them, are as worthy of study as the extraordinary objects found in archaeological digs. He is very nearly moved to poetry by 'the thousand and one things which surround us from the first glimpse of the sleepy dawn to the last yawn and the feel of the pillow and the ticking of the clock in the night'.[41]

Butter represents plenty, and it must be rich and golden. A strange sense of mystery cloaks cheese – the subtle appreciation of cheese is on a par with the appreciation of art. Chicken is much less masculine than steak – the expression 'chickening out' is symbolic of this fact. Citrus fruits have always been symbols of abundance in a variety of cultures, their roundness and warm colours suggestive of the life-giving Sun. Cookies are feminine and must always be displayed in large quantities. As Carl Jung observed, the Phoenician goddess of fertility was called Ichthys, which means Fish, and for many people, not just Catholics, eating fish still has hidden religious connotations. Messiness and childishness are among the many psychological obstacles confronting jams and jellies. The act of cutting meat and tearing it with our teeth is more important to us than the meat's meatiness. Prunes are entirely without prestige, like desiccated spinsters, and they call to mind immediately and unfortunately their use as a laxative. Raisins, however, represent a return to nature. Rice suggests a strong, young fertile woman, particularly because it expands while cooking, and this partly explains why we fling it joyfully at newlyweds. Soup is thought to be endowed with magic, rejuvenating power. Spaghetti suggests family fun – but not canned spaghetti, which is associated with indignity in the minds of the upwardly mobile. Yogurt is a personal as opposed to family food, bought for private rather than shared consumption, more medicinal than nourishing. While cake is the most feminine of foods and meat the most masculine, roast chicken and oranges are in fact bisexual.[42]

All of that is the merest snippet of Dichter on fine form, teasing out the psychological meaning of various foods. In the book, he takes up clothing, household items, cosmetics, drugs, toys, cars, flowers, alcohol, cigarettes, and much more. Whether or not you think he's on to anything in all this, his studies changed the way products were marketed, presented, packaged and advertised, to people all over the world.

Ivory soap was among the first products to get the Dichter treatment. He interviewed 100 people, visited bath houses, and conducted research on the ritual meaning behind bathing, soap, cleanliness and purification. He discovered that the Saturday night bath had erotic overtones – some women told him that 'you never know what might happen' on a Saturday night. Bathing was also one of the few times a person had 'permission' to caress him or herself, and there was a kind of primal pleasure in the smooth, slippery soapiness of that gratifying contact. As he put it some years later, 'bathing, in its old, ritualistic, anthropological sense, is getting rid of all your bad feelings, your sins, your immorality, and cleansing yourself, baptism, etc'.[43] He suggested a slogan that might play on all this: 'Be Smart, get a fresh start with Ivory Soap.'

In a study for Chrysler he revealed that, 'to most people, a convertible is a symbol of perennial youth, of adventurousness, raciness, and boldness'.[44] While a man of a certain age knows his days of youthful adventure are behind him, he still likes looking wistfully at the convertible and dreaming a little, even though he'll eventually calm down and buy the much more reasonable sedan. Dichter discovered that a man in the market for a car settles on the sedan through 'a psychological process similar to the one a man goes through when he decides to give up his alluring mistress and marry a plain girl who will make a good wife and mother'.[45] Dichter told Chrysler that if they really wanted to sell more sedans they should give the prime display space to the curvaceous and racy red convertibles. Men will come in for the tempting little red number but come to their senses and leave with respectable sedans.

*

In trying to think your way through the meaning of this part of the shift from argumentation to psychologically-informed, largely covert persuasion, you can do a lot worse than to start with the objections first raised when these new tactics became known in the wider world. We are in a way used to all this now, or maybe numb to it, and hearing from those who first found it new and shocking might well snap us out of it.

Dichter clearly had shaky views about women, and a number of early objections to motivation research came from feminists in the early 1960s. Despite the changing times, Dichter was in favour not of gender equality but a sort of gender complementarity, the idea that men and women complement one another by fulfilling different roles in a relationship – men are the bread-winners and women are housewives and mothers, mostly helpmates to the man of the house.

It led him to think that consumer motivation itself was gendered and that products were also secretly gendered in the minds of shoppers. A masculine product was therefore doomed if it were advertised in a feminine way – as one observer put it, the worry was that anything 'too gay' would never sell.[46] He counselled against an advertisement showing a woman handing men their cigars – cigars being phallic, it was as if the men were being given permission to be men by the woman, and that would never resonate in the mind of a man who likes the idea of his well-proportioned cigar and its smoke powerfully taking over the room, making those around him uncomfortable.[47]

He thought the gender of toys might be more pronounced as well, eventually making recommendations that led to the absurd dimensions of the Barbie Doll. 'He interviewed girls about what they wanted in a doll', Hedy Dichter, his wife, recalled some years later. 'It turns out that what they wanted was someone sexy looking, someone that they wanted to grow up to be like. Long legs, big breasts, glamorous.'[48] Mothers didn't like the dolls from the start, and Dichter advised that they be sold on the idea that Barbie would help their children learn how to accessorise while they were young, so when they were older, fashion and make-up would be easier for them to understand.

Betty Friedan's *The Feminine Mystique* launched the second wave of feminism in the United States, and in it is an early critique of psychological manipulation in advertising. The book is about 'the problem that has no name', a vague feeling of unhappiness and frustration some women had, despite being financially well off and married with children. That kind of life was supposed to make women happy. 'The feminine mystique says that the highest value and the only commitment for women is the fulfillment of their own femininity', Friedan writes. 'The mistake, says the mystique, the root of women's troubles in the past is that women envied men, women tried to be like men,

instead of accepting their own nature, which can find fulfillment only in sexual passivity, male domination, and nurturing
maternal love.'[49] But many women actually wanted something
more than a husband and a family – some were in fact miserable housewives. The feminine mystique was a lie or at least an
illusion. The trouble is that motivation research and psychological advertising were reinforcing it on an extraordinarily
large scale.

In a chapter called 'The Sexual Sell', Friedan argues that the
facts as she had them do not add up. Women are miserable,
feeling trapped in the roles of mother and housewife, but all
this at a time when they have more opportunities than ever
before to pursue other kinds of lives. The explanation: 'some-
body, something pretty powerful must be at work.'[50] Part of
that power was branding and advertising. It pushed an image
of women as happy only when managing the home, doing
housework, looking after children – and buying the various
consumer goods required to accomplish all this. Women made
the vast majority of everyday purchases for the home. It made
sense to nurture in them a certain sort of self-image, create a
set of needs that could be satisfied by making purchases.

Friedan had the opportunity to sift through some of
Dichter's reports in his headquarters and discuss matters with
the man himself – one can imagine her eyes widening as she
turned over page after page of analysis reinforcing the stereotypes she believed perpetuated the feminine mystique. 'I
learned *how* it happened', she writes, 'when I went to see a man
who is paid approximately a million dollars a year for his professional services in manipulating the emotions of American
women to serve the needs of business.'[51] As Friedan saw it, the

advertising world deliberately endeavoured to keep women thinking of themselves as housewives, because those engaged in motivational research believed that women with a particular kind of self-image can be given 'a sense of identity, purpose, creativity ... the self-realization, even the sexual joy they lack – by the buying of things'.[52]

Friedan pulled no punches. Corporations and advertisers didn't create the idea that women could be happy only as wives and mothers, but they certainly kept it going, maybe strengthened it in the minds of women: 'it is their millions which blanket the land with persuasive images, flattering the American housewife, diverting her guilt and disguising her growing sense of emptiness.'[53] Perhaps 1950s depth research really did get in the way of the liberation of women and, if Friedan is right, a number of human lives were much less fulfilling than they might have otherwise been as a result. But extrapolate from that possibility to today, and you might be able to think of a vast number of types, not just housewives, but all of us – sports fans, hipsters, conscientious consumers, career women, and a thousand other 'lifestyles' – all of them reinforced and kept slightly miserable by the message that they can be made happy only 'by the buying of things'.

There was, and perhaps still is, a need to create a certain kind of consumer to fit the products mass-produced, and in the 1950s and 60s that meant pushing on women the notion of a dutiful housewife and devoted mother. Perhaps as bad as this was the cultivation and manipulation of guilt in the minds of women who might have already had their own misgivings about finding non-traditional roles. This might be a special case of a more general objection to this kind of modern persuasion

– the perpetuation of stereotypes and anxieties in an effort to increase consumption. We'll see it again in a moment.

In a critical piece on motivation research that appeared in 1953, the writer Robert Graham raised two solid concerns of his own. 'First, the social scientist is the inheritor of three thousand years of western man's effort to understand himself. The psychologist of today stands on the summit of a great mountain whose mass is composed of immense boulders, the brains of Aquinas and Leonardo and Descartes and Jefferson and countless others. At the very peak, it would appear, squats the head-shrinker, intoning unctuously, "Madam, tell me what you really think of this plastic commode."'[54]

Graham's objection is, as he puts it, 'a charge of common prostitution', but I think there's more to it than that. The long conversation humanity has been having with itself – the ongoing attempt that began with the Greeks, the hope that we might be able to understand ourselves and our place in the universe – is in a way one of the most extraordinary things about us, one of the most valuable features of human nature and human culture. It's precious, and its value is lost when it is used merely instrumentally, to get into our heads and sell us stuff we don't need. It's not just the squatting head-shrinker who's demeaned, *pace* Graham, it's all of us.

Packard comes near to wondering what this use of our cultural heritage does to us too: 'All this probing and manipulation has its constructive and amusing aspects; but also, I think it fair to say, it has seriously antihumanistic implications. Much of it seems to represent regress rather than progress for man in his long struggle to become a rational and self-guiding being.'[55] It is, Packard suspects, sometimes a struggle to turn away from our dubious, perhaps base desires for mere self-gratification, towards the better angels of our nature, the higher things in a happy, flourishing human life. We really are only recently down from the trees. Persuasion that leans on our non-rational levers puts ever more pressure on us to listen to the darker parts of ourselves. If being reasonable is a kind of effort for us nearly hairless apes, given the kind of creatures we are, then manipulating us by treating us as unreasonable bundles of hidden desires is more than a step backwards in that struggle. It diminishes us much more than we think.

Graham goes on: 'The second point concerns the fact that the social scientist knows a great deal about the workings of the human mind. He knows of certain things that might be called national neuroses – the excessive and almost morbid desire for security, for example. Suppose the social scientist tells the adman how to play upon these neuroses … If prejudice or anxiety is played upon it may be increased or it may even be inculcated when it was not present in the first place.'[56]

Maybe this is a kind of broadening of Friedan's worry or a variation on it. It's not only gender stereotypes that are being exploited and cultivated, but general human fears and anxieties. The social scientist in the pay of big business has a kind of edge, knows what makes us tick. By playing on our insecurities, those very insecurities might be enhanced, or shaped into new kinds of imbalances. Hearing a large number of messages from advertisers who know what really bothers us, what we're afraid of, must increase our insecurities. It might create new ones too. It certainly can't do our sanity much good.

Packard ends his book by asking how certain uses of motivation research can possibly be morally justified.[57] How can it be morally right, he wonders, to encourage someone to be irrational and impulsive when buying food for their family? What's the moral justification for manipulating children with advertising, long before they have the critical faculties that might protect them? Echoing Friedan and Graham, he asks, 'What is the morality of playing upon hidden weaknesses and frailties – such as our anxieties, aggressive feelings, dread of conformity, and infantile hangovers – to sell products?' How can it possibly be right to encourage wastefulness through the mechanism of psychological obsolescence, particularly when some human beings have so very little?

For his part, Dichter responded to at least some of these criticisms. He also did very well from the exposure brought to him by Packard's various attacks and wrote a letter thanking him for the welcome new business. Dichter thought that there was nothing wrong with identifying real human desires, nothing wrong with living a hedonistic lifestyle. Part of his mission, as he saw it, was to give us permission to enjoy ourselves following the deprivations of war. As we consume, both our lives and our economy improve. It's important that we never quite have everything we want. Unleashing desire, increasing our wanting and striving, all this is the secret to the good life, or so Dichter believed. As he put it: 'Our role, as scientific communicators, as persuaders, is one of liberating these desires, not in an attempt to manipulate but in an attempt to move our economic system forward and with it our happiness ... The real definition of happiness is what I call constructive discontent. Getting there is all, not just half, the fun. Stress and insecurity and whatever its labels may be, are the most beneficial movers and springs of our life: Trying to reach a goal but having the goal recede is the real mystery of happiness.'[58] If we got everything we wanted we'd be miserable. A world stoked by advertising – creating and not quite fulfilling desires, endlessly cultivating stresses that can be satisfied only by the buying of things – this offers human beings the prospect of true happiness.

But with hindsight it now looks as though the opposite is true. 'Compared with their grandparents, today's young adults have grown up with much more affluence, slightly less happiness and much greater risk of depression and assorted social pathology', as David G. Myers, professor of psychology, sees it. 'Our becoming much better off over the last four decades has not been accompanied by one iota of increased subjective well-being.'[59] There is in fact a lot of evidence, appearing since the mid-1980s, for the conclusion that people with materialistic values are actually psychologically worse off than people who value other sorts of things. And materialism undermines not just individual happiness, but social cohesion as well.

Researchers Tim Kasser and Richard Ryan prepared a questionnaire designed to measure what really matters to people, called 'The Aspiration Index'. In it they present a number of different goals: such things as feeling safe, helping others, and having good family relationships, on one hand, and being your own boss, having a job that pays well, and buying whatever you want on the other. Respondents were asked to rate each one: is it not at all important, somewhat important, or extremely important? They were also asked questions aiming to assess positive feelings of well-being and negative feelings associated with depression and anxiety. The results were straightforward: 'When financial success is relatively central to [our] aspirations, low well-being, high distress, and difficulty adjusting to life are also evident. Although we cannot be sure from these results whether materialistic values cause unhappiness, or whether other factors are at work, the results do suggest a rather startling conclusion: the American dream has a dark side, and the pursuit of wealth and possessions might actually be undermining our well-being.'[60]

A large number of studies undertaken with British, Danish, German, Indian, Romanian, Russian and South Korean people replicate this result: 'Strong materialistic values are associated with a pervasive undermining of people's well-being, from low life satisfaction and happiness, to depression and anxiety, to physical problems such as headaches, and to personality disorders, narcissism, and antisocial behaviour.'[61]

Does advertising and the inculcation of materialistic values actually *cause* unhappiness or do they just sometimes go together for some unknown reason? It's possible that a childhood of deprivation leads both to materialistic values and unhappiness; in other words, they're both caused by something else. Maybe the causal arrow points in the other direction: unhappy people try to do something about it by pursuing wealth and surrounding themselves with things. It's also possible that people who are materialistic tend to be unhappy not because of the values they have but because the pursuit of wealth and objects crowds out the time they might spend on other things that would make their lives better. The relationship might be mutually causal: unhappiness leads to retail therapy, which leads back to unhappiness, which is temporarily relieved by another round of shopping, and so on. Some maintain that having lots of material comforts and getting used to the finer things in life itself undermines the pleasure one might have taken in ordinary things – if you've done a lot of fine dining you might not appreciate a cold beer as much as someone who eats more simply than you do. It's also worth remembering that all of this applies only to people who have attained a certain standard of living. Pursuing money and things might lead to unhappiness and anxiety, but only if you're some way clear of poverty in the first place.

A series of recent studies suggest that materialistic values really do cause an undesirable raft of anti-social behaviour, narcissistic feelings, anxiety and unhappiness.[62] Perhaps more unsettling, it appears that a materialistic mind-set can be temporarily activated in anyone exposed to a certain sort of cueing.

Researchers showed one group images of luxury goods – high-end electronics, jewellery, cars and the like – while another group viewed just natural scenes. Merely seeing images associated with high consumption resulted in increased reports of depression, anxiety, self-dissatisfaction, and a lower interest in social activities than the control group. But it's not just feelings that are affected. In another study designed to explore the social ramifications of what researchers called 'situational materialism', subjects were presented with a water shortage problem that required some rationing and possibly collaboration with others. Some heard language that framed the problem as affecting either local individuals or local consumers. Merely characterising the problem as one for consumers resulted in a reduction in feelings of personal responsibility, lower trust in other people, and a reduction in willingness to cooperate.

The implications are worrying for people like us, people who are exposed to advertising almost constantly. As the authors of that study put it: 'The kinds of cues that triggered situational materialism in these experiments are highly analogous to features of everyday life that are extremely commonplace in contemporary postindustrial societies. Advertising, which depicts an endless parade of desirable commodities, is highly similar to the pictorial primes we used ... Framing information in terms of its relevance to consumers (rather than, e.g., citizens), as is very common in media discourse, is analogous to the framing manipulations we employed.'[63] It's not much of a stretch to conclude that even a person who does not think of herself as particularly materialistic will nevertheless have that undesirable raft of anti-social behaviour, narcissistic feelings, anxiety and unhappiness activated whenever she is exposed to advertising. And while the effects might be temporary, 'it probably is not long until another [cue] comes along to reignite materialistic concerns and their negative implications for affect and social engagement'.[64]

If Dichter and the captains of industry pushing consumption in the middle of the twentieth century were wrong about human happiness, they were certainly right about the economy. Creating in us the desire to consume more than we need, activating psychological obsolescence and all the rest of it actually has built an enormous market in the West, a market that has lately expanded to the East and the South, creating new consumer desires along the way. We spend an astonishing amount of money on this literally depressing project. At the moment, global advertising spending is expected to pass half a trillion dollars within a year.[65] It might well cost us a very great deal more than that in terms of well-being, environmental degradation, and losses to the social world. We got the market right at the cost of getting human happiness all wrong.

Left to Our Devices

'We live in a society exquisitely dependent on
science and technology, in which hardly anyone
knows anything about science and technology.'

CARL SAGAN

The girl's father could see no reason to be stoic about it. He appeared at his local Target, a department store somewhere on the outskirts of Minneapolis, and confronted the store's manager in person. 'My daughter got this in the mail!' he shouted. 'She's still in high school, and you're sending her coupons for baby clothes and cribs? Are you trying to encourage her to get pregnant?' The manager didn't know anything about it, but he apologised on behalf of the store. Maybe it was some sort of computer glitch, but in any case it wouldn't happen again. The manager called some days later, to follow up and apologise for a second time, but the father was now contrite. 'I had a talk with my daughter', he said. 'It turns out there's been some activities in my house I haven't been completely aware of. She's due in August.'[1]

The coupons were no coincidence, and there certainly was no computer glitch. Target knew about the girl's pregnancy before her father did. Like most large retail chains, Target has been storing and analysing data about its customers for many years, perhaps decades. Target assigns each shopper a 'Guest ID Number' and uses this to track every purchase, and ties this information to other facts about us. It's hard to be sure, as stores are understandably unwilling to admit to much, but major stores track such things as credit card details, a customer's marital status, whether or not a shopper has children, email addresses, the point of sale, and the time of day purchases are made. All of this can be coupled with much more finely-grained and personal information – political interests, credit ratings, past bankruptcies or legal troubles, education history, charitable donations, and now much more nuanced information gleaned from our social media profiles, search histories and other virtual interactions – all of it purchased from suppliers in the business of acquiring and selling data. It's not known for sure how much shops like Target know about us. What's clear is that it's in their interest to know as much as they can.

This is because Target also knows an important fact about our general behaviour as consumers. Once we settle into buying habits, we tend to keep them. If the toothpaste is acceptable, given that we're creatures who stick with defaults, we're likely to use it for as long as we've got teeth. But marketing teams know there are fabled moments of flexibility in a human life, instances in which purchasing decisions become gloriously unmoored from the habits of a lifetime, and new customers can be won over. Buying a house, starting a degree, marriage, divorce, losing a job and the death of a family member all offer the salesperson superb moments of intervention, a chance to sell new products and ingrain new kinds of habits. But the possibilities associated with the birth of a first child are very nearly endless. A huge number of new purchasing decisions must be made – nappies, formula, cribs, clothing, car seats, blankets, toys and on and on – all of it under some duress and on the basis of almost no previous experience. It's the stuff of a salesperson's dreams.

Target, along with almost every other large company interested in selling you something, devotes considerable resources to 'predictive analytics'. In part, this entails the use of a vast range of computer models and algorithms geared to crunch numbers and identify who might be most easily persuaded to buy something. It's used for many things, from improving customer retention to cross-selling, the practice of selling you something more when you make an initial purchase. Buying shoes? Why not pick up some shoe polish too? But more than this, it's now known that people with a certain profile are more likely to succumb to a certain sales pitch than others – not just the buyers of shoes, but suburban mothers with eleven-year-old boys, recently retired widowers, college students or newly married couples. Finding out who you are and what people like you might purchase is now the business of PhDs in the employ of large marketing firms.

For its part, Target put a statistician called Andrew Pole on this particular case, charging him with identifying pregnant shoppers. Anyone can locate parents – they're the ones with the children – but identifying a pregnant woman well before it all gets obvious and she is on the verge of changing the shopping habits of a lifetime – that is exceptionally valuable from a sales point of view. In an exposé for *The New York Times*, Charles Duhigg writes: 'Target has a baby-shower registry, and Pole started there, observing how shopping habits changed as a woman approached her due date ... Many shoppers purchase soap and cotton balls, but when someone suddenly starts buying lots of scent-free soap and extra-big bags of cotton balls, in addition to hand sanitisers and washcloths, it signals they could be getting close to their delivery date.'[2]

Pole found that an interconnected analysis of 25 products enabled him to assign each shopper a 'pregnancy prediction score'. He could also forecast due dates with considerable accuracy. Pole's programmes were set loose on Target's national database, and this enabled delighted marketing teams to home in on tens of thousands of women who were very probably pregnant, and tailor messages directly to them.

This, apparently, is what happened to the pregnant teenager in Minneapolis. It's part of a relatively new form of persuasion, and it exists not just in the retail world – political messages are also focused in this way, particularly during election campaigns. Regardless of their actual views, candidates can direct the most persuasive images and words at precisely the subset of the voting public likely to be moved by them. Religious families in southern US states could hear a campaign pitch entirely different from the one pointed to Midwestern farmers or those loading container ships in Seattle. If your computer's history and your digital footprint tells one story, a website requesting a donation to a political party will appear differently to you than it might to me, and the calls and emails we receive in the run-up to a vote might make different claims too.

The value of a grip on demographics has been known for some time, but this looks at least relatively new, a souped-up and remarkably powerful descendant of a practice once called 'narrowcasting' to distinguish it from broadcasting. Years ago, advertisers and others could get their messages out by simply 'road blocking' the few major television or radio networks – showing the same ad at the same time across all channels, ensuring everyone saw it. But as the devices and the methods we use to encounter content shift and change, as the techniques to gather data about us become more refined, as individuals discover ways to dodge traditional forms of messaging, and as information technology in all its forms evolves, persuasive messages can now be broadcast not just generically to everybody, but very specifically, very individually, directly to us precisely when and where the statistics and computer models indicate that we are most vulnerable to them.

Target quickly learned to camouflage adverts meant to appeal to pregnant women by including coupons for other things like lawnmowers and tool-sets in their offers. It makes the store appear less creepily prescient while still delivering the message to its intended audience, albeit on the sly. This, it seems likely, points to the future shape of persuasion, at least in the short term. At the end of this chapter, we'll finally engage in some obligatory but, I admit, entirely ill-advised reflection on new persuasive practices, what they are now and where they seem to be headed.

Our speculations here can only be guesses, but maybe you can get a feel for the future by considering a part of the contemporary landscape of persuasion that you encounter almost daily – the retail world. Target's predictive power is just a small sliver of it. Those who sell us things have created a number of very heavily funded persuasion laboratories, all engaged in a high-stakes arms race, creating and discovering new ways to influence us. Here you can find the latest thinking about persuasion, informed by and realised in new technology. Something as simple as the layout of a store, and your behaviour in it, is now subject to a great deal of testing and theorising. In a carefully conceptualised shop, nothing, not even what seems to you like an impulse buy, is left to chance.

*

The entrance to a shop is called the 'landing strip', 'decompression zone' or, for those who prefer their terminology a bit more sinister-sounding, the 'Gruen Transfer', named after the Austrian architect Viktor Gruen, who had views about the entrances of shopping malls. Consumer psychologists have discovered that, as you walk along the city streets or make your way into a store from the car park, you move at a particular pace, your mind is alert and focused on the navigational task at hand, and it takes a moment to downshift from that accelerated mental and physical speed to the slower, more meandering steps you take as you walk along the aisles browsing the displays of a store. As one expert puts it, the mind needs time and space to make 'a switch from rational and attentive thinking to a more impulsive and automatic mode of thought'.[3] The landing strip is therefore almost entirely worthless from a retail point of view, because shoppers have not yet made the transition to shopping mode and will probably not notice any merchandise displayed within it.

So you might find a large stockpile of trolleys and baskets, checkout aisles, bag recycling bins and customer information desks there. In some shops the landing strip might seem like empty space, but in fact its bright carpeting is meant to serve as a visual edge or psychological speed bump that might slow you down to shopping speed. Others wisely attempt to blur the space and accelerate your transition from walker to shopper by arranging merchandise outside, around the entrance. Some stores try to snap you out of it by placing something striking in your way – brightly coloured flowers, a rack of newspapers you might linger over, or a so-called Power Wall emblazoned with lurid special offers and the trigger word 'SALE' prominently displayed in bright, arresting colours.

If the store is remotely on top of things, the rest of the place will also have been meticulously planned and tested, down to the location of items on individual shelves and the shape and colour of those items. When you enter a shop and make the transition through the decompression zone, you have given yourself over to retail persuasion. Like nudging, it's persuasion without an obvious message – there's nothing for you to deliberate about, but your mind is nevertheless changed. It's persuasion built into the architecture itself.

Consider first those carts and baskets – they raise questions in the minds of careful store-planners. According to research informed by the notion of embodied cognition that we have already encountered in the chapter on political persuasion and metaphor, which object you choose, cart or basket, might well make a difference to the number of 'vice' or 'impulse' buys you end up with at the counter. The physical movements associated with using a basket, when you lift and carry it, are similar to those you make when you pull something close to you. It's called 'arm flexion', as opposed to 'arm extension', which is the movement you make when you push something away. Compare a bicep curl to a press-up and you'll see the difference. Entirely unconsciously, you have been subjected to a lifetime of classical conditioning when it comes to moving your body in these two ways. You have learned to attach positive associations to pulling things close and negative associations to pushing things away.

There is a lot of experimental evidence in support of this connection between thought and movement. In one representative study, some subjects were asked to press down on a desk top, while others were asked to press upwards on the bottom of a desk. Both groups were then presented with novel stimuli – in this case, a series of Chinese ideograms – and asked simply if they liked or disliked what they saw. The ones pressing up, engaged in arm flexion, rated many more of the images positively than those pressing down, engaging in arm extension.[4] Similar changes to attitudes can be created, bizarrely, by putting a pen in your mouth in various ways. Bite down on it with your teeth and you simulate the muscular contractions associated with smiling; use your lips to hold it, and you mimic a frown. In one experiment, people holding pens in these ways came to different conclusions about how funny cartoons were. Those simulating smiles 'reported more intense humor responses' than those mimicking frowns.[5]

Researchers conducted a number of tests to determine what effects carrying a basket and pushing a trolley have on purchasing decisions. They found that carrying a basket increases the likelihood of 'purchasing vice products' like chocolate bars rather than fruit, as well as a preference for 'smaller, sooner' over 'larger, later' monetary rewards.[6] It turns out that those pushing trolleys are more risk-averse and long-termist, while those carrying baskets are inclined to live in the moment – all tended to make purchases accordingly. (While you are likely to buy more when you push a trolley, it might be worth using one if you're trying to lose weight.) The authors speculate that even the design of a shop's front door can influence purchasing decisions: 'Our studies also suggest that pulling a door to enter a building, rather than pushing that same door, could lead to purchases of products that entail immediate benefits ... Shops selling vice products or companies selling insurance may want to consider how a customer needs to open a door.'[7] They go so far as to wonder whether driving a car with a manual transmission or an automatic plays some role in the number of burgers we order at drive-through windows.

The number of items you actually buy in a store is largely dependent on a single variable: how much time you spend shopping. The longer you shop, the more likely you are to succumb to impulse buying. Whether or not you make an impulsive purchase itself largely depends on the perception, accurate or otherwise, of the existence of a sale item, something regarded as a deal. It almost goes without saying that it's the shops that helpfully identify such deals. Estimates vary, but it's thought that 40 per cent of groceries are sold as part of some sort of sale or special offer, and as supermarket sales are worth something in the region of £160 billion a year, the temptation simply to create artificial promotions is perhaps overpowering.[8] It's hard to say how widespread fake sale prices and confusing promotions are, but the independent consumer organisation Which? recently filed a 'supercomplaint' with a regulatory body in the UK, following on from years of careful research, outlining what it called 'misleading and opaque pricing practices in the grocery market'.[9]

Large-name supermarkets were found to offer products at a

'reduced' cost for far longer than at what they claimed was the 'standard' price. Sainsbury's, to take one of many examples, sold handwash for £1.80 for seven days before generously offering it as 'Was £1.80 now £1' for the next 84 days. Asda sold a pack of rice for £1, but put up the price to £1.58 precisely when it established a 'multibuy sale price' of two packs for £3, in effect making it 50p more expensive per pack while creating the illusion of a sale. Which? uncovered a very large range of other dubious methods used to increase revenue, including seasonal offers that depended on higher pricing when the product was out of season and not being purchased anyway, shrinking package sizes without a corresponding drop in price, and inconsistent, even illegible unit prices, making comparison shopping very difficult. They conclude that misleading pricing alone could dupe UK consumers out of £1 billion a year.[10]

Estimates of how much we spend on impulsive purchases, including such 'deals', are all over the place – some surveys indicate that 40 per cent of us spend more than we intend on any given shopping trip;[11] one estimates that 60 to 70 per cent of purchases made in supermarkets are unplanned;[12] one report has it that the average British person spends more than £71,000 on impulse purchases in a lifetime;[13] another found that even during the recession UK shoppers spent £1.2 billion a year on kitchen gadgets, exercise equipment, clothing and accessories they never or rarely use.[14] Whatever it is, those looking into it agree that it's a lot of money. Very few of us leave a shop carrying only the items on a shopping list.

So efforts are made to keep you in the store for as long as possible and to tune the environment as required to maximise the chances of your making a purchase. Even minor changes, rolled out nationally across a brand or throughout a chain, can result in tens of millions more in revenue. It's well known that the items you probably need – like bread and milk in grocery stores and prescription medication in pharmacies – are deliberately placed at the back, to force you to spend more time in the presence of products you might be tempted to buy. No doubt it's also obvious that shops are trying to make a good first impression by placing fresh fruit and vegetables, flowers or high-quality items up front, rather than toilet paper and bin bags. (Toilet paper, tampons and nappies are often sequestered together on the same aisle to limit our exposure to them and thus avoid the so-called 'yuk factor', which has been found to lead to less spending.) And putting a lot of special offers, eye-catching, novel 'seasonal' items, sweets or newspapers and magazines around people who are bored, hungry, tired and stuck waiting to check out is another obvious tactic.

But what's perhaps less well-known is a recent change in shops' understanding of how to structure absolutely everything – from the location and appearance of items on individual shelves to the shelves, displays, departments and stores themselves. In the last few decades or so, retail planners have had recourse to the new discipline of consumer anthropology and, even more recently, neuromarketing.

*

In the late 1970s, Paco Underhill was among the first of a new sort of market researcher who applied insights from anthropology and environmental psychology to human behaviour out in the wild of retail environments. He observed shoppers, as an anthropologist might observe some newly encountered tribe, and learned what he could about their behaviour. As he puts it in his account of his discoveries, *Why We Buy: The Science of Shopping*, his subject matter is vast: the way consumers interact with 'every rack, shelf, counter and table display of merchandise, every sign, banner, brochure, directional aid and computerized interactive informational fixture, the entrances and exits, the windows and walls, the elevators and escalators, and stairs and ramps, the cashier lines and teller lines and counter lines and restroom lines and every inch of every aisle'.[15] He and a team of 'trackers' watch and record the movements of shoppers in extraordinary detail – measuring how long they study labels, exactly how they move through stores, how and when they pick up items, what signs and labels they read and how much time they spend reading them, sometimes using slow-motion video to capture every nuance. They hide behind potted plants and peer around corners, armed with stopwatches, video recorders, computers and questionnaires, following shoppers, taking note of everything they do – countless data points are cross-referenced and analysed.

Human beings pick up persuasive messages not just in traditional advertising, Underhill says, but by walking around and being influenced by the aisles and displays while shopping. A store is, as he puts it, 'a walk in container for words and thoughts and messages and ideas'.[16] The thing, if structured correctly, exerts a large influence on those who move within it.

In a few years, by Underhill's estimate, he and his teams have measured 900 'different aspects of shopper-store interaction'. He has discovered a very great deal about our shopping behaviour, and much of this has been used in various ways by his corporate clients to change the way shops affect us, and of course to increase sales. A number of his discoveries have to do with gender differences. For example, 65 per cent of men who try on jeans in fitting rooms will end up purchasing them, compared to 25 per cent of women – it is therefore a good idea to encourage men to try things on.[17] 86 per cent of women look at price tags, but only 72 per cent of men do – a retailer might therefore be more likely get away with mark-ups on some items aimed at men rather than women. A woman shopping with a female companion spends on average 8 minutes and 15 seconds in a store, but a woman hurried along by a man spends just 4 minutes and 41 seconds shopping. If you want to keep women in your store, you should find ways to distract their men.[18]

Many of Underhill's discoveries are simply about how we move around in shops. People slow down near mirrors and walk faster past banks. In general, we drift right when we walk through a shop and tend to pick things up that we find on our right – so stores ought to put what they want to shift most in the front right of a store, just past the landing strip. The space to the right of a top seller on any shelf is valuable for similar reasons.[19] People tend to walk as far down an aisle as they must in order to find what they want, typically retreating back out the way they came – hardly anyone marches all the way down every aisle – so shops are advised to place the most desirable items in the middle, to ensure that we walk at least half way in. Because we walk facing forwards, we have to turn our heads to see what's on offer in the aisles, so there's no guarantee that we'll spot everything that's stocked. But the 'endcaps' or displays on the ends of aisles are right in front of anyone on the approach to an aisle. They're extremely eye-catching and therefore lucrative spaces – so stores load them with sale items and impulse buys.[20]

But it's not just our own movements that affect how we think and feel in a shop. It turns out, for example, that tie racks placed too close to an exit can underperform because people browsing them are sometimes bumped from behind by others making their way out of the store. People are unlikely to carry on examining ties because the jostling from behind makes them uncomfortable, and they move on. Underhill has named the phenomenon 'butt-brush'.[21]

Since Underhill's early days of following people around, a large number of consultancies and marketing departments are now devoted to dissecting and analysing consumer behaviour *in situ*. We are now the object of intensive scientific study, like any other naturally occurring object, and with a certain degree of knowledge comes a level of control. As psychology professor and author of *The Power of Persuasion* Robert Levine concludes, 'consumer anthropologists know more about your habits than you do. They can bounce you through a store like a billiard ball.'[22]

*

When parts of the brain become more active, blood vessels dilate, and blood flows in with much-needed supplies of the brain's fuel, oxygen and glucose. Blood contains iron atoms, and their movements create changes in the magnetic field surrounding them. Functional magnetic resonance imaging (fMRI) detects the changes associated with increased blood flow and therefore brain activity. In short, fMRI scans tell you which part of the brain is active, and if you also know something about which bits are associated with which mental functions – such things as memory, perception, pleasure and pain, judgement, emotion, planning and so on – then you can begin to make educated guesses about what a person is thinking and feeling when exposed to products, packaging, advertising messages and web pages. This is the hope held out by practitioners of neuromarketing. It's suggested by some that fMRI scans can spot mental activity below the threshold of conscious awareness, revealing facts about our minds that have effects on what we think and feel and do but that are introspectively unavailable to us. By understanding and finding ways to affect these subconscious processes, it's possible that persuasive messages, if it's still right to call them that, can bypass whatever conscious defences we might have and influence us without our knowledge.

In a seminal paper published in 2004, researchers performed a variation on the Pepsi Challenge on subjects in an fMRI scanner – they conducted blind taste tests as well as tests in which subjects knew what they were drinking – and discovered what many take to be the neural correlates of the mighty effects of brand power. Coke and Pepsi are, the authors point out, 'nearly identical in chemical composition, yet humans routinely display strong subjective preferences for one or the other'.[23] In anonymous taste tests, they found that there was almost nothing in it. A nearly equal number of people preferred Pepsi as preferred Coke. So Pepsi should have had an equal market share, but instead it trailed Coke by a substantial margin. When subjects were given brand information, when they knew that they were drinking Coke, they suddenly had a strong preference for it. What explains this shift in attitudes?

The results of the fMRI scans got attention in marketing circles and beyond. The researchers found that different parts of the brain were active in the anonymous trials and in the branded trials. When all subjects had to go on was an anonymous taste, a part of the prefrontal cortex was active, the bit associated with appetite and reward (both drinks are physiologically rewarding, in so far as they're both sugary, so this is unsurprising). But when subjects knew it was Coke, entirely different parts of the brain swung into action, the parts associated with memory, emotion, thinking, judging, and, the authors speculate, 'recalling cultural information that biases preference judgements'.[24] Here, perhaps, was proof of the power of the Coke brand as revealed in the indisputable results of a brain scan. Taste a sugary brown liquid and part of your brain reacts to the taste. Drink a Coke, however, and the experience is enhanced, processed by different parts of your brain, transformed by brand messaging, by everything you have been made to think and feel about Coke. It is, after all, 'the real thing', and although it's true that all real things, including cans of Pepsi, are also real things, the fact that Coke is a real thing somehow matters very much to us. The commercial application of this kind of information was not lost on those in the business of branding and selling.

In 2001, there were just two firms billing themselves as experts in the techniques of what is now called neuromarketing – the word 'neuromarketing' appeared only in 2002. There are now more than 300 such companies, alongside neuromarketing departments in more traditional research companies. There are university degrees in the subject.[25]

Neuromarketers make use of much more than just fMRI technology.[26] Electroencephalography (EEG) is the measuring and recording of electrical activity on the scalp. Neurons are electrically charged, and when enough of them are active, they shift a lot of positively charged atoms around. The resulting electrical activity can be detected by monitors just outside the skull. There's disagreement about how to break it all down, but different electrical frequencies appearing in different places on the head are thought to be associated with particular mental events. While an fMRI scan requires a subject to remain motionless, flat on her back in a large machine, an EEG can operate on someone who is sitting comfortably, even moving around, inconvenienced only by the wearing of a shower cap of electrodes. The things can be worn in a store, most of the machine slung in a backpack, with the results recorded in real time, weighed microsecond by microsecond against a subject's every move as she shops.

This is thought to be particularly useful information when synchronised with the results of eye-tracking devices – what you are thinking and feeling can be correlated with what you are looking at. Some trackers follow the eye by following objects embedded into specially made contact lenses. Others bounce infrared light off the cornea and keep tabs on the reflection with a tiny video camera. Such devices measure where and how long the eye fixates and how it moves from fixation point to fixation point. A resulting track of fixations and movements can be used to generate 'scan paths' or 'gaze plots' that show exactly how the eye travels over, say, a magazine advert, television commercial, website, aisle, package or shop front. Data from a number of individual plots can be brought together and turned into 'heat maps', tracing multiple eye tracks over advertising imagery, representing where the visual action is by lighting up hot-spots with red, indicating a lot of interest from a lot of people, down to blue for much less. More information about pupil dilation and blink rate – both associated with attention and arousal – can be gathered at the same time by more sophisticated machines.

Yet more can be discovered by monitoring the mostly automatic, purely biological responses we have to what we sense around us, responses that are closely associated with the experience of emotion. Finger pulse meters and blood pressure monitors detect changes to the heart rate – a quickened pulse belying emotion and excitement. Saliva swabs might be taken to determine quantities of cortisol, a steroid naturally present when we experience stress. Facial electromyography can be used to monitor the sometimes very small, nearly undetectable electrical impulses associated with the voluntary and involuntary contraction of facial muscles. These tiny muscular twitches are thought to indicate both conscious and unconscious emotional reactions. The electrical conductance of the skin varies with the amount of sweat we produce, and this too can be measured and used to gauge our emotional state.

How is all of this information actually used? There's a lot of variation among practitioners. Some focus on the brute elements of perception. As David Lewis, one of the pioneers of neuromarketing, has it, 'the Givens are everything the consumer can see, hear, feel, touch, smell and possibly taste about a product. Neuromarketing can help identify which aspects of the Givens are most likely to appeal and which to appal.'[27] This is most valuable at the prototype stage. Using the many devices at her disposal, a neuromarketer can place variations on packaging and advertising before test subjects and attempt to gauge, for example, where and how our eyes move around the page or product; whether our emotional responses are positive or negative; whether the images are memorable, exciting, disgusting, or sexually arousing; and whether our critical faculties are engaged or offline. The prototype advert or product that pushes the best buttons might then be recommended and rolled out.

Some of the results Lewis cites are not at all predictable or easy to explain. Consider the first of his Givens, what we see. Something as basic as colour and lighting can have unexpected effects on our shopping experience, as revealed by brain scans and heart rate monitors. Lewis found that changing the colour of the hat on a child's plastic bath duck from purple to blue, for example, somehow increased interest, and increased sales by one third.[28] Neuromarketers have found that shops decked out in blues and greens are experienced as relaxing, but where orange dominates, customers feel stimulated. A lot of red and yellowish green results in negative emotions and the desire to leave a shop. Dark colours can make us feel aggressive.[29] Curiously, printing bargain messages in red can make men believe that they 'will save a lot of money', but the effect vanishes when they are asked to think carefully about the offer – for what it's worth, women seem largely unaffected by the colour of sales messages.[30] The effects of store lighting, on the other hand, are so very pronounced that researchers 'found it was possible to control the time customers spent examining products and the number of items they looked at purely by adjusting the level of brightness'. Dim lighting mellows us out and makes us feel relaxed enough to browse, but in general bright lights intensify our interest in what we see and can lead to higher sales.[31]

Lewis discovered that even something as innocuous as the

look of the font used in a product's description can make a substantial difference to our perceptions. Two groups sampled the same soup, from the same can, described in each case as 'rich and creamy tomato soup' – but one group read that description in the comparatively stylish font Lucida Calligraphy, and the other was presented with the much less refined Courier. Those in the Lucida Calligraphy group were more likely to describe the soup as tastier, fresher and more enjoyable, and they were twice as likely to say they would buy some, as compared to the Courier group.

What we hear while shopping affects us too, and this is largely determined by the background music the store chooses to play – it's often a very carefully made choice, and professional music profilers are on hand to help. Lewis reports that music can have an effect on how much and even on what we end up buying, and most of the time we have no idea this is the case. One study showed that baby boomers were more likely to make purchases with classic rock in the background, even though, when asked a bit later, two-thirds couldn't remember what music was playing. Slow tempo muzak can slow shoppers down, increasing time spent shopping and boosting sales. What we buy can be manipulated by music too. When a wine store switched from Top 40 to classical music, people spent more money buying more expensive wine.[32] Sounds also come into play in the form of jingles and the music used to set moods in commercial messages. Again, neuromarketers claim to be able to study our responses and identify the jingles most likely to stick in our heads and the music liable to affect us on an emotional level.

Even touch can have effects on our financial decisions.

Researchers discovered that particular sorts of physical contact can increase our tendency to take risks with money – good news to those hoping to make us part with it. The idea again depends on the view of the mind as embodied: from an early age we associate a gentle touch with comfort and security, and even in later life a maternal hand on our shoulder can feel reassuring and have effects on our decisions. In one experiment, subjects were led into a cubicle by a woman, where they were asked to make a series of choices: risky gambles or safer options resulting in immediate but smaller payoffs. Half were ushered to their seats merely verbally; the other half also received a light and fleeting touch on their backs as they made their way in. It's thought that those touched felt safer and were therefore more likely to take risks.[33] It's worth wondering how this might translate into a sales environment. Certainly a reassuring, feminine touch before a sales pitch might do the trick, but some researchers have found that even an unobtrusive brush of the hand when you receive your change at the checkout can make you feel more positive about both your purchases and the store.[34]

*

Other neuromarketers are moved by thoughts about the dual systems approach to the mind we encountered in our consideration of nudging and Kahneman's work on decision-making. You'll recall the fast, automatic, intuitive thinking characteristic of System 1 and the slow, reflective, rational thinking characteristic of System 2. The hope here is that System 1 might be prodded in subtle ways, increasing the perceived value of a product, which in turn might influence our purchasing decisions.

Phil Barden, neuromarketing guru and author of *Decoded: The Science Behind Why We Buy*, cites a study led by the neuroscientist Brian Knutson.[35] Subjects were shown images of products, followed by prices. They were then asked to press a button if they thought they would buy the product at that price – their neural activity analysed all the while using fMRI. Knutson found that some images of products activated the brain's 'reward system', and just as in the Pepsi Challenge test, brand value seemed to have a lot to do with how positive subjects felt towards the products they saw. If a strong brand appeared, the reward centre was more active and the perceived value of the product increased. But when prices were subsequently shown, the parts of the brain that process pain kicked in. The trick, it would seem, is finding ways to tip the balance in favour of reward over pain – if the gain outweighs the loss, we seem inclined to make the purchase. 'Inclined' might not be strong enough. Knutson actually goes so far as to maintain that the patterns of activation he found 'independently predicted decisions to purchase'.[36] On some interpretations of the data, Knutson knew whether or not subjects would buy products before they did.

All of this leads Barden to a marketing strategy: 'we have two levers to influence consumer decision making – reward and pain … In order to make consumers buy, we can increase reward and at the same time decrease pain.'[37] This can be done explicitly and to some extent clumsily by lowering the price of something or increasing the reward, say by adding more product. But neuromarketing holds out the possibility of doing something else entirely: discovering ways to make subtle changes to the appearance of both the product and the price that can alter our perception of value and pain. Under the influence of systems theory, Barden claims that decision-making sometimes happens explicitly – out in the open, consciously, under the gaze of System 2. But the unconscious processing carried out by System 1 has a much greater effect on our choices than we realise and therefore gives the neuromarketer far more opportunities to change our minds.

Our automatic system, Barden argues, picks up on almost everything, so even the subtlest cues can make a difference to perceived reward and pain: 'The autopilot processes every single bit of information that is perceived by our senses. It has a huge processing capacity of 11 million bits per second, roughly the size of an old floppy disk ... no matter whether we're aware of this input or not. And every input is processed by the autopilot and can potentially influence our behaviour.'[38]

This processing capacity is contrasted with the 40 bits our working memory can handle, a rough guesstimate of the limits of our deliberative System 2. 'Even if we wanted to decide reflectively', Barden concludes, 'our very limited capacity constrains us from doing so.'[39] What's more, there's not much room for manoeuvre when it comes to explicit value – as he puts it, 'in mature markets, the quality at the product level hardly offers a perceivable and big enough difference between competing products'.[40] All drain cleaners clean drains. So the action is mostly at the implicit, or hidden level. That's where *perceived* value can be added, and where the *perceived* pain of price can be minimised. Consider value first.

The reward centres of the brain might well be affected by creating a large number of positive associations with the brand in question through advertising. Whether we're aware of it or not, this line of thinking goes, the mere appearance of a logo or a jingle might well send System 1 into free association mode. If the brand is strong and its advertising has done its work, this creates positive undercurrents in our neural networks, triggering more action in our reward centres, outweighing the pain of parting with money, and finally shifting us into buying behaviour. It's why one brown, sugary liquid can be as good as another, but once brand names get in on the act, people have strong preferences and a strong sense of value. It's also partly why we might be willing to pay £3 for a single cup of Starbucks' coffee and £3 for an entire bag of ground coffee that can brew 30 perfectly decent cups. Implicit triggers overwhelm us, and System 2 never gets the chance to compare the reward we're actually getting for the money we're spending.

But value might be enhanced in other, considerably more sneaky ways. Barden's example is packaging specifically designed to set off subtle, subconscious cues, in this case, the persuasive symbols built into a bottle of Dynamic Pulse Shower Gel. All shower gels smell fine and clean the skin well enough, but by designing the container so its colour and shape are suggestive of motor oil packaging, a number of cues get picked up by our all-seeing System 1 and pump up the perceived value of the stuff. The bottle has a solid grip line up the side and the cap clicks audibly and firmly – all of this implies the kind of manly control we might associate with top-of-the-line car engines. It communicates the gel's power to energise and kick-start the day in what must be an extremely refreshing and spectacularly masculine morning shower. System 1 spots all this, processes it, and value is added to the product implicitly, without our awareness. So too with the sophisticated packaging of Voss bottled water. The bottle looks more like an expensive table decoration, a kind of chic water feature, than bottled water. People are willing to pay five times as much for it as for bottles that send less urbane signals.

Flowery descriptions that strike us as ridiculous on reflection also seem to have measurable effects on how much value we place on products, and therefore how much we're willing to spend. Calling sandwiches 'freshly cut' might seem idiotic to System 2, but System 1 could nevertheless be moved. A number of studies involving menus with different descriptions of the food on offer – 'seafood fillet' versus 'Succulent Italian Seafood Fillet' – show that food temptingly described is ordered more often and perceived as better-tasting. Customers are even willing to pay more for food cooked with the same ingredients and using the same recipe if its description is alluring enough.[41]

What's perhaps less obvious is the malleability of our perception of price. Perhaps prices were once set by plotting demand curves. The thought was that people will buy more as the price drops, and buy less as the price rises. Set the price too high and you'll price yourself out of the market; set it too low and you'll never break even. The aim was to find the right price, somewhere in the middle, a price that most people are happy to pay but that still results in a decent return. Some prices, in long-lost corners of Mom and Pop stores, were even fixed by the notion of fairness. But now pricing consultancies offer all sorts of advice that has more to do with how our brains work than actual bottom lines. Probably everyone has noticed that a very large number of prices end in the number 9. There's disagreement about why this works on us – maybe we anchor on the first number and ignore the others – but a raft of studies show that we perceive, say, £2.99 as a much better price than £3.

More recent work on pricing has much to do with the heuristics discovered by those working in behavioural economics. Price consultants now might try to play on our inbuilt reaction to scarcity by using 'limited time offers', manipulate our natural tendency to discount the future with the suggestion that we could 'buy now and pay later', or use the power of reciprocity to encourage us to buy more by offering us free gifts. This should all be familiar from the chapter on nudging.

But many other, less obvious factors influence our experience of price. How the price is presented to us is enough to change our perception of it. Again, using restaurant menus, researchers tried several variations: an entirely numerical version with a dollar sign (e.g. $10.00), the same numbers but without a dollar sign (10.00), and finally a version with the price written out, using no numbers at all (ten dollars). People who saw the price without the dollar sign spent significantly more – it's thought that the dollar sign is processed by System 1 as an extremely reliable pain signal.[42] Even colours and swooshes and glittering stars can make a difference to how we perceive a price. A price printed in black and white is perceived as more expensive than the same price presented with the words 'discount price' on a blue background. The same number with the words 'special price' against a red background seems like even more of a bargain.[43]

However, what appears to have the biggest effect on our perception of price is context, and in particular contrast. We don't really know how much something is worth to us unless we have something to compare it to, and that something can be presented to us by those who wish to influence our experience of cost. The best example of this, made famous by the author and professor of psychology Dan Ariely, is an unusual offer made by *The Economist*. Their website presented these options: an online subscription for $59, a print-only subscription for $125, and a print and online subscription, also for $125. Why would anyone go for the print-only subscription when you can have a print and an online subscription for the same price? If no one would ever take it, why bother offering it?

It turns out that simply including the duff offer changes how we perceive the value of the other two options and actually pushes more people into making the more expensive choice. The relative merits of an online-only subscription and a print and online subscription are hard to compare – it's hard to know how much we ought to pay for each – but contrast print-only with print and online for the same price, and suddenly one looks like a good deal. Ariely demonstrated this effect by offering 100 students at MIT the original three options and another 100 students just two, the online and the print and online options. With just two options, 68 chose the cheaper online subscription and 32 chose print and online. But if they also saw the print-only option, just sixteen chose online only and 84 now opted for the more expensive print and online offer.[44]

Price consultants advocate the use of 'decoys' like this whenever products are difficult to compare.[45] Say two competing phone-makers are selling phones with a range of different features – Phone A has an excellent battery life, Phone B has a good camera; Phone A has a bigger memory, but Phone B has a wider screen. It's hard for us to work out what matters most in this mess, but if you're selling Phone A, it makes sense to offer a decoy product, Phone A Minus, the same phone with a slightly smaller memory and a slightly higher price tag. If it's hard for consumers to compare the two competing phones, it's easy to compare Phone A and Phone A Minus, and a lot more people will end up buying Phone A as a result. Decoys like this appear almost everywhere, from high-priced items on wine lists and extravagant travel options to alarmingly expensive electrical equipment and overpriced cars – all of it is intended not to sell itself but to sell something else.

*

In the summer of 2011, France made this addition to its bioethics code: 'Brain-imaging methods can be used only for medical or scientific research purposes or in the context of court expertise.' That's one way to deal with it. The move effectively bans the use of brain imaging for commercial purposes. The worries voiced in France at the time can be heard in Anglophone discussions now.

Some argue that the claims of neuromarketing are wildly overblown. There's a lot of debate about the interpretation of brain scans. It's often a complicated and finely grained thing, even with expensive equipment in well-funded labs. So the pronouncements of a small team working on the cheap in less than ideal conditions might be taken with a grain of salt. Certainly it's reasonable to be suspicious when presented with the proposition that one can literally 'see' something like memory or desire or brand value instantiated in brain structures. Retired doctor and author Raymond Tallis is among the more outspoken critics of this kind of thing, an aspect of something he calls 'neuromania'. Although consciousness requires a brain in good working order, he argues, a mind is not the same thing as a brain, and therefore facts discovered about a brain are not facts discovered about a mind.[46] For what it's worth, the idea he's attacking is a philosophical position called mind-brain identity theory, and while it might be innocently presupposed by marketers, almost nobody holds it in philosophical circles. It was knocked over in the late 1960s by the philosopher Hilary Putnam, who argued that brain states cannot be identical to mental states, because a mental state might be 'multiply realised' in different brain states. If that's possible, mind and brain can't be the same thing. If you think a Martian and a human could both experience the same mental state, say pain, but have completely different brain chemistries (carbon-based for us and maybe silicon-based for them), you get the point of the objection.[47]

There's really no need to bother Putnam. Some claims made at the particularly enthusiastic end of neuromarketing just can't be right. Brain scans are said to have revealed that eating chocolate is better than kissing. Everywhere and at all times? All chocolate, compared to every possible kiss? How could something like that possibly be proved? This is, incidentally, the result of an investigation underwritten by Cadbury's. Elsewhere, neuromarketing methods have disclosed the formula for the perfect holiday. Really? For every human being? And again, this is, incidentally, the result of an investigation underwritten by Holiday Inn. As one sceptic observed, 'the research that's involved appears to be little more than PR in an ill-fitting science suit – advertising guff interspersed with vague references to the brain.'[48]

But other objections start with the real possibility that at least some neuroscience can reveal commercially useful facts about how our minds work – the question then is whether or not morally problematic manipulation is going on. It's a question that ought to become more and more pressing as our theories of how the brain works approach correctness. Almost none of the discussion around the 'ethics of neuromarketing' on the part of practitioners themselves concerns such moral questions. Instead, there's the promise that neuromarketers will not hoodwink their clients in the business world by exaggerating their ability to peer into our minds. The 'core principles' of the Neuromarketing Science and Business Association's code of ethics, if that's anything to go by, contains just this, plus the promise not to bring the profession into ill repute and to use only 'accepted scientific principles'.[49] There's no reflection on human dignity, the right to privacy, and whatever we mean when we say we value human freedom. To ask a plain question, taking advantage of an understanding of the way a human mind works and using that to get us to pay more money for something – is that a decent thing to do? Whether it is or it isn't, it's something that happens to you and to me, every day.

But you don't need to be Descartes to think that the mind is something other than the brain, and so wonder how much the study of the brain can really tell us about a human being's thoughts and hopes and fears – maybe a very great deal, but not everything, and not without a lot of careful interpretation and theorising coming along for the ride. And you don't need to be Kant to worry that some of the practices recommended by neuromarketers seem to treat a human being merely as an object, a thing to be studied and manipulated for financial gain, rather than a person with goals of her own, someone owed our respect. There's something to both points, and there are replies to be made, but I'll leave it there. What interests me now is the meaning of modern retail persuasion and what it might tell us about where we're headed.

You can make a start by thinking of neuromarketing as the contemporary inheritor of Dichter's depth probing – it too offers the promise of bypassing the conscious mind and getting inside the heads of consumers, persuading us without our knowing that our minds have been changed. This, in a way, echoes the promises made by past masters of persuasion. Think again about Ivy Lee's art of steering heads inside and Edward Bernays' engineering of consent. There's a hope in all of this that a bit of arcane knowledge enables the initiated to change the minds of the masses. It's possible that human beings have always had this hope, this desire to find a shortcut that persuades others, without bothering with facts and reasons. Maybe we've just moved on a bit from incantations and love potions to Freudianism, behavioural economics, and now neuroscience. You can suspect that such an old hope is going nowhere fast, and the future of persuasion will almost certainly have its share of characters cashing in on it – some of their methods efficacious, some not.

So if the past is anything to go by, the persuasive techniques of the future will depend on the theories we devise about what makes us tick – if you have ideas about what those theories might be, you have your own guess about where we're headed. Persuasion has always surfed along with what are at the time fresh ideas about, say, the mechanics of crowd psychology, the herd instinct, and more recently, the dual systems approach, embodied cognition, and the nature and persuasive power of metaphor. If there's a trend in the theories of our age, it's reductive – from explaining conscious desires in terms of subconscious urges and fears to understanding decision-making in terms of a set of heuristics or mental shortcuts. We've been burrowing down into our mental life for so long that the basic unit of persuasion is now very nearly the neuron. And what has figured centrally in all this, relatively recently anyway, is emotion. Professional persuaders, from the propagandists of the last century to contemporary advertisers, know very well that emotion moves us more deeply and more surely, faster and farther than any set of facts and figures. Maybe we'll discover even more powerful forms of persuasion that play on our emotions in unforeseen ways. We've been headed in that direction, and away from reasoned argument, for a while.

As David Lewis sees it, people in the advertising business were once interested in what people were thinking, not what they were feeling. If you wanted to persuade someone to buy something, you appealed to their reason. Give people the facts and a clear sales pitch and they'll buy your product. However, he writes, 'Psychological and neuroscientific research over the past 30 years has shown these confident beliefs to be profoundly mistaken ... emotions are more important than thoughts in influencing shopping behaviour [and] emotions can be successfully engineered without consumers ever becoming consciously aware of how their minds are being manipulated.'[50] The near future of persuasion, anyway, seems likely to be bound up even more tightly with the manipulation of emotion.

It would be short-sighted to ignore the fact that there's now a lot of data about every one of us available to those who wish to persuade us – and it's likely that our data-gathering capacities will only improve and expand. It's also possible that knowing everything about our past puts pressure on us to learn more about our present. There's talk of 'moodvertising' in the air at the moment, finding ways not just to monitor a person's present emotional state but to respond to it and even change it, tailoring messaging to us in real time. As Gemma Calvert, managing director of the neuromarketing research agency Neurosense writes: 'Given the multitude of new communication platforms and ubiquity of mobile devices, could the past age of static advertising be succeeded by campaigns that are far more empathetic, interactive and literally adaptive to our shared emotional states?'[51] Twitter and other forms of social media might be monitored, identifying the feelings of those in a particular place. Messages could then be tailored accordingly. Facial recognition software might do a similar job from existing security cameras.

Facebook got into trouble for taking part in an enormous experiment (689,000 users were unwittingly involved) that proved it could make people feel more positive or negative by filtering the content of their news feeds in various ways – playing up or playing down the happy or sad posts of their friends. The authors of the study concluded that 'emotional states can be transferred to others via emotional contagion, leading people to experience the same emotions without their awareness'.[52] The emotions that our Facebook friends feel and express online influence how we feel – and that influence can be manipulated, on a massive scale, by changing what comes to us via our social networks. Some wonder whether Facebook could steer an election to a desired outcome, sow political dissent, or quell rebellion by influencing the emotions of its 1 billion active users. Certainly it can change how we feel.[53]

Others say that Facebook could swing an election by much less subtle means. Researchers found that by sending a

Facebook message urging people to 'Get Out And Vote' on election day, very many people who might not have voted actually acted on the message, an effect that could influence the 'real-world voting behaviour of millions of people'.[54] It's raised the prospect of something called digital gerrymandering: aiming the 'Get Out And Vote' message at the supporters of just one candidate in places where the vote is likely to be close, and thus deciding the outcome.

There is also a worry about the power of search engines to control not just how we vote, but what and how we think about all sorts of things. Researchers created a site that mimics Google and skewed sets of search rankings to favour Candidate A, Candidate B, or neither candidate. Subjects were asked questions about whether or not they liked or trusted the candidates – they were also asked which one they would vote for. They were then given fifteen minutes to do some online research about the candidates, and while each group had access to the same search results, the rankings were different: one group's results were biased towards sites favourable to Candidate A, another group had results with a bias towards Candidate B, and the control group was exposed to random rankings.

'When our participants were done searching, we asked them those questions again', the lead researcher, Robert Epstein, writes, 'and, voilà: On all measures, opinions shifted in the direction of the candidate who was favored in the rankings. Trust, liking and voting preferences all shifted predictably.'[55] They estimate that the voting preferences of 20 per cent of undecided voters could be shifted in this way, and given how close many national elections are, they say that 25 per cent of all national elections, worldwide, including recent US presidential elections, could be changed by alterations to Google's algorithms. Because the nature of those algorithms is kept secret by Google, it's very unlikely that anyone would know if Google were actually rigging elections. The authors note that 'when people are unaware they are being manipulated, they tend to believe they have adopted their new thinking voluntarily'.[56] Obviously it's not just votes. Our thoughts about anything we could conceivably search for online can be altered in this way.

It's not hard to imagine a future where information comes to us not through links ranked on a page, but far more personally, via something a generation beyond the merely visual representations delivered by Google Glass. Those who make choices about whatever it is that will govern the flow of information in the future, whatever supersedes page rank algorithms, will be in an extraordinarily strong position to change what we think. And, again, if we don't know we're being manipulated, we'll believe that we've adopted new thoughts entirely voluntarily. Something tells me the future of persuasive messaging will be much more detailed than the simple suggestion that I 'Get Out And Vote'.

It might be said that these slightly spooked and certainly dark thoughts about the future of persuasion are what they are because we're living in post-Snowden times – anyone who tries to think about the future is affected by the present, and our present is a little preoccupied with the surveillance capabilities of our governments and corporations. No doubt that's true. But it's also true that persuasion has always worked best against the backdrop of inside information. The obvious next step, the thing that follows on from knowing a great deal about your customers and your adversaries and your citizens, is using that knowledge to change their minds.

The sociologists Zygmunt Bauman and David Lyon use the words 'liquid surveillance' to try to come to terms with what surveillance is today. They write: 'In today's liquid modern world, the paths of daily life are mobile and flexible. Crossing national borders is a commonplace activity and immersion in social media increasingly ubiquitous … Surveillance spreads in hitherto unimaginable ways, responding to and reproducing the slippery nature of modern life, seeping into areas where it once had only marginal sway.'[57]

Maybe 'liquid persuasion' is the right way to think about where we're headed. Persuasion that's much more mobile and flexible than anything we've encountered so far, persuasion that responds to our feelings, changes them, empathises with us, moment to moment, and so influences us subtly but profoundly, rapidly, persistently and without our knowing. Persuasion that targets us with just the right messages at precisely the right time, when statistics show we're most open to them – orders of magnitude more carefully measured and refined than Target's efforts to win over new mothers or standard pop-up adverts that know something about our browsing histories.

Every mobile device, every system into which we have integrated our thoughts, perhaps our bodies, their signs and signals, could be whispering to each of us differently but in just the right key, maybe in concert, resonating precisely with our mood, changing it, turning on jealousy here, calming down dissent there, all the while with us thinking that our conclusions are entirely our own. Pushing buttons in us that lead us to buy or to vote or to dream, to be less cautious, less critical, perhaps more trusting. Liquid persuasion that flows around us and with us, through us, very nearly part of us, wherever we are.

The Lost Art of Argument

'The public use of one's reason must always be free, and it
alone can bring about enlightenment among human beings.'

IMMANUEL KANT

The *Iliad* begins with a father begging for his daughter's life.
Agamemnon has taken the beautiful Chryseis as a war
prize. Her father offers a ransom and pleads for her release. 'Old
man', Agamemnon sneers, 'I will not free her. She shall grow old
in my house at Argos far from her own home, busying herself
with her loom and visiting my couch; so go, and do not provoke
me or it shall be the worse for you.' The old man slinks away.

The *Iliad* and its sequel the *Odyssey* are in a sense the West's
first true documents, the earliest real insights we have into the
minds of the Greeks alive almost 3,000 years ago. Whatever else
we can glean from these poems, they are packed with exchanges
like this – quarrels, disagreements, threats, pleas and the odd
bit of straightforward begging. A threat like Agamemnon's is
a reason for action, in a sense, perhaps a pragmatic reason – if
you don't want your head kicked in, then you'll do what he
says. But it's not a rational reason, not a premise being offered
in support of a conclusion. Agamemnon isn't reasoning with
anyone. He's getting what he wants, or else 'it shall be the worse

for you'. To keep these two kinds of persuasion clear, I'll now reserve the word 'argument' for the higher thing – not threats and quarrels and the like, but the giving of good reasons shoring up a conclusion. It's hard to find an argument, in this sense, in Homer's poems, but they're shot through with the lowbrow, quarrelsome stuff.

By the time we get to Plato, at large around 400 BCE, it's as though we're dealing with a different species. There are still arguments that appeal to authority, the occasional suggestive analogy, but in Plato's dialogues we find page after page of serious argumentation – premises piled high on premises, carefully crafted, honed pieces of analysis and reasoning, much of it so complex that you have to read it over and over to get to grips with it. No one threatens anyone with anything. Everyone's in the reasoning business.

It's easy to think that giving reasons for conclusions is a fundamental feature of our humanity – being reasonable in this sense, according to all sorts of traditions, is part of what makes us human, what separates us from all other creatures. Man is a rational animal – that's how it is with Aristotle, the Neo-Platonists, Catholic philosophers in the medieval period and beyond, Enlightenment thinkers, even to some extent, and slightly surprisingly, Freud. More recently, as people like Richard Dawkins would have it, what marks us out from the other apes is our big brains and what we do with them. But being reasonable, insofar as that means constructing arguments, might well be something we had to learn how to do. If that's so, if it's not a natural part of the human factory specification, it's something that we can also forget how to do, something that can largely pass out of our understanding as a people.[1]

What explains the transition from Agamemnon's threats to Plato's arguments? As Walter Ong describes it in *Orality and Literacy*, scholars since the eighteenth century have gradually worked out the answer to a moderately embarrassing question: Why were Homer's poems, well, bad? They are wonderful in many ways, of course, but they are also filled with repeated stock phrases, cliché, bad plotting, cheap characterisation and painfully predictable story arcs. The classicist Milman Parry found the answer with a combination of insight and a close reading of the text.[2] It looks like bad writing to us because we're enmeshed in a literate culture. Homer wasn't. The poems were part of an oral tradition, passed down and probably altered by many poets over many generations. For all we know there never was an actual poet called 'Homer'.

What looks like bad writing to us was something once crucial to the continued existence of the poems themselves: mnemonic devices. Because they weren't written down, they had to be remembered, mostly, although there was room for improvisation on the speaker's part. Trying to keep so much in your head was no mean feat. The *Iliad* is 15,693 lines of verse, and the *Odyssey* is 12,110 lines. Without the aid of writing, Ong explains, 'knowledge, once acquired, had to be constantly repeated or it would be lost: fixed, formulaic thought patterns were essential'.[3] It's hard to remember a string of sentences in a written paragraph, but it's easy to recall a song word for word as you sing it, with its chorus, repeating phrases, rhythms, familiar character types and predictable narrative. The poets who sang Homer's poems made things easy on themselves with similar tricks.

The Homeric epithet is perhaps the best known, slightly

puzzling feature of the poems, which makes sense once you see it as an aid to memory. Hera is usually 'white-armed Hera'. Athena is 'grey-eyed Athena'. Achilles is 'fleet-of-foot'. Odysseus is 'much-suffering Odysseus' or 'crafty Odysseus'. The sea is 'wine-dark'. The dawn, however wonderful, is most often 'rosy-fingered'. Why do you never encounter mildly-annoyed Achilles or angst-ridden Athena? The stock phrases can be slotted in as needed to get the metre right, but they also instantly remind both poet and audience of the subject at hand. Of course, it's fleet-footed Achilles we're talking about again – I remember him.

What explains the transition from Homer to Plato is the invention of written language, the shift from an oral culture to a literate one, and the enormous change to thinking this brought with it. Writing probably has its roots in numbers and pictures drawn to help memory – maybe symbols used to keep track of commerce, drawings recording important events or marking out special places, and pictures serving religious functions. It's thought that this kind of thing appeared in different places, eventually turning into different kinds of written representations of sounds and concepts. But alphabetic writing – the use of symbols to represent individual sounds – was invented just once, by Semitic peoples living in the Levant, around 1500 BCE. It's thought that all or nearly all alphabets can be traced back to this time and place.

The Greek alphabet appeared around 700 BCE. It's called the first true alphabet, because while its precursors used symbols mostly just to represent consonants, the Greek version put vowel sounds on an equal footing. This innovation did something remarkable to human culture, because it was now able to grow in a new way, by piling up wisdom in a storehouse of scrolls and eventually books. It did something remarkable to human beings too. Instead of having to save everything worth remembering in formulaic songs and poems in our heads, we had the mental space to do a new kind of free thinking. We weren't stuck imagining Achilles just as fleet of foot. We were free to think of everything else in new ways too. 'By Plato's day', Ong writes, 'a change had set in: the Greeks had at long last effectively interiorized writing … The new way to store knowledge was not in mnemonic formulas but in the written text. This freed the mind for more original, more abstract thought.'[4] With knowledge secured out there in the world rather than filling up our heads, we had the bandwidth required for entirely new kinds of cognition. Among other things, the written word made argument possible.

*

To understand the nature of argument, it makes sense to linger a while over its beginnings. Like the alphabet, argumentation might well have been a kind of discovery, perhaps also appearing in just one place and at one time, maybe even the act of a single genius. It's hard to say it with much confidence, and reasonable people can disagree about this, but it's entirely possible that the ability to argue came to humanity around 500 BCE in a dream, a rational revelation. The dreamer was Parmenides.

There were of course other early philosophers advancing views before him, and in the fragments that have come down to us you can piece together the beginnings of reasons and arguments here and there. But it really is hit and miss. Thales, for example, is thought to be the first philosopher, credited with thinking that everything is made of just one substance, water, and that 'all things are full of gods'. It's tacky to suggest it, but I'll do it anyway. You can wonder whether this kind of thing is really philosophy, careful argumentation backed up by reasons. Even Aristotle, who had access to a lot more evidence than we do, struggled to understand Thales' reasons for saying what he said. It's not entirely clear that he produced any.

But even if others sometimes gave reasons for their views – the mystic musings of the Pythagoreans and the obscurities of Heraclitus are also in the running – Parmenides might have been the first to do so explicitly and carefully. At least he tells you that's what he's doing by distinguishing between a 'path to truth' that depends on the giving of reasons and the mere assertion of opinion. He chooses to express what might be the West's first full-blooded arguments in a poem that is almost entirely lost to us now. The loss of Parmenides' poem is not necessarily a bad thing. He was an awful poet.

His poem begins with the daughters of the Sun appearing in a dream and carrying him on a whirling chariot up into the heavens. They arrive before a great gate leading to the paths of night and day. The daughters persuade another divine being, Justice, to unbolt the gate, and there a mysterious, gentle and remarkably talkative goddess takes Parmenides by the hand and begins his long instruction. She promises to reveal everything: 'reality' on one hand, and 'the opinions of mortals, which contain no genuine proof' on the other. It's his emphasis on proof that's interesting, here and elsewhere – it's at the very centre of his thinking.

Brace yourself for some of Parmenides' poetry. The goddess begins by telling him that there are just two kinds of inquiry:

'Two ways there are of seeking how to see
One that it is, and is not not to be –
That is the path of Truth's companion Trust –
The other it is not, and not to be it must.'[5]

As the philosopher Anthony Kenny puts it, 'I must ask the reader to believe that Parmenides' Greek is as clumsy and as baffling as this English text'.[6] A slightly more forgiving translator, John Burnet, renders it this way:

'Come now, I will tell thee – and do thou hearken to my
saying and carry it away – the only two ways of search that
can be thought of. The first, namely, that It is, and that it is
impossible for anything not to be, is the way of conviction,
for truth is its companion.

The other, namely, that It is not, and that something must
needs not be –
that, I tell thee, is a wholly untrustworthy path.
For you cannot know what is not – that is impossible – nor
utter it;'[7]

Put both translations together, squint, and you can just about see a recognisable argument.

Some of this is controversial, but what's clear is that Parmenides believes that there are two 'ways of search', two ways of 'seeking how to see' – two ways to try to get at the truth about the world. One works, and one doesn't. The distinction rests on his claim that thinking must have an object of thought that really exists. Strictly speaking, 'what is not', nothing, is not something you can actually think or talk about – 'you cannot know what is not'. So 'the path of Truth' is thinking about what is, thinking about things that really exist. Thinking about nothing is a mistake, because 'that is impossible'.

Parmenides claims that this point has unexpected implications. Whatever exists cannot come to be, because that would require us to think about a nothing out of which the something appeared – and thinking about nothing is impossible. Whatever exists cannot cease to be either, for just the same reason. Therefore, whatever exists has always been and always will be.

Fair enough, maybe, at a stretch, you might think, but Parmenides draws a few more remarkable conclusions. Again strictly speaking, there can't really be gaps or spaces between things – gaps and spaces are instances of nothing. So Parmenides says there's no movement, or anyway that movement must be illusory. How could there be movement if logic tells us that there are no empty spaces, no nothings, into which things might move? And if there are no spaces between things, technically there really are no different things – the existence of separate objects must also be illusory. So there must just be one big thing. The universe is a single, coherent, permanent, unchanging, seamless whole. And it's round. Parmenides thinks it has to be round.

But the world as we encounter it doesn't look round or single or permanent or unchanging. It looks like a disconnected mess of changing objects, moving in and out of those spaces Parmenides says we can't think about. How can he possibly mean to talk us out of what we can plainly see everywhere? There's an answer given by Diogenes Laertius, the third-century biographer, gossip and author of *Lives and Opinions of the Eminent Philosophers*. Diogenes tells us that, in antiquity, Parmenides is best remembered because he 'used to say that argument was the test of truth; and that the sensations were not trustworthy'.[8] The power of argument trumps even what you can see.

Or as Parmenides would have it, with his reassuringly consistent lack of clarity:

> 'For never shall this be proved, that things that are not are;
> But do thou hold back thy thought from this way of enquiry …'

So far, so good – a repetition of his principle that 'nothing' is not something you can think about. Do hold back your thought about this, he counsels, because it's a mistake to try to think about nothing. But he goes on. Don't let what everyone else thinks, or your past experience, lead you astray either, because what matters is where the argument leads, even if it's a difficult conclusion to accept.

> 'Nor let custom, born of much experience,
> Force thee to let wander along this road thy aimless eye,
> Thy echoing ear or thy tongue; but do thou judge by
> Reason the strife-encompassed proof that I have spoken.'[9]

It doesn't matter what you see. Maybe the proof is tough to swallow. Think about it and make up your own mind, but 'Do thou judge by reason'. Maybe that line means a very great deal in the history of argumentation.

The word translated here as 'proof' is *logos* in the original

Greek. To the ancients, logos meant many things – its most basic meaning is simply 'word', but the concept could expand to include plea, opinion, a gathering of thoughts together, giving an account or justification or reason for belief, or simply reasoned discourse – eventually, it meant argument. It could also be used to refer to an underlying order or governing principle hidden behind ordinary things. Just as thoughts are the order behind words, logos is the rational principle behind the created world. Maybe Parmenides had something like that sense in mind: logos as the divine, creative idea. It's a notion exemplified much later in the Gospel of John. 'In the beginning was the Word, and the Word was with God, and the Word was God.'

The power of argument might have seemed like magic to those who first felt its force. It's not easy for us even to throw ropes over to so ancient a conception of argument, but it was once something divine, the gift of a goddess, a power in tune with the creative energy behind all that exists.

But if argument began with Parmenides, it reached a new height within his lifetime, in Socrates, the undisputed master of argument in the ancient world. Even now, when you read Plato's dialogues, you're right there, sitting in the Athenian sun, joining Socrates as he asks his endless questions, springs traps, draws out implications, and follows the arguments wherever they lead. It really is a million miles away from Agamemnon.

Socrates' argument style is called the *elenchus* – the Greek translates as refutation, cross-examination, testing or scrutinising – and his facility with it was unmatched. As his contemporary Xenophon puts it, 'in argument he could do what he liked with any disputant', but he didn't simply win arguments.[10] He used argumentation as a method for acquiring self-knowledge.

Losing an argument to Socrates was not at all a straightforward thing. It could be a kind of enlightenment.

Most of us regard losing an argument as a failure, maybe the worst kind of failure, an instance of being outdone or outshone by someone mentally more agile, but those gathered around Socrates saw things differently. They thought that when you're tripped up in an argument, there's a weightless moment as you float free of the mental rut you were in – you stop, your eyes narrow, and no words come to you. The Greeks didn't necessarily feel humiliation in this experience, although it's true that Socrates sometimes duffed up opponents who certainly didn't enjoy it. What they occasionally felt was freedom, a rare opportunity to move in new intellectual directions, grasp new possibilities. They called this feeling *aporia*, literally 'no path'. There's no comparable word in English. Imagine walking along, lost in thought, looking up, snapping out of it, stopping mid-stride and realising that you're in unfamiliar territory. You don't know where you are, and you don't know where to go next. That realisation, that feeling, is aporia. Rather than avoid the experience of losing an argument at all costs as we do, the Greeks got together and argued for hours, seeking the freedom of thought that followed aporia. Sometimes they must have smiled when they felt it.

The usual pattern for Socrates was to begin with an agreed goal, usually a question aiming at a definition: What is truth, or justice, or piety, or courage? Someone offers a definition, and Socrates picks it apart, setting up common ground on the hoof, often in the form of procedural rules and arguments by analogy. He's astonishingly slick when it comes to finding ways to show an opponent that, for example, by his own understanding of justice, his proposed definition fails.

In Plato's masterpiece, *Republic*, Socrates asks Cephalus, an old businessman, what he thinks justice is. Cephalus offers this definition, an encapsulation of the traditional Greek view: justice is living up to your legal obligations and telling the truth. Socrates provides a test case that immediately lands Cephalus in difficulty. Suppose you borrowed a knife from a friend who's since gone off the rails, has murder in mind, and wants it back. Would it be just to live up to your legal obligations, tell the truth, and return what you borrowed, even if that act would result in the deaths of his innocent victims? Cephalus concedes that would be unjust, and in so doing discovers that by some deeper conception of justice he has yet to articulate, his original definition can't be right. By the end of the book, several definitions are considered and rejected, as the conversation leads them all to a better understanding of what justice is.

Here's another good example of Socrates in action. Plato describes an encounter between Socrates and a relativist who's famous for holding the view that all opinions are on a par, and if you think something is true, then it's true for you – there's no deeper, objective fact of the matter. Socrates dismantles the whole thing with a single, smooth question: if you believe that everybody's opinions are true, what do you think about someone of the opinion that you're completely wrong about that? If it's true that everyone's opinions have an equal claim to truth, then the opinion 'Relativism is false' must itself be true, no?

Socrates goes further. If you're a relativist, he argues, you're committed to the idea that the opinions of others are just as valid as your own, including the opinion that you're wrong. So, as a relativist, you have to take on board the idea that relativism is false. Relativists must see truth in the views of those who disagree with them, so they must disagree with themselves. And if both proponents and opponents of relativism think it's false, no one thinks it's true. You can imagine Socrates leaning forward as he says it: 'Since it is therefore disputed by everyone', he concludes, 'the truth of relativism is true to nobody – to the relativist no more than to anyone else.' Socrates calls this 'a really exquisite conclusion', and that's just what it is.[11] By a relativist's own understanding of truth, relativism is false for absolutely everybody, relativists included.

We can disagree about how and where it started, but there's no doubt that argument was thriving in Plato's day, and that it reached new heights with Socrates. However, it took the work of a different sort of genius to formalise argumentation. Thanks to Aristotle, argument became a skill one might acquire – it became teachable, something anyone could study and learn how to do.

The ancients thought that only a certain sort of education would do for a free person, as opposed to a mere slave or foreigner. With this training an individual could do anything worth doing: learn any vocation, fight well for their country, understand the nature of virtue, live a good and decent life, and, crucially, take part in public debate while looking after themselves intellectually. To secure all this, they taught their children just three things, the *artes liberales*, the liberal arts, the skills required to live a free, human life: grammar or the mechanics of language; logic or the rules of right reasoning; and rhetoric, the art of persuasive public speaking. The formal study of both logic and rhetoric really began just after argument was itself getting under way.

John Locke, writing in the seventeenth century, was quite right to reach for hyperbole: 'God has not been so sparing to men to make them barely two-legged creatures, and left it to Aristotle to make them rational.'[12] Aristotle invented logic, the systematic study of the rules of correct reasoning. No significant advance on his logical works, collectively called the *Organon*, meaning the Tool, was made until Gottlob Frege's concept script appeared in the last century.[13] For perhaps 2,000 years, a large part of humanity took Aristotle's writings as the very blueprint for rationality.

His focus is deductive argument: 'A deduction is a discourse in which, certain things being stated, something other than what is stated follows of necessity from their being so.'[14] The 'certain things being stated' are the premises of an argument. The conclusion is the 'something other' that 'follows of necessity'. Premises are built up out of subjects and predicates, and premises can either affirm or deny that the subject has a predicate. When it all lines up, and the conclusion follows, you've got what Aristotle called a syllogism.

The most famous example of an argument will make all this more clear.

> Socrates is a man.
> All men are mortal.
> Therefore, Socrates is mortal.

The expression, 'Socrates is a man', is a premise that says of the particular subject Socrates that he has the predicate or property of being a man. The expression, 'All men are mortal', says of the general term 'men' that all such things have the property of being mortal. The conclusion follows necessarily, and that just means that if the premises are true, the conclusion has to be true too, given the formal structure of the premises. They are, and it is: therefore, Socrates is mortal.

Aristotle discovered that when premises hang together in a number of different ways, new truths have to follow. He mapped all of this out, showing which constructions preserve truth and which do not. Armed with this, you can tell whether or not almost any argument is logically valid or truth-preserving – you can tell that if its premises are true, the conclusion has to be true too. It was an enormously powerful discovery.

He had a nearly equal influence on rhetoric. Others addressed the topic before him, manuals existed and professionals offered to teach the art of public speaking before he took up the subject, but it's Aristotle's treatment that had the greatest impact. As he puts it, 'Rhetoric may be defined as the faculty of observing in any given case the available means of persuasion'.[15] He explains exactly how to understand, evaluate and cultivate this faculty.

In persuasive speech, the first thing to notice is that not just the argument itself is in play. There's also the speaker and the listener. Aristotle writes: 'Of the modes of persuasion furnished by the spoken word there are three kinds. The first kind depends on the personal character of the speaker; the second on putting the audience into a certain frame of mind; the third on the proof, or apparent proof, provided by the words of the speech itself.'[16]

In public speech, you have to establish your credibility as a speaker almost instantly, or no one will listen to you. As Aristotle has it, 'We believe good men more fully and more readily than others'.[17] So you have to display a certain degree of prudence, the kind of practical wisdom that comes with experience. You also can't seem remotely shifty – speakers must be perceived not just as knowing what they're talking about, but as having a good character. And the crowd has to think the speaker has good intentions. Notice, by the way, that all of these things have to come across in the speech – it's not enough that you have a good character or are well-intentioned – all of this must be perceived by those who hear you. Only then, Aristotle says, will a crowd find you credible.

But credibility isn't enough, because Aristotle recognised that 'our judgements when we are pleased and friendly are not the same as when we are pained and hostile'.[18] There are different interpretations of Aristotle on this point, a few quite mercenary. It's sometimes thought that Aristotle advocates the deliberate arousal of emotion on the part of the speaker to gain rhetorical advantage, but others say that Aristotle's long and in-depth treatment of emotion suggests that an understanding of it is all he's advocating. A point about knowing your audience, recognising its mood and speaking against that backdrop, might well be all he intends.

Finally, there's the argument itself, and here Aristotle recognises room for manoeuvre compared to the rigorous world of formal logic. In a logical deduction, certain premises are supposed and a conclusion follows of necessity. But in rhetorical speech, we are dealing not with logical syllogisms, but what Aristotle called *enthymemes*, from the Greek verb 'to consider', which suggests these sorts of arguments put propositions up for consideration, rather than establish them necessarily. An enthymeme is an incomplete demonstration or, as Sam Leith helpfully calls it in his history of rhetoric, 'a half-arsed syllogism; typically one that, rather than having its premises right out in the open, had a hidden assumption somewhere'.[19] A rhetorical argument establishes truth, not necessarily, but 'for the most part'. If an audience was convinced of the credibility of a speaker and in the right mood, a conclusion that held 'for the most part' was probably quite enough for them.

Within a few decades, argumentation seems to have come into existence and, thanks to Aristotle, became the kind of thing one might study, learn, hone and perfect. While I'm only nearly sure about all that, it's enough to make me entertain an intriguing possibility. Just as alphabetic writing appeared just once, maybe argument appeared just once too. It's clear that something happened between Homer and Plato, and scholars are probably right to point to the shift from an oral tradition to literacy as at least a large explanation of the change. It's all this that makes me hang a bit looser, conceptually, when it comes to the connection between being reasonable and being human.

Perhaps the capacity for rationality, insofar as that consists in listening to reason and understanding the power of arguments, is not a fundamental part of human nature, whatever that is. It seems to have started somewhere. We had to learn how to do it. It's had a bumpy history since – sometimes venerated, sometimes all but ignored. Once you start to see it like this, you might be open to the idea that the capacity to follow and formulate arguments is something that might well have been largely lost in recent years, just because we have forgotten how to do it, perhaps because we don't value it particularly highly, perhaps because we've found other kinds of persuasive tactics that meet our needs. Socrates and his gang had a flair for it. Maybe we no longer do.

*

The more we've learned about argument, the more we've come to understand its limited power, in our lives anyway, and this has also contributed to how and where arguments now figure into public life. Maybe Enlightenment thinkers put their trust in the individual's capacity to think things through for herself, but recent research has shown that argument has only limited effects on us – I'll leave open the question of whether that's a new fact about human beings or whether we've always been only marginally affected by argument. Either way, we've got a deeper understanding of the limits of argument now. Maybe many of us would view that Enlightenment trust as misplaced.

Probably the first careful study of the actual persuasive power of argumentation was undertaken by Carl Hovland and his colleagues during the Second World War. Hovland was working as a psychologist at Yale when he was recruited by the Experimental Section of the Research Branch of the US Army's Information and Education Division. The government began producing propaganda material, films like the series *Why We Fight*, aimed at rallying new soldiers to the cause, and Hovland was charged with understanding how effective all this was. Test groups watched *The Battle of Britain*, and their responses to questionnaires were compared to those of control groups who hadn't seen the film. It turned out that the test group picked up some facts about the war, but seeing the film didn't change their general attitude towards the war itself, and it certainly didn't do much to motivate them to fight.[20] What sorts of arguments would bring about opinion change? When do arguments work, and when do they fall on deaf ears? Hovland and others in the division spent large parts of their working lives answering variations on these questions.

What are the effects of letting your audience draw its own conclusions as opposed to stating your conclusion yourself? Some people won't follow you, so maybe you should spoon-feed them, but on the other hand the conclusion might really sink in if you give people the room to come to it themselves. Hovland recorded two presentations in favour of devaluing the US currency during wartime. One group heard the final conclusion that the evidence adduced pointed to: that this was a desirable course of action. The other didn't. He found that 'over twice as many subjects changed their opinions in the direction advocated by the communicator when the conclusion was explicitly drawn as did when it was left to the audience'.[21] When arguing, you should take pains to spell it all out.

Is presenting both sides of an argument a good idea? If you want to bring people around to your view, is it better to present only arguments favouring your conclusion or should you also discuss and dismiss the case against? You might think that suspicions would be aroused if you offer only a one-sided presentation, but then again just mentioning reasons on the other side might actually reinforce belief in the view you're trying to undermine.

Two groups of Hovland's soldiers heard arguments pushing the conclusion that the war with Japan would be a long one – so be prepared to continue the fight, boys – but one also heard arguments for the view that the war might be over soon, followed quickly by a refutation of those arguments. Both approaches changed minds, but Hovland found that what really mattered was the initial stand of the listener. The message taking up both sides of the argument was much more effective on men who were initially opposed to the desired conclusion that the war would be long, while the one-sided message was more effective on those who already agreed with it. If you're preaching to the choir (or speaking at the Democratic Primary), stick to gospel. But if you hope to persuade people who disagree with you, it will help your case if you engage with arguments in favour of their view.

Hovland also found that presenting both sides of the argument is more effective on people who are better educated. And he discovered that hearing about and ultimately rejecting the opposing position seemed to inoculate soldiers against the effects of counter-propaganda. Those exposed to both sides of a position were better able to shrug off counter-arguments they heard later. Thinking about an argument and rejecting it once seems to strengthen one's resolve against future attacks.

The order of the presentation of arguments was another topic for investigation. If you're trying to build a case, should you bring out your best arguments early or save them for a rousing conclusion? So called 'climax order' presentations reserve the big guns for the finale, while 'anti-climax order' presentations start with strong arguments and conclude with weaker ones. Both tactics have recommendations, but Hovland found that the effects of the ordering depend ultimately on the listeners. If they're bored and have little interest in the topic, it might be best to try an anti-climax order, to at least get your message across before they drift off. But when the audience is both attentive and concerned about the issues involved, when what you are talking about matters to them, Hovland found that a slow build can be much more effective than an anti-climax.

Hovland is with Aristotle in thinking that facts about the audience make a difference to the persuasive power of an argument. And while he also investigated the power of adding emotion to an argumentative appeal (it turns out a little fear is sometimes a good thing), his focus was on group identity. Someone who is a self-identifying member of a group, who values the group highly and conforms to the group's beliefs about how members are supposed to behave, might be particularly resistant to arguments that come into conflict with the group's norms. To test this, Hovland's researchers gave questionnaires to twelve Boy Scout groups in an effort to gauge their positive attitudes towards such things as woodcraft skills and camping. A week later researchers subjected them to 'a standardized communication, criticizing woodcraft activities and suggesting that in the modern world boys would profit more from learning about their cities'.[22] Harsh, perhaps, but the Scouts generally responded as Scouts should: those who placed the most value on group membership and 'Boy Scout norms' were the least likely to be influenced by arguments critical of their traditional skills.

Hovland was also with Aristotle in thinking that the way the speaker is perceived by the audience plays a large part in whether or not an argument is thought to be persuasive. But he departed from Aristotle by backing his views up with considerable experimental evidence. The two main factors that determine the credibility of the speaker, Hovland found, were 'the extent to which a communicator is perceived to be a source of valid assertions (his "expertness")' and 'the degree of confidence in the communicator's intent to communicate the assertions he considers most valid (his "trustworthiness")'.[23]

In one study, groups of college students read identical articles – the same arguments for the same conclusions – but one group was told the papers were written by a high-credibility source and the other from a low-credibility source. One article, for example, was a consideration of whether an atomic submarine might be built with existing technology. One group saw this article as the highly reliable work of theoretical physicist Robert J. Oppenheimer, and the other saw this as the alarmingly dubious work of *Pravda*, at the time the mouthpiece of Cold War Russia's Communist Party. The very same arguments were perceived as 'less fair' and identical conclusions were regarded as 'less justified' if they came from the less credible source. 96 per cent thought Oppenheimer's arguments were compelling, while just 36 per cent found the very same arguments compelling when presented by *Pravda*. The source of an argument is sometimes considerably more important, when it comes to persuasion, than the argument itself.

Hovland's work was only the beginning. In the years since his pioneering studies, a whole range of theories have been formulated and studies undertaken, all attempting to explain and predict the hidden mechanisms that underlie 'attitude change'. Orators through the ages have certainly had their share of tricks, but it's only been in the last half century or so that a speaker has had so much to go on. Cicero was good, but he had nothing like the kind of theoretical understanding that a contemporary communications specialist has at her disposal. Perhaps one hundred years ago a politician or business leader might make a case to the public by laying out an argument, maybe going so far as to believe that those listening would see reason, be persuaded and go along with the conclusion. That approach is hard to imagine now. No one who knows what they're doing would ever leave so much to chance.

In the middle of the last century, we began to see experimental evidence suggesting that arguments are persuasive only in a certain range of cases – we are clearly not pure enquirers, idealised thinkers sitting in the sun with Socrates or at the bench with Aristotle, following valid arguments to their necessary conclusions. Sometimes what swings it is whether or not the conclusion is explicitly drawn. The same argument will be rejected or accepted not on the strength of the reasons given but on the perceived credibility of the speaker. The order of the presentation can make all the difference. The listener's ideas about the kind of person she is, her self-identity, can also get in the way – thoughts about cognitive dissonance should figure in here too. Once we began to pick argument apart in this new way and understand its limitations, and certainly once we got a better grip on how decision-making actually works in the world, perhaps we also began to see the advantages of other sorts of persuasive practices, like those sketched in this book. At least some of the changes to the way we persuade one another have been at the expense of our interest in being reasonable. As a result, we're changing not just our minds, but our lives, and our social world as well.

*

Finally, a bit of stock-taking. I know that it's easy to say that argument is a lost art, but there is of course another possibility, and in the end I think I have to leave it open. It seems to me that we've moved away from the giving of reasons, as a culture, partly because we've found new ways to persuade one another that are easier to scale up or that simply work more reliably than giving reasons. But it still might be true that argument has always had only a tenuous hold over us. Maybe the thought that we're rational animals, creatures who do what we do for good reasons – maybe all that is just another myth that we live by, to borrow Mary Midgley's useful phrase. We've always been exactly as irrational as we are now, you might think, but sometimes we interpret ourselves and our actions through the lens of rationality, and sometimes we don't. I don't buy it, but it's still a live option.

The other possibility, the one we've been contemplating in this book, is that the way we persuade one another has changed relatively recently. If that's true, there's reason to think that it's part of what's making our society less democratic and less equal than it might otherwise be. The ability to engineer public opinion, mass produce it like any other commodity, is something that has concentrated power in the hands of corporations, or anyway people with money. I think the rise of the darker side of public relations and lobbying is more than coincident with the decline of real democracy in the West. And it's probably true that the appearance of a class of professional persuaders effectively crowds out the rest of us amateurs. Anyone can say anything in our mostly free online world, but an ordinary person can almost never really get a message across – we're mute compared to the persuasive power of the professionals. There are books that will tell you how to persuade others, but compared to the influence of a multinational public relations firm or seriously well-funded lobbying group, it's hard for me to think that 'persuasion' is the right word for what you and I might do.

It also seems clear to me that modern persuasion compromises freedom in various ways. The more we discover about the heuristics and biases that partly shape our thinking, the more we might be nudged in various ways, pushed towards conclusions by well-meaning, paternalistic choice architects – or possibly those with less agreeable agendas, maybe people in the employ of big businesses, dubious governments or other powerful concerns. In some cases, nudges appear benign, even helpful, but so-called hard shoves raise difficult questions. The conception of freedom operative in a lot of this literature seems to boil down to something quite thin: a lack of coercion. But power can be exercised, for good purposes or evil ones, even when nobody is literally forced to do anything. (Don Vito Corleone is not forcing you to accept his offer, but that doesn't mean you're exactly free to refuse either.) A full-blooded conception of freedom, the kind of freedom that's worth preserving anyway, requires much more: something closer to understanding the choices we ourselves make as we act, owning those choices, knowing and feeling that what we do flows from our own, carefully chosen purposes and goals. If that's the kind of freedom you value, maybe that is compromised, even by a well-meaning nudge.

Questions about freedom appeared in our discussion of buying and selling as well. The sorts of objections raised by Vance Packard when he encountered the hidden persuaders pulling strings in the marketplace still resonate when we reflect on neuromarketing and the precision targeting of contemporary persuasive messaging. To remind you of just a part of it, how can it be right to encourage irrationality and impulsiveness when it comes to buying a family's food? Aren't we all demeaned when an understanding of how our minds work is used merely to exploit us commercially? There are more,

perhaps deeper worries, to do with human dignity and whatever right we might think we have to privacy, both in our
homes and in our heads.

We ought to go further. Setting up a world with never-
ending buying cycles and fashions, driving a market through
rendering perfectly good products psychologically obsolete –
all that is an extraordinarily bad idea on a finite, increasingly
crowded planet. It's yet another part of contemporary persuasion that creates ever greater inequality. It pushes the haves and
the have-nots further apart, and there are good reasons to think
that a less equal world has a lot more unnecessary suffering in it
than a more equal one.[24] What's more, the materialistic worldview built into persuasive advertising makes us less happy and
less cooperative individuals every time we encounter it, and we
encounter it almost constantly. At least some research shows
that persuading us to buy things by playing on our anxieties
makes us a bit more depressed, anxious, and even narcissistic and anti-social. In all this, it's important to look the trade-
off square in the eye: human happiness, human well-being, is
undermined in exchange for a growing market and better lives
for the already much better off.

We've found that the use of framing effects in political messaging raises its own set of hard questions. There's the obvious
tangle associated with the way politicians now speak to us – in a
sense dancing backwards while somehow still leading – polling
us and using those polls to tease out the words that are most
likely to push the right buttons in our heads and keep them
in power. It's hard to see speeches and interviews as opportunities for politicians to say what they think or be in some
sense accountable to us. Instead, it's a chance to engage in mere

tactical phrasing, persuading by repetition, which, for what it's worth, certainly works. It's also no part of a real, accountable democracy.

The less obvious tangle has to do with the fluidity of our beliefs and the possibility that our thoughts are so dependent on context that democratic decision-making is, in some sense anyway, itself suspect. Knowing that the crowd will respond in one way to crime framed as a beast on the loose and in another as a disease in need of treatment puts those who might pull our thoughts in one direction rather than another at a clear advantage. But it also means there might be no fact of the matter about what we really believe when it comes to dealing with crime. How to proceed, in the light of that unnerving possibility, is not at all clear to me.

As non-rational forms of persuasion take the place of persuasion by argument, some say we can expect other sorts of changes and losses. Ruth Grant's illuminating book *Strings Attached: Untangling the Ethics of Incentives* takes up the persuasive power of offering money or rewards of some kind in an effort to change behaviour. Governments present tax breaks to businesses that relocate within their borders. Those accused of a crime might be inclined to plead guilty to a lesser charge in exchange for a reduced sentence. There are conditions attached to International Monetary Fund loans, including the introduction of austerity measures. The subjects of experimental research are offered financial compensation for taking part. Children are presented with cash in exchange for better test scores. Maybe it's persuasion by bribe, but it's certainly not persuasion by argument. What does this kind of thing do to us?

For one thing, Grant argues that incentives can 'crowd out'

moral and other kinds of values.[25] She offers a number of examples. British women are 50 per cent less likely to give blood when offered cash incentives to do so. People in Switzerland were less likely to accept a nuclear waste storage facility in their neighbourhood when offered monetary compensation. Children given money to solve educational puzzles in the classroom perform less well and lose interest more quickly than other children. What explains all this?

In some cases, perhaps like giving blood, people do what they do for their own good, altruistic reasons, and the offer of money is a kind of insult that makes them disinclined to be so generous. Paying someone to do something good makes that good act selfish and therefore not really worth doing anymore. It's insulting because it presupposes that your motives were never moral in the first place, that you'll do the right thing only if there's something in it for you. The same goes for the Swiss citizens who might have thought it was their civic obligation to take some of the country's nuclear waste. Maybe they'd do it out of a sense of duty, but they refuse when asked to do it for money. Children learning for the sake of it are, again, doing it for their own good reasons, but paying them shifts the goals, the emphasis, onto something lesser, something not really worth pursuing at all. As Grant explains: 'The incentive, or extrinsic motivation, diminishes the intrinsic motivation. It turns play into work, decreasing both enthusiasm for the task and the level of performance ... Moreover, incentives undermine altruism, reciprocity, and other non-self-interested motives in a manner similar to the way in which they undermine intrinsic motivation.'[26]

Grant suspects that there's a spill-over effect too. If you pay your child to mow the lawn, rather than encourage her to help out for better reasons, she's likely to want a bit of cash for doing the dishes too. Grant argues that if people are regarded as self-interested incentive-seekers, that's just what they become. The more we are treated as one-dimensional creatures, motivated by selfish cost-benefit analyses and little else, the more we 'get used to an "incentivized" environment … the assumption of incentives – that people are primarily moved by calculations of extrinsic benefits and costs – becomes self-fulfilling.'[27] When we're treated like robots, we can turn into robots. Incentives can make us 'passive, self-interested, predictable and manipulable.'[28]

What's true of incentives is probably true of a number of non-rational sorts of persuasion, and I think Grant's conclusions here can be generalised. Any sort of persuasive method that moves us without giving us good reasons diminishes the power of reasons on us. When we're nudged, anchored and incentivised, not reasoned with, we become less reasonable people, more easily manipulated, more self-interested. As persuasion changes, we change, and not at all for the better.

But pan out for a moment, from the effects of modern persuasion on the character of individual people to what it might be doing to us nationally or even globally. The philosopher Martha Nussbaum, for her part, warns that the decline of argumentation in our culture is part of 'a crisis of massive proportions and grave global significance' brought on by changes to the way we now educate children and young adults.[29] As budgets tighten, as governments worry about competing with one another economically, she claims that the humanities are being put aside in almost every nation. With a focus on vocational skills rather than the liberal arts, the world is producing 'generations of useful machines, rather than complete citizens who can think for themselves'.[30]

Nussbaum devotes a chapter in a book on the future of education to the importance of learning to argue in the Socratic tradition. Socrates saw himself as a gadfly, stinging the sluggish horse of democracy into action with his critical questions about justice, truth and goodness. Democracy needs citizens with the sorts of skills Socrates had, Nussbaum argues, just because they're central to democratic citizenship, even constitutive of it. Critical thinkers capable of following arguments are more likely to listen to reason than defer to authority or go along with the mob. People who can argue are far harder to manipulate than those who can't spot fallacies and sophistry. Being able to tease out the truth, she says, is fundamentally anti-authoritarian, essentially democratic, and when history is moving in a certain direction, that kind of thing can matter enormously. A failure to see through demagoguery has led human beings to awful places. Argument is a kind of intellectual self-defence at the very heart of people power. Lose it, and we stand to lose what it protects.

Nussbaum also suggests that the loss of the ability to argue is behind the lack of respect we now show one another in public discourse, and that's partly responsible for our failure to move forward together politically. It can only get worse as nations become more multicultural and people from diverse backgrounds with competing values rub shoulders with one another. She likens public debate in the minds of many of those taking part to a sporting contest. Participants aim only to score points, seeing those on the other side as merely enemies or opponents they hope to defeat by almost any means. No one is expected to seek common ground in a football match, and so no one is likely to compromise or find room for give and take in a debate that's not informed by the norms of reasonable argumentation. But, as Nussbaum points out, Socrates knew better: 'Socrates' attitude towards his interlocutors, by contrast, is exactly the same as his attitude toward himself. Everyone needs examination, and all are equal in the face of the argument. This critical attitude uncovers the structure of each person's position, in the process uncovering shared assumptions, points of intersection that can help fellow citizens progress to a shared conclusion.'[31]

As we lose our grip on the ability to argue, our prospects for building an interconnected, peaceful world can only diminish. It's perhaps the largest cost associated with losing the ability to argue.

*

We're left with what now looks like an urgent question. What can we do about modern persuasion? I think it's important to recognise that there probably is no 'it', in a sense, no single problem of persuasion, no one force or factor steering our world in a particular direction. As we've seen, there are a number of theories, methods and tactics, and an array of interests, all pushing persuasion from different angles. So I don't think there's a single answer to it, just because there's no single problem. It's also important to notice that persuasion itself is not the only thing out there making the world less equal, less democratic, and all the rest of it. You should always be suspicious of anyone reducing anything complicated to a single explanatory principle, and I am certainly not trying to do anything like that.

But when we do try to find ways to cope with new persuasive practices, we run into a unique kind of conceptual trouble. As the techniques of persuasion have evolved, the moral outlook we use to understand them has not kept pace. We understand what to do with a lie, just because lies have always been around and over time we've worked out how to think about them and respond to them. But we're not so sure about spin, much less a nudge or a price anchor. I'm starting to think that new persuasive practices have brought new wrongs into the world, perhaps enormous new wrongs, and we haven't worked out how to think about them yet, how to see them as wrong. Until we do, we won't really know how to judge modern persuasion and therefore how to respond to it. Some of the suggestions on the table already might therefore not go far enough, perhaps because the wrongs in play are not yet obvious to us. It's a reason to go further, push harder against what persuasion has become.

So we should do more than just condemn the worst of lobbying and public relations work – we should consider laws and regulations that make it illegal, punishable by something a whole lot worse than a fine. Should we go so far as to contemplate prison terms for offenders and the dissolution of wayward firms? If we break up monopolies because they're unfair, shouldn't reflection on fairness lead us to rethink PR and lobbying and the concentration of power that comes along with it? If that sounds excessive, maybe we need a new thought in this neighbourhood: a very great many human lives might be lost if a country is pushed into war or away from banning hazardous products, just because people with know-how manage to swing votes or win hearts and minds to a cause. Jeremy Bentham was one of the first to argue that the punishment we attach to a crime ought to be tied to the damage it does to us, individually or collectively. We ought to think about the harm and death caused not just by dangerous corporations and governments, but by those who enable them to get on with their awful work. There are bloody hands all around, and our response ought to be equal to the size of the wrongs perpetrated.

Advertising should be judged in new ways too, ways that keep up with changes to advertising itself. When advertising is condemned, it's often because it's misleading, misrepresenting the product it sells. Sometimes we take offence at advertising when it's insulting, sexist, racist, or just in bad taste. We also worry when it targets children, and perhaps here there's room to expand our thinking. Advertising aimed at children is arguably wrong because children are, in a way, defenceless or anyway more easily manipulated than adults. The more I've discovered about my own defences when it comes to contemporary persuasion, particularly in the retail world, the more I'd welcome a little more protection myself in this connection. I am as vulnerable as a child when placed up against an industry that is in the business of triggering my emotions, playing on my anxieties, and taking advantage of glitches in the heuristics I think with. This kind of manipulation is a new wrong in the world, ushered in by a new understanding of the mind, and it ought to be considered and dealt with as such, at the very least by much better-informed advertising watchdogs and policy-makers.

Another suggestion by some in Martha Nussbaum's camp is a change in education. It might be said that we ought to ensure that critical thinking has a central place in schools and universities – if not a return to grammar, logic and rhetoric, then at least a new emphasis on thinking clearly and well. The ability to argue is teachable, and the more one learns about it, the easier it is to resist the persuasive pressure placed on us.

But we must go further here too, and demand not just a revolution in education, but a kind of continuing education that keeps up with changes to persuasive practices. It's not a new idea. In the run-up to the Second World War, the Institute for Propaganda Analysis was founded. You can find a short history of it in Aldous Huxley's discussion of 'Education for Freedom', which is itself not a bad idea, in *Brave New World Revisited*: 'The Institute was founded in 1937, when Nazi propaganda was at its noisiest and most effective, by Mr Filene, the New England philanthropist. Under its auspices analyses of non-rational propaganda were made and several texts for the instruction of high school and university students were prepared. Then came the war – a total war on all the fronts, the mental no less than the physical. With all the Allied governments engaging in "psychological warfare," an insistence upon the desirability of analyzing propaganda seemed a bit tactless. The Institute was closed in 1941.'[32]

But before it closed, the Institute published books, a regular bulletin and pamphlets, and targeted not just students but opinion-leaders and all interested adults. They warned of common propaganda devices – cherry-picking facts, using vague slogans, name-calling, testimonials from popular figures and so on – and analysed and undermined examples as they surfaced. It was a kind of logical rapid reaction force, and something like that is needed today. An independent body of people who are good at spotting and attacking the worst of modern persuasion could do the world a lot of good.

But top-down responses to modern persuasion are hard levers to pull. Changing advertising legislation, ending the culture of lobbying, outlawing the worst of public relations, a renewal of education – there's too much money and power in the way, or so you might think. Thoughts like this have led me to consider bottom-up solutions, actions an individual might take in the course of an ordinary life, and here I've had a little success in my own experiments. For what it's worth, my main strategy is to try, whenever possible, to bring about the boomerang effect.

Sometimes an attempt at persuasion backfires and leads one to believe the opposite of what's intended. Carl Hovland himself encountered this worrying effect in the 1950s, but the psychologist Jack Brehm is credited with coining the phrase 'psychological reactance' a decade later, and this notion might explain what's sometimes going on when persuasion fails. As he puts it, 'if individuals feel that any of their free behaviours … is eliminated or threatened with elimination, the motivational state of psychological reactance will be aroused. This reactance state is directed toward the restoration of the threatened or eliminated behaviour.'[33] Freedom to choose is fundamental to survival, Brehm argues, and any threat to it mobilises us, awakens us, and makes us want to fight to restore it or at least ensure it's not eroded further. It's partly why telling your child to wear a hat makes her disinclined to wear a hat, and why some motorcyclists fight against mandatory helmet laws. Psychologically, it's a powerful thing.

We encountered it when we saw that the Behavioural Insights Team got a negative reaction to an organ donor message coupled with a stock photo of a happy crowd. People saw through it, suspected it was a marketing gimmick designed to influence them, and were less inclined to go along with the request as a result. When we see through modern persuasion, spot it for what it is, we feel manipulated, and to restore a sense of freedom we sometimes deny the message and choose something else for reasons of our own. This might be going on with women offered money to donate blood or children being paid to do exercises in school – they feel manipulated and are therefore less inclined to comply. Ruth Grant sees a strategy here as well: 'The sense of insult that incentives can provoke is worth cultivating.'[34] So too, I'd argue, with one's reactions to all forms of non-rational persuasion.

*

If I work hard enough in the morning I think it justifies going out for a coffee and possibly a sandwich. I have to pass over a road usually occupied by charity workers seeking donations. Sometimes it's a cancer research charity, and while I'm all in favour of their good work, the volunteers wear mock lab coats. I think immediately of Stanley Milgram's experiments* and Leonard Bickman's work on authority, compliance and attire. I see it as an attempt to manipulate me and feel the pleasing

---

* Milgram's famous experiments show that ordinary people are willing to administer what they believe are fatal electric shocks to others so long as an authority figure presses them to do so. Milgram found that compliance increased when the person in authority wore a lab coat. Bickman discovered that twice as many people obey simple requests if made by a person in a guard's uniform compared with the same person making the same requests in ordinary clothing.[35]

indignation of the boomerang effect. Sometimes it's a different charity, asking me just to send a text message in support of their cause. Again, I've read something about escalating commitments, the so-called 'foot in the door technique'. (In one study, people who first signed a petition were twice as likely to say yes when asked to give money to the cause as those who were simply asked for a donation. You'll be unsurprised to learn that I no longer sign petitions.[36]) I usually do make it past the charity phalanx, but not always. Amnesty International has been getting a regular donation from me for some time now.

The place I go to for coffee is a chain that's actually called 'EAT', and whether or not it's deliberate, I see Walter Dill Scott's direct command approach to advertising all around me. Their own-brand bags of crisps are labelled 'EAT Crisps', yoghurt pots are called 'EAT Yoghurt' – the word 'eat' appears hundreds of times all around me. Nice try, I think, as I decide that I won't buy anything to eat here today.

In another coffee shop I'm offered a loyalty card, and the cashier helpfully gives me two free stamps towards my next coffee, but I refuse to take it. She looks at me sideways, but I've read a study about the endowed progress effect, which shows that people are more inclined to fill up a loyalty card that's already got some stamps on it, than one without – it turns out that even 'artificial advancement increases effort'.[37] But not in my case, just because I know about it, see it as manipulative, and for a moment find the very idea of a loyalty card insulting.

When I shop in the evening, I switch myself on by deliberately taking a second to judge the Gruen Transfer of every store I enter. My local big name supermarket has a particularly nice one – a massive Power Display with seasonal offerings, magazines and flowers. Nice endcaps too. There are soothing images of happy cows and wholesome grains, which I suspect are also there for a reason. They even do a kind of social-proof/ reciprocity/Gruen hat-trick extravaganza, by enabling only Club Card Members to stop for a free cup of coffee by the front door. Seeing it for what it is, I'm quietly pleased not to have that coffee, knowing as I do that the enormous power of reciprocity is not something I want hanging over me in this kind of environment. I consult my shopping list and take care not to deviate from it, but it isn't easy. I try when I can to recognise that everything I see – from the colour of the apple on the carton of juice to the shape of the shower gel bottle – has probably been tested and trialled so as to trigger desire in my brain. Some shops route us through an incredibly insulting impulse-buy chicane on the way to the checkout, but not here, just a few entirely resistible chocolates and biscuits. A man ahead of me in the checkout line reaches over and puts two bags of chocolate footballs in his basket – the sign says 'Two For One' in red lettering on a white background. I wonder if it was the colouring that did it.

I have less luck with political and corporate messaging, because I rarely know when it's coming so I'm often unprepared for it. When I hear a spokesperson for anything making a statement, on television or in a newspaper, I try very hard to identify actual reasons given in support of a conclusion. Having a background in philosophy means I know something about informal fallacies, so those are easy to spot when I'm switched on and thinking. The most common seems to me to be a failure to address the issue at hand – doing everything possible to change the subject if a difficult question is asked. Appeals to emotion stand out (they're not arguments), as do personal anecdotes offered as evidence for some position that actually requires a lot of evidence. Presidents and Prime Ministers go in for this a lot, telling a story about someone they met on a farm somewhere, presumably in an effort to connect with us emotionally. Now that I know that's what they're trying to do, I feel manipulated, the boomerang effect kicks in, and their effort to change my mind falls entirely flat.

My enemy in all this is something we've encountered before: ego depletion. You might think that self-control and will-power are stable character traits, but it turns out that everyone's mind is like a muscle, subject to fatigue, and the more we use it the less able we are to control ourselves.[38] A number of studies have shown that it's a robust feature of our mental lives. To take just one of many examples, subjects were asked to view a film clip – something funny, or maybe a tear-jerker.[39] Some were told to control their emotional responses and others simply watched and reacted however they liked. Both groups were then given anagrams to solve. Those who earlier had to try to control themselves solved 50 per cent fewer anagrams. Half their brain power was just gone. Our mental energy is limited, and when we use it, we become impaired in various ways. We simply can't keep our guard up all the time.

I know in my own case that just being asked a number of questions by a salesperson is enough to wear down my will-power and make me vulnerable to a purchase I wouldn't make otherwise. I can actually feel myself caving in. So I try to conserve energy. I've got into the habit of thinking of my wallet or credit card as a trigger, and whenever I touch it, whenever

I'm about to hand over cash, I make myself stop and try to pay attention.

But ego depletion is just a small part of it. We have hidden enemies too. I'm aware that I'm likely to over-estimate my ability to resist persuasion, but I also now know that all sorts of ridiculous things can influence my thinking in entirely absurd ways. Some of the studies I've encountered in trying to come to grips with persuasion have unsettled any thoughts I might have had about my own rational faculties. It turns out that my political views will probably tilt in a conservative direction if I'm asked about them in close proximity to a hand sanitiser.[40] I know I'm more likely to find someone persuasive if they happen to share my initials or my birthday.[41] I'm less likely to go along with what others say if there's a screensaver with dollar bills on it in the room.[42] I'm more inclined to comply with requests spoken into my right ear than my left.[43] My ability to negotiate a good deal on a car is significantly compromised if I'm sitting in a well-cushioned chair.[44] I'm more inclined to believe propositions that rhyme. (I know this thanks to a paper with the glorious title, 'Birds of a Feather Flock Conjointly'.[45]) I know I'm more likely to believe messages that are easy to read – written clearly, on nice paper, and expressed in simple words.[46] I'm also not entirely sure what to do with all these odd facts.

When I spell out some of these quirks of persuasion to friends in the pub, sometimes lamenting the fact that we're such malleable creatures, I'm often reassured by those who find knowing about all this not debilitating, but empowering. The more we know about persuasion, the better able we are to see through it, some say, and I have to agree. But maybe I'm actually with those who get a little angry when I tell them about Nayirah's 'testimony' about the Kuwaiti babies, Edward Bernays and the engineering of consent, a politician's mind-benumbing message discipline, the manipulation of desire in the marketplace, Frank Luntz's Republican Playbook, decoy pricing, Dichter's dubious views about women, bogus psychometric tests used by a government to manipulate its citizens, politicians creating the illusion of approval by paying for crowds on demand, push polling, stores predicting pregnancies, and the changes contemporary persuasion is making to the nature of democracy, social equality, freedom, and even our prospects for living happy, flourishing, decent human lives in an open and interconnected, peaceful world.

I've felt that anger too, many times, while trying to understand what persuasion has become and what it's doing to us. There's a special kind of anger that it's possible to feel, resentment attached not just to being manipulated, but being manipulated casually, by people who are as good as untouchable, who do a lot of damage to us in exchange for nothing more than money, a salary. We have plenty of movements, and probably the world does not need another lobby that lobbies against lobbying. But if you are now asking yourself what you can do about modern persuasion, it's sometimes enough to think that if a critical mass of us learns to listen to reason again, maybe then we'll realise that there's power in the simple but very difficult act of withholding assent and insisting on good reasons. Sheer numbers can change things. They always do.

I'm reminded of that line in Aristotle's *Ethics*: 'Anybody can become angry – that is easy, but to be angry with the right person and to the right degree and at the right time and for the right purpose, and in the right way – that is not within everybody's power and is not easy.' I'm not yet sure what we will do to fight this shift in persuasion, but I know I'm against it, and the paradoxical heart of it, for me anyway, is the fact that emotion can rise to the defence of reason. It's in a kind of measured, focused, thoughtful anger that a strategy of struggle lies.

Epilogue: Post-Truth Politics

The days just before the 2016 US presidential election now seem like a sunnier, innocent, distant age. As I write this, it was just last week, but it already feels like a very long time ago.

To remind you of how it all seemed then, Hillary Clinton was consistently ahead in the polls, had a blue firewall of solid support and a lead in most swing states, and many viable pathways to the White House. Even Donald Trump seemed to write himself off, saying he'd contest the election if he lost and thought it was somehow rigged. In the final days his campaign looked disorganised, angry, defensive and erratic, trying to sprint to as many states as possible, while Clinton calmly focused on key battlegrounds. Trump's team spent more money on hats than polling – which, given how wrong the polls were, doesn't look so ridiculous now, but it did then. Clinton had been through this before and knew what she was doing. She summoned the star power of the Obamas, Madonna, Barbra Streisand, Samuel L. Jackson and Lady Gaga at her rallies. Trump had the support of a crotch-grabbing Ted Nugent and the star of *Superbabies: Baby Geniuses 2*, Scott Baio. Despite the FBI looking again at her emails, it really did look like she'd win, maybe by a landslide.

The long election year was a like a nasty circus, but despite it all, Americans were expected to snap out of it and reject the hate and divisiveness of Trump's campaign when it mattered. Somehow they didn't. Tens of millions turned out and voted for him – many holding their noses, but others rejoicing at the prospect of a Trump presidency.

The other half of the American population, and a good portion of the wider world, was simply shell-shocked. Writing in *The New Yorker*, a slightly hysterical David Remnick called Trump's election 'a tragedy for the American republic … a sickening event in the history of the United States and liberal democracy'. It is impossible, he wrote, 'to react to this moment with anything less than revulsion and profound anxiety'.[1] *The Guardian* was alarmed. In an unrestrained opinion piece entitled 'Will Donald Trump Destroy America?', Jonathan Freedland wrote: 'This is a political and cultural cataclysm that few believed would really happen … Americans have done a very dangerous thing this week. Because of what they have done we all face dark, uncertain and fearful times.'[2] Gérard Araud, the French Ambassador to the United States, meekly tweeted as if from a darkened, post-apocalyptic bunker: 'A world is collapsing before our eyes.' #RIPAmerica trended on Twitter. Canada's immigration website crashed. Tens of thousands of people took to the streets to protest in more than 25 cities across the United States, night after night. Some chanted, 'No Trump! No KKK! No fascist USA!'

Alongside all this is a struggle to understand not just the meaning of what happened, but how it could have happened in the first place. Conservatives and liberals were equally startled. A part of the answer, I think, is the long-term trend sketched in this book, the shift away from giving reasons in public life, away from praising evidence and facts and arguments, towards something else, something that operates outside of reason. The persuasion revolution has left us with a political discourse that depends more on insults and lies than reasons and good argu- ments – and in this kind of atmosphere, all sorts of awful things can thrive.

The insults slung around in this campaign were breathtak- ing – but maybe the kind of thing to be expected in a world that's forgetting the give and take of argument. *The New York Times* published a list of 'The 279 People, Places and Things Donald Trump Has Insulted on Twitter'.[3] It runs to many, many pages, which is arresting when you think that each tiny nug- get of abuse can be no more than 140 characters long. Rival Republican candidates certainly got an earful. Jeb Bush is vari- ously described as 'a basket case', 'phony', 'weak', and 'clueless'; Ted Cruz is a 'loser', a 'choker', and 'a nasty guy'; and Rick Perry 'should be forced to take an IQ test'. Barack Obama is 'insane', 'incompetent', and 'ridiculous'. Naturally Hillary Clinton gets the most attention. Scanning the list for as long as I could stand it, I counted something approaching 500 individual insults aimed just at her, with repeated appearances of the words 'crooked', 'bad judgement', 'not qualified', 'fraud' and 'dumb'.*

* Wading through all this, it's hard not to think about psychological projection, the theory that people sometimes cope with worries about their own shortcomings by seeing them in others and denouncing them out there, where it's safe for them to do so. It can make you think again about the words that come up a lot in Trump's tweets: 'dumb', 'incompetent', 'ridiculous', 'crooked', 'fraud', 'not qualified', 'total hypocrite' and all the rest. By the way, the 'things' he insulted include baseball ('so ridiculous') and a podium at the White House ('looks odd', he tweeted, 'not good').

It's not just Trump who stooped to something other than reasoned reflection on the issues – it was one of the least inspiring campaigns in American history on almost every side. Republican primaries included discussion of the size of a candidate's penis and mooning, along with regular shouting matches and name-calling. In the middle of one debate, the moderator explained his interruption by saying, 'I want to get the facts straight for the audience'. He was loudly booed by them for his trouble. I found myself thinking again about the grand London debates of the late eighteenth century, and wondering what to make of where we are now.

The presidential debates were also largely untroubled by substantial policy matters. Trump pressed Clinton on her husband's infidelities. Clinton focused on Trump's mistreatment of women, tax dodging, and his racist and sexist remarks. Clinton's team interviewed Tony Schwartz, ghost-writer of Trump's bestselling *The Art of The Deal*, and consulted a panel of psychologists, all in an effort to work out what might get under Trump's skin and trip him up during the debates. With any luck they might really get him to lose it, live on television.[4] In the final days of the campaign, Clinton ramped up references to Trump's talk of assaulting women until she nearly lost her voice. Trump called her a criminal and promised to put her in jail if elected. That was the finale of American political discourse in 2016.

Certainly a presidential candidate's character is important to voters, and so it should be, but it also almost goes without saying that personal attacks have absolutely nothing to do with real policy matters, actual positions on the economy, the climate, healthcare, foreign policy, gun control, immigration, energy, education and a hundred other things that will have serious effects on millions of real human lives in the next four years and beyond. This part of the persuasive language on both sides amounted to what philosophers call *argumentum ad hominem* – an attack on the person, not their position. It's a logical fallacy, and when people who understand argument hear it, they put it to one side as irrelevant to the question at hand. Your opponent might be a bigot or a liar, but pointing that out has no bearing on whether or not their arguments and policies are any good. The candidates should never have gone there, and voters should have ignored it as best they could or insisted on something better from presidential candidates, but those insults landed solidly.

Just as insult has begun to push reasoned argument out of the centre of our political discourse, lies have a much larger place in politics than they ever had. There's no doubt that politicians have relied on mudslinging and lies in the past, but there's a feeling that something new is happening. Catching a politician in a lie has hitherto ended campaigns and careers. Now, both politicians and citizens seem less concerned with what's true and what's not. Again, something we might expect as we become less reasonable people.

A fact-checking website called Politifact rated 144 of Clinton's claims as true or mostly true, but found 40 to be mostly false, another 28 to be completely false, and a worrying seven statements earned the lowest score, 'Pants on Fire', indicating what the site calls 'ridiculous lies'. Only 47 of Trump's claims were either true or mostly true, with 166 of his assertions characterised as mostly false or false – 54 landing in the 'Pants on Fire' category.[5] *The Washington Post*'s fact checkers gave their lowest ranking, Four Pinocchios, to 70 per cent of Trump's claims that they examined.[6] Politifact monitored everything both Trump and Clinton said across all platforms over five days of campaigning. Trump averaged a lie about every three minutes in five hours of speaking and tweeting. In one and a half hours of statements over the same week, Clinton averaged a lie every twelve minutes.[7]

It's said that we've entered an era of post-truth politics – 'post-truth' is the Oxford Dictionary's word of the year. The idea first received real attention in a 2010 blogpost for *Grist* written by David Roberts. The original thought was that we've strayed some distance from the Enlightenment ideal of how a voter ought to operate: one should gather facts, draw conclusions based on the facts, come to a reasoned political position with a grounding in those conclusions, and then lend support to the political party which promises to enact policies in line with one's considered views.

But Roberts claims we now do more or less the reverse. We start by choosing a party whose representatives seem to share our values, people we feel we kind of like, people who are like us, people we identify with, people who 'tell it like it is'. We then support whatever positions they and their party advocate, and only then, if pressed, do we try to come up with reasons and arguments, finally cherry-picking just the facts that support those arguments and the positions we already hold – mostly ignoring anything contradictory. As a result, Roberts writes, 'we live in post-truth politics, a political culture in which politics (public opinion and media narratives) have become almost entirely disconnected from policy (the substance of legislation).'[8]

Seeing the election in this way – as having a lot to do with feelings and not with facts, good reasons and arguments – can help us understand why insults mattered and truth was put to one side. It can also help us answer the earlier question, repeated by dazed Democrats and well-wishers abroad: what were Trump supporters thinking? If the place of reason in public life really is on the wane, what matters isn't what Trump's supporters were thinking, but what they were feeling.

No doubt that's a complicated matter, and feelings were different for different people, but some Trump followers expressed themselves plainly enough. They were angry: angry with the establishment, with career politicians lining their pockets, with East Coast elites whose liberal policies were responsible for closed mines and factories, with Washington insiders on first-name terms with fat cat bankers, with a biased media, and with political correctness full stop. In a wide-ranging analysis of Trump's personality, professor of psychology Dan P. McAdams concludes that 'the emotional core around which Donald Trump's personality constellates is anger ... Indeed, anger may be the operative emotion behind Trump's high extroversion as well as his low agreeableness ... And anger permeates his political rhetoric.'[9] If political support now follows feeling, and if the American voter's anger is understood alongside Trump's personality, some part of his victory can start to make sense, even seem inevitable.

It's worth noticing that it might work this way for many on the other side of the aisle too. A lot of Democrats supported Obama because of how they felt about who he was, what electing an African-American might mean, rather than clear-headed reflection on his policies. As the comedian Larry

Wilmore put it at the White House Correspondents' Dinner, 'I've always joked that I voted for the president because he's black. And people say, "Well, do you agree with his policies?" And I always said, "I agree with the policy that he's black." I said, "As long as he keeps being black, I'm good." They'd say, "What about Iraq?" I'd say, "Is he still black?"'[10]

Look beyond America and you'll find other politicians playing on feeling and putting the truth to one side too. According to *The Economist*, '"post-truth" politics – a reliance on assertions that "feel true" but have no basis in fact' has taken hold in a growing number of countries.[11] Officials in the Polish government have made political capital out of the claim, unsupported by evidence, that President Lech Kaczynski did not simply die in a tragic plane crash but was assassinated by the Russians. Politicians in Turkey have suggested, again with no grounding in fact, that the CIA was behind the recent failed coup. Carbon laws were repealed in Australia following political campaigning grounded in not much more than outright lying. 'The scaremongering was almost completely without substance', one observer noted. 'Mining leaders openly acknowledged that the debate had moved beyond rational discourse.'[12]

The United Kingdom might have moved beyond rational discourse too. Lies and unfounded claims formed the backbone of both sides of the debate on membership of the European Union. Those pushing for the UK to remain warned of alarming consequences for a vote to leave. An emergency Brexit budget would make previous austerity budgets look generous, and it would have to be implemented immediately. The economy would quickly fall into recession and businesses would flee, leading to catastrophic job losses. There was even talk of World War Three and, according to the European Council's President, Donald Tusk, the destruction of 'Western political civilisation in its entirety'.[13] By the end of 2016, not only was there was no recession and no world war, unemployment hit an eleven-year low and the UK's GDP grew by 0.5 per cent. It was among the best results for any of the world's leading economies.[14]

Those pushing a vote to leave the EU offered to 'give our NHS the £350m the EU takes every week' – the slogan was famously painted on the sides of the Leave battle bus and repeated by campaigners. It was just as famously denounced as misleading by several reasonable sources, not least the UK Statistics Authority – the sum failed to take into account the many millions that flow back into the UK through such things as farm subsidies and research grants. Advocates of Leave knew the figure was wrong – they were pressed on it and presented with the actual numbers – but they carried on repeating what they knew to be a lie.

In a televised interview, Michael Gove, then Justice Secretary and a leading Leave campaigner, was presented with a list of world leaders, banks and other financial institutions, UN secretary generals past and present, and trade union officials – all had reasons for supporting Remain. When asked why the public should trust a handful of Tories rather than so many authorities of international standing who probably knew what they were talking about, Gove said: 'I think the British people have had enough of experts.'[15] The thing is, he's probably right.

*

It's never easy to understand your own times, but that hasn't stopped a lot of speculation about the times we're in now.

The explanations in the air at the moment tend to pick some large, new feature of the world and point to that as the odd thing now in existence that explains what's going on. So some look to technology. The thought is that Facebook newsfeeds and search engine algorithms tend to silo us, keep us stuck in filter bubbles along with other like-minded people, saying the same things to one another, reinforcing and entrenching ever more extreme views. It can help explain a country turning inwards politically or becoming ever more polarised. It can partly explain why we talk past one another.

Some point to the fear and insecurity that's followed the recent financial crash and argue that it could lead voters to tough-talking leaders promising security. A recent study examined 800 general elections over 140 years in twenty economies. It found that after a serious financial crisis, 'voters seem to be particularly attracted to the political rhetoric of the extreme right, which often attributes blame to minorities or foreigners'. They concluded that, 'on average, extreme right-wing parties increase their vote share by 30% after a financial crisis'.[16]

Others say the current tilt towards nationalist, populist movements worldwide can be explained by recent demographic shifts. In the Netherlands, Hungary, France, Poland, Turkey and Germany, nationalism is on the rise or taking charge – Trump's talk fits the mould, as does some of the language around the Leave campaign. Whatever this kind of populism is, it depends on thoughts about in-groups and out-groups, us versus them. Race can figure enormously in this kind of equation. The 'us' both in the US and Europe is often 'us white people', and the 'them' might be anyone from drug dealers, Mexicans and Muslims, to Black Lives Matter protesters, Eastern Europeans,

Syrians, and Africans. Those who see our times by these lights have a straightforward explanation of the contemporary political scene: we're hearing the 'death rattle of angry, fearful white men'.[17]

To all of these new possibilities, add the very long-term trend we've considered in this book, the slow-motion shift in persuasion that seems to have changed both our minds and our social world. As modern persuasion sways us without giving us good reasons, as being reasonable loses its place among our core values, the power of reason over us really does seem to diminish. When we're not reasoned with, as we saw in the last chapter, we become less reasonable people, more easily manipulated, more self-interested, more likely to go along with the crowd rather than question what's being thrown at us. We're certainly less likely to engage critically with one another. Unless we do something about it, both the US election and the EU referendum are a glimpse of the future that might now lie ahead.

I'll say again what seems to me to be an increasingly important point. The ability to argue, to think critically, spot fallacies and work together towards the truth is a kind of intellectual self-defence at the heart of democracy. If we lose that, we lose what it protects – and, ultimately, what it protects is us from all sorts of horrors. We must recover the art of argument, sound political discussion, and reasoned debate. A lot hangs on it.

It's widely agreed that Trump's election and the vote for Brexit were protests, reactions by people fed up with the way things are, willing to have anything but the status quo, almost no matter what the new reality might be. But real solutions to this much discontent have to go beyond protest, and anyway our troubles probably won't be solved by Trump or by Brexit.

Instead, we could do a lot worse than to try to think again about what matters to us when we reflect on what democracy is. Not only should we insist on a lot better than insults and lies from our leaders, we've all got to recognise that our duties as citizens are not discharged by retweets and online petitions. We have to learn to talk to one another again and follow the discussion and the argument wherever it takes us. We have to recognise that the point of politics in the public sphere isn't to win over the other side to our way of thinking, but to move forward together.

A real political conversation is harder to sustain than a stream of insults, and thinking through the facts, openly and honestly, is more difficult than just going along with whatever feels right. Finding a way through this mess won't be easy, but it's still within our grasp if we learn to listen to reason again.

November 2016

Notes

Preface

1. The lecture was about the problem of universals. How can universal properties like redness exist in many places at once – in fire engines, rubies and roses? The don argued that universal properties exist as ideas in God's mind. There's really just one Red, a single idea in God's mind that is somehow partly reflected in the red things we see in the created order all around us. If that's right, I argued, so too with everything that shares a property, everything that's of a kind. Not just all red things, but all dogs are dogs because God has the idea of Dog in his mind. All trees are trees because God has the idea of Tree in his mind. The question I asked was, 'If all God's ideas are the same kind of thing, namely ideas, what makes *them* the kind of thing that *they* are?' It's a version of an old objection to Plato's metaphysics, owed to Aristotle, called the third man argument. The professor's proposed solution led to an infinite regress, a series of further questions and replies, and it was therefore no solution at all.

Chapter 1: The Robin Hood on Butcher Lane

1. This account of the London debating societies depends very much on Donna T. Andrew (1994), 'Introduction', *London Debating Societies 1776–1799*, VII–XIII, and Andrew (1996), 'Popular Culture and Public Debate: London 1780', *The Historical Journal*, 39, 2, pp. 405–23.
2. Andrew (1994), p. 407.
3. *Ibid*.
4. Andrew (1996), pp. 407–08.
5. September 1778, *Gazetteer*, cited in Andrew (1994).
6. For an account of the repression of public debating societies, see Mary Thale (1989), 'London Debating Societies in the 1790s', *The Historical Journal*, 32.1, pp. 57–86; and Iain McCalman (1987), 'Ultra-Radicalism

and Convivial Debating-Clubs in London, 1795–1838', *The English Historical Review*, Vol. 102, No. 403, pp. 309–33.

7. Michael Sandel, 'The Lost Art of Democratic Debate', www.ted.com/talks/michael_sandel_the_lost_art_of_democratic_debate.

8. Lee Siegel (2010), 'The Lost Art of Argument', *Wall Street Journal*, 13 November 2010.

9. Bertrand Russell (2008), *The Problems of Philosophy* (Rockville, MD: Arc Manor), p. 101.

Chapter 2: The Art of Steering Heads Inside

1. As reported in *O'Dwyer's PR Services Report*, January 1991, p. 10.

2. 'Faked Kuwaiti Girl Testimony', video, viewed 26 March 2014, youtu.be/LmfVs3WaE9Y; the following quotations come from her testimony.

3. George H.W. Bush (2009), *Speaking of Freedom: The Collected Speeches* (New York: Simon & Schuster) p. 162.

4. Amnesty International, 'Iraq/Occupied Kuwait Human Rights Violations Since 2 August', 19 December 1990, p. 56.

5. John R. MacArthur, 'Remember Nayirah, Witness for Kuwait?', *The New York Times*, Monday, 6 January 1992.

6. 'Deception on Capitol Hill', *The New York Times*, 15 January 1992.

7. John MacArthur, interview in Neil Docherty (director) (1992), *The Fifth Estate: To Sell A War: Gulf War Propaganda*, viewed 26 March 2014, youtu.be/nrwUgWpv4qA.

8. Craig Unger (2004), *House of Bush, House of Saud: The Secret Relationship Between the World's Two Most Powerful Dynasties* (London: Scribner), p. 136ff.

9. John Stauber and Sheldon Rampton (1995), *Toxic Sludge is Good for You! Lies, Damn Lies, and the Public Relations Industry* (Monroe, ME: Common Courage Press), p. 169. This account of the activities of Hill and Knowlton and Citizens for a Free Kuwait depends on Stauber and Rampton; Docherty; David Miller and William Dinan (2008), *A Century of Spin: How Public Relations Became the Cutting Edge of Corporate Power* (London: Pluto Press), especially Chapter 7; and Stuart Ewen (1996), *PR: A Social History of Spin* (New York: Basic Books), p. 28ff.

10. Dee Alsop, representative of the Wirthlin Group, interviewed in Docherty (1992).

11. *Ibid.*

12. John R. MacArthur (2004), *Second Front: Censorship and Propaganda in the 1991 Gulf War* (Berkeley: University of California Press), p. 247.

13. Docherty (1992).

14. Aziz Abu-Hamad, 'Kuwait's "Stolen" Incubators', report for Middle East Watch, dated 6 February 1992.
15. PRSA, 'What is public relations?', www.prsa.org/AboutPRSA/PublicRelationsDefined/#.U1pxQfldWSo, accessed 23 April 2014.
16. 'Public Relations Firms in the US: Market Research Report', *IBIS World*, December 2013.
17. Chris Grimshaw (2007), 'A Tour of the United Kingdom's Public Relations Industry', in William Dinan and David Miller (eds), *Thinker, Faker, Spinner, Spy: Corporate PR and the Assault on Democracy* (London: Pluto Press) p. 34.
18. John Sullivan, 'PR Industry Fill Vacuum Left by Shrinking Newsrooms', *ProPublica*, 1 May 2011.
19. Grimshaw (2007), p. 33.
20. These and nearly 150 more examples can be found at sourcewatch.org/index.php/Front_groups#Examples, accessed 23 April 2013.
21. David Lee, 'Wikipedia investigates PR firm Bell Pottinger's edits', bbc.co.uk, 8 December 2011.
22. 'The Transcript: "David Cameron raised it with the Chinese Prime Minister"', *The Independent*, 6 December 2011.
23. Bernard Williams (2001), *Truth and Truthfulness: An Essay in Genealogy* (Princeton: Princeton University Press), p. 96.
24. 'P.R. Firm Had No Reason to Question Kuwaiti's Testimony', *The New York Times*, 7 January 1992.
25. Clifford Krauss, 'Congressman Says Girl Was Credible', *The New York Times*, 12 January 1992.
26. Edward L. Bernays (1928), *Propaganda* (Brooklyn: Ig Publishing), p. 50.
27. Amanda Amos and Margaretha Haglund (2000), 'From social taboo to "torch of freedom": the marketing of cigarettes to women', *Tobacco Control*, 9, pp. 3–8.
28. 'May Woman Smoke In Auto?; Not in Fifth Avenue, Says Bicycle Policeman – Trouble Follows', *The New York Times*, 26 September 1904.
29. 'Few hotels have rules against women smokers', *The New York Times*, 16 March 1919.
30. *New Mexico State Tribune*, dispatch from the United Press, 1 April 1929. These and other quotes from Miss Hunt appear in Larry Tye (1998), *The Father of Spin: Edward L. Bernays and the Birth of Public Relations* (New York: Henry Holt and Co.). Chapter 2 is particularly enlightening.
31. Edward L. Bernays (1965), *Biography of an Idea: Memoirs of Public Relations Counsel Edward L. Bernays* (New York: Simon & Schuster), p. 383.
32. Details of the plans behind the campaign are spelled out in Tye (1998), p. 28ff.

33. Tye (1998), p. 29ff.
34. Anne Marie O'Keefe and Richard W. Pollay (1996), 'Deadly Targeting of Women in Promoting Cigarettes', *Journal of the American Medical Women's Association*, 51, pp. 1–2.
35. 'Sun Smiles on New Yorkers in Easter Parade', *Chicago Daily Tribune*, 1 April 1929. I'm helped here by useful pointers from Michael Kliegl on Science Comma Blog, blogs.kent.ac.uk/sciencecomma.
36. 'Fair Smokers Go on Parade', *Los Angeles Times*, 1 April 1929.
37. Tye (1998), p. 33.
38. Tye (1998), p. 8. The following account of Bernays' career and the rise of PR is owed to Tye (1998); David Miller and William Dinan (2008), *A Century of Spin: How Public Relations Became the Cutting Edge of Corporate Power* (London: Pluto Press); and Stuart Ewen (1996), *PR! A Social History of Spin* (New York: Basic Books).
39. As quoted by Ewen (1996), p. 132, from Ivy Lee (1924), 'The Meaning of Publicity' (unpublished manuscript).
40. Edward L. Bernays (1928), p. 27.
41. Ewen (1996), p. 132.
42. Bernays (1965), p. 167.
43. Gustave Le Bon (2002), *The Crowd: A Study of the Popular Mind* (Mineola, NY: Dover Publications), p. 8; I'm helped here very much by Ewen (1996), Chapter 7.
44. Le Bon (2002), p. 34.
45. *Ibid.*
46. Wilfred Trotter (1919), *Instincts of the Herd in Peace and War* (New York: Macmillan), p. 36.
47. Ivy Lee, 'Publicity', address before the American Electric Railway Association, 10 October 1916, as quoted in Ewen, p. 74.
48. Ray Eldon Hiebert (1966), *Courtier to the Crowd: the Story of Ivy Lee and the Development of Public Relations* (Ames: Iowa State University Press).
49. Walter Lippmann (2004), *Public Opinion* (Mineola, NY: Dover Publications), p. 8.
50. Lippmann (2004), p. 136.
51. Lippmann (2004), p. 170.
52. Walter Lippmann (1927), *The Phantom Public* (New York: Harcourt Brace and Co.), p. 155.
53. Bernays (1928), p. 1.
54. *Ibid*, p. 9ff.
55. Bernays interviewed by Adam Curtis in 'Happiness Machines', *The Century of the Self*, Part 1.

56. Alex Carey, quoted in David Miller and William Dinan (2008), *A Century of Spin: How Public Relations Became the Cutting Edge of Corporate Power* (London: Pluto Press), p. 56.

57. Miller and Dinan (2008), p. 57.

58. William Dinan and David Miller (eds) (2007), *Thinker, Faker, Spinner, Spy: Corporate PR and the Assault on Democracy* (London: Pluto Press), p. 11.

59. For a good discussion, see Randal Marlin (2013), *Propaganda and the Ethics of Persuasion* (Peterborough: Broadview Press), p. 197.

60. Ewen (1996), p. 412ff.

61. *Ibid.*

62. Marlin (2013), p. 339.

63. Dinan and Miller (2007), p. 299.

64. *Ibid.*

65. Andrews Perez and David Sirota, 'Election 2016: Jeb Bush Speech Denouncing Lobbyists was Organized by Corporate Lobbying Group', *International Business Times*, 1 July 2015.

66. Stefania Vitali, James B. Glattfelder, and Stefano Battiston (2011), 'The network of global corporate control', *PLoS ONE*, 6(10): e25995. doi:10.1371/journal.pone.0025995.

67. The image is owed to John Cavanaugh, *et al.* (2002), *Alternatives to Global Capitalism: A Better World is Possible* (San Francisco: Berrett-Koehler), p. 124. Cavanaugh makes a number of other good suggestions for coping with corporate power through law-making. I'm grateful to Randall Curren for pointing me to it.

Chapter 3: On Second Thoughts

1. Richard H. Thaler and Cass R. Sunstein (2008), *Nudge: Improving Decisions about Health, Wealth, and Happiness* (London: Penguin), p. 6.

2. This account of the two systems relies on Daniel Kahneman (2011), *Thinking, Fast and Slow* (London: Penguin), p. 19ff. Thaler and Sunstein are also in the mix.

3. These examples can be found in Shane Frederick (2005), 'Cognitive Reflection and Decision Making', *Journal of Economic Perspectives*, 19.4. See Kahneman (2011), pp. 45 and 65ff, and Thaler and Sunstein (2008), p. 23ff.

4. Kahneman (2011), p. 420. It's worth mentioning that the discovery of many of these biases pre-dates the two systems approach, and some suspect that the interaction between the systems is not as straightforward as I'm making it – I'm using systems language throughout anyway.

5. Kahneman (2011), p. 146ff. A very large number of studies confirm a halo effect when it comes to political candidates.

6. See Kahneman (2011), p. 128ff.

7. The study appears in A. Tversky and D. Kahneman (1973), 'Availability: A heuristic for judging frequency and probability', *Cognitive Psychology*, 5 (1), pp. 207–33.

8. See Michael Ross and Fiore Sicoly (1979), 'Egocentric Biases in Availability and Attribution', *Journal of Personality and Social Psychology*, 37, pp. 322–36; discussed in Kahneman (2011), p. 131.

9. Franklin Templeton Investments (2012), 'Investors Should Beware The Role of "Availability Bias"', *Business Insider*, 6 October 2012.

10. Bureau of Consular Affairs, US Department of State (2012), 'Terrorism Deaths, Injuries, Kidnappings of Private US Citizens, 2011'.

11. D.L. Hoyert, J.Q. Xu (2012), 'Deaths: Preliminary data for 2011', National Vital Statistics Reports, Vol. 61, No. 6 (Hyattsville, MD: National Center for Health Statistics).

12. See T. Mussweiler and F. Strack, (1999). 'Hypothesis-consistent testing and semantic priming in the anchoring paradigm: A selective accessibility model', *Journal of Experimental Social Psychology*, 35, pp. 136–64.

13. G.B. Northcraft and M.A. Neale (1987), 'Experts, amateurs, and real estate: An anchoring-and-adjustment perspective on property pricing decisions', *Organizational Behavior and Human Decision Processes*, 39, pp. 228–41.

14. T.D Wilson, C.E. Houston, K.M. Etling and N. Brekke (1996), 'A New Look at Anchoring Effects: Basic Anchoring and Its Antecedents', *Journal of Experimental Psychology*, 125.4, pp. 387–402.

15. L. Baker and R. Emry (1993), 'When Every Relationship is Above Average: Perceptions and Expectations of Divorce at the Time of Marriage', *Law and Human Behavior*, 17, pp. 439–50.

16. Robert Levine (2006), *The Power of Persuasion: How We're Bought and Sold* (Oxford: Oneworld), p. 8ff.

17. Kahneman (2011), p. 416.

18. Thaler and Sunstein (2008), p. 9.

Chapter 4: When Push Comes to Shove

1. David Cameron, 'The Next Age of Government', TED Talk, February 2010, www.ted.com/talks/david_cameron.

2. From the BIT's website, www.behaviouralinsights.co.uk/about-us.

3. It's a lot more complicated than this. See Laura Haynes, Owain Service, Ben Goldacre, and David Torgerson (2013), 'Test, Learn, Adapt:

Developing Public Policy with Randomised Controlled Trials', Cabinet Office.

4. Cabinet Office Behavioural Insights Team (2011), 'Behaviour Change and Energy Use', p. 11.

5. Reported in *The Guardian*, 'The Nudge Unit – Has It Worked So Far?', 2 May 2013.

6. Behavioural Insights Team (2013), 'Applying Behavioural Insights to Organ Donation'.

7. This discussion draws on Robert B. Cialdini (2009), *Influence: Science and Practice* (Boston: Pearson), Chapter 4, and Thaler and Sunstein (2008), p. 58ff.

8. Solomon Asch (1995), 'Opinions and Social Pressure', in Elliott Aronson (ed.), *Readings About the Social Animal* (New York: W.H. Freeman).

9. Richard S. Crutchfield (1955), 'Conformity and Character', *American Psychologist*, 10, pp. 191–8.

10. Hunt Allcott (2011), 'Social Norms and Energy Conservation', *Journal of Public Economics*, 95.9, pp. 1082–95.

11. Behavioural Insights Team (2013), 'Applying Behavioural Insights to Organ Donation', p. 4.

12. Tversky and Kahneman (1991), 'Loss Aversion in Riskless Choice: A Reference-Dependent Model', *The Quarterly Journal of Economics*, 106.4, pp. 1039–61.

13. Kahneman (2011), p. 279ff.

14. See Cialdini (2009), Chapter 2; and Levine (2006), Chapter 3.

15. Alvin W. Gouldner (1960), 'The Norm of Reciprocity: A Preliminary Statement', *American Sociological Review*, 25, pp. 161–78.

16. R.T. Regan (1971), 'Effects of a favor and liking on compliance', *Journal of Experimental Social Psychology*, 7, pp. 627–39.

17. Leon Festinger (1957), *A Theory of Cognitive Dissonance* (Stanford: Stanford University Press); see also T. Freijy and E.J. Kothe (2013), 'Dissonance-based Interventions for Health Behaviour Change: A Systematic Review', *British Journal of Health Psychology*, 18.2, pp. 310–37.

18. www.organdonation.nhs.uk; accessed June 2014.

19. Behavioural Insights Team, 'Annual Update 2011–2012', www.gov.uk, accessed 17 June 2014; also reported in *The Guardian* (2013), 'The Nudge Unit – Has It Worked So Far?'.

20. The story was revealed by the blog Skwawkbox and picked up widely; see *The Guardian*, 'Jobseekers made to carry out bogus psychometric tests', 30 April 2013.

21. www.behaviourlibrary.com/strengths.php; accessed 18 June

2014. The test has been taken down, but you can still find screengrabs at Skwawkbox: skwalker1964.wordpress.com/2013/04/18/fake-dwp-psych-test-reveals-sinister-govt-mind-control/.

22. *The Guardian*, 'Jobseekers psychometric test "is a failure"', 6 May 2013.

23. *Ibid.*

24. *Ibid.*

25. So argues Andrew Orlowski, 'Nudge Unit Flies into Nesta's Arms', *The Register*, 6 February 2014.

26. Cass Sunstein (2013), *Simpler: The Future of Government* (New York: Simon & Schuster), p. 2.

27. *Ibid.*, p. 3.

28. Sunstein discusses some of this himself in Sunstein (2013), p. 20ff; for videos and quotations, see: mediamatters.org/blog/2013/03/21/cass-sunstein-received-death-threats-after-fox/193182.

29. Sunstein (2013), p. 100.

30. William Samuelson and Richard J. Zeckhauser (1988), 'Status Quo Bias in Decision Making', *Journal of Risk and Uncertainty*, pp. 7–59.

31. Discussed in Sunstein (2013), p. 103.

32. Sunstein (2013), 'Impersonal Default Rules vs. Active Choices vs. Personalized Default Rules: A Triptych'; available at SSRN: ssrn.com/abstract=2171343, or dx.doi.org/10.2139/ssrn.2171343.

33. Sunstein (2013), p. 130ff.

34. *Ibid.*, p. 142ff.

35. Thaler and Sunstein (2008), p. 24.

36. Some people do argue against it, or at least argue that following a few simple rules can get us out of trouble. See Gerd Gigerenzer (2014), *Risk Savvy: How to Make Good Decisions* (New York: Penguin).

37. Thaler and Sunstein (2008), p. 5.

38. *Ibid.*

39. *Ibid.*

40. Sunstein (2013), pp. 191–2.

41. See Sunstein (2013), Chapter 9 and Sunstein (2012), 'The Storrs Lectures: Behavioral Economics and Paternalism', *Yale Law Journal*, Vol. 122, pp. 1826–99.

42. Sunstein (2013), p. 192.

43. *Ibid.*, p. 194.

44. See discussions in Thaler and Sunstein (2008), Introduction; and Sunstein (2013), Chapter 9.

45. Sunstein (2013), p. 187; see also Sunstein (2014), *Why Nudge?: The Politics of Libertarian Paternalism* (Yale: Yale University Press); and Sunstein

(2012), 'The Storrs Lectures: Behavioral Economics and Paternalism', *Yale Law Journal*, available at SSRN: ssrn.com/abstract=2182619, or dx.doi.org/10.2139/ssrn.2182619.

46. Sunstein (2012), 'The Storrs Lectures', p. 45.
47. Sunstein (2013), p. 200.
48. *Ibid.*
49. See the discussion in Sunstein (2012), 'The Storrs Lectures'.
50. Isaiah Berlin (2002), (Henry Hardy, ed.), *Liberty* (Oxford: Oxford University Press), p. 178.
51. Edward L. Glaeser (2006), 'Paternalism and Psychology', *University of Chicago Law Review*, 73.1, p. 155.
52. Sunstein (2013), p. 10.
53. The study was undertaken by Mark J. Whitehead, Professor of Geography at Aberystwyth University, and details can be found at changingbehaviours.wordpress.com/2013/11/04/globalising-nudgew/.
54. BBC (5 February 2014), '"Nudge unit" sold off to charity and employees'.

Chapter 5: Lost for Words

1. Matt Bai (17 July 2005), 'The Framing Wars', *The New York Times*.
2. Richard Wolffe (11 October 2004), 'Trail Mix: Between the Numbers', *Newsweek*.
3. Bai (2005), 'The Framing Wars'.
4. George Lakoff (2004), *Don't Think of an Elephant: Know Your Values and Frame the Debate* (White River Junction: Chelsea Green Publishing), p. 3ff.
5. Kahneman and Tversky (1981), 'The Framing of Decisions and the Psychology of Choice', *Science*, New Series, Vol. 211, No. 4481, pp. 453–8; see discussion in Kahneman (2011), p. 368.
6. Kahneman (2011), p. 368.
7. Herbert Hyman and Paul Sheatsley (1950), 'The Current Status of American Public Opinion', in J.C. Payne (ed.), *The Teaching of Contemporary Affairs*; Twenty-first Yearbook of the National Council of Social Studies; and more recently Howard Schuman and Stuart Presser (1981), *Questions and Answers in Attitude Surveys* (New York: Academic Press). I'm helped here by a good discussion in Jamie Terence Kelly (2012), *Framing Democracy: A Behavioral Approach to Democratic Theory* (Princeton: Princeton University Press), Chapter 1.
8. See Richard Gooding (November 2004), 'The Trashing of John McCain', *Vanity Fair*; and Ann Banks (January 2008), 'Dirty Tricks, South Carolina and John McCain', *The Nation*.

9. www3.norc.org/GSS+Website/.

10. Kenneth Rasinski (1989), 'The Effect of Question Wording on Public Support for Government Spending', *The Public Opinion Quarterly*, Vol. 53, No. 3, pp. 388–94; see Kelly (2012), p. 17ff.

11. *Ibid.*

12. Sam Howe Verhovek (6 November 1997), 'The 1997 Elections: Affirmative Action; Referendum in Houston Shows Complexity of Preferences Issue', *The New York Times*.

13. Lewis F. Powell, Jr. (1971), 'Attack on American Free Enterprise System', Washington and Lee School of Law, Powell Archives, law.wlu.edu/powellarchives, p. 1.

14. *Ibid.*, p. 2ff.

15. *Ibid.*, p. 6ff.

16. *Ibid.*, p. 10.

17. *Ibid.*, p. 15.

18. *Ibid.*, p. 16.

19. *Ibid.*, p. 26.

20. *Ibid.*, p. 30.

21. This is a quotation from the Heritage Foundation's website, www.heritage.org/about.

22. The Heritage Foundation and Affiliates (2013), 'Consolidated Financial Report'.

23. Nick Cohen (10 December 2006), 'How a celebrity pollster created Cameron', *The Guardian*.

24. www.luntzglobal.com/.

25. PBS interview, www.pbs.org/wgbh/pages/frontline/shows/persuaders/interviews/luntz.html.

26. Frank Luntz (2010), 'The Language of Financial Reform', www.docstoc.com/docs/23808095/Language-of-Financial-Reform.

27. Frank Luntz (2009), 'The Language of Healthcare', thinkprogress.org/wp-content/uploads/2009/05/frank-luntz-the-language-of-healthcare-20091.pdf.

28. Oliver Burkeman (4 March 2003), 'Memo exposes Bush's new green strategy', *The Guardian*.

29. Frank Luntz Research Companies (2006), 'The New American Lexicon'; I have made corrections to grammar and inconsistent usage in the text.

30. *Ibid.*, p. 10.

31. *Ibid.*, p. 11.

32. *Ibid.*, p. 24.

33. *Ibid.*, p. 24.
34. *Ibid.*, p. 63.
35. *Ibid.*, p. 165ff.
36. George Lakoff and Mark Johnson (1980), *The Metaphors We Live By* (Chicago: University of Chicago Press), p. 3.
37. Lakoff and Johnson (1980), p. 5. The following discussion also depends on Lakoff (2004), Lakoff and Johnson (1999), *Philosophy in the Flesh: The Embodied Mind and Its Challenge to Western Philosophy* (New York: Basic Books); Lakoff (2003), *Moral Politics* (Chicago: University of Chicago Press); Lakoff (2006), *Whose Freedom? The Battle Over America's Most Important Idea* (New York: Farrar, Straus & Giroux).
38. Paul Thibodeau and Lera Boroditsky (2011), 'Metaphors We Think With: The Role of Metaphor in Reasoning', *PLoS ONE*, Vol. 6, Issue 2.
39. Lakoff and Johnson (1999), p. 17.
40. 'Forward', youtu.be/1WbQe-wVK9E, published 30 April 2012.
41. P. Brinol and R.E. Petty (2003), 'Overt head movements and persuasion: A self-validation analysis', *Journal of Personality & Social Psychology*, 84, pp. 1123–39.
42. Dan Schneider (22 July 2015), '1-800-Hire-A-Crowd', *The Atlantic*.
43. crowdsondemand.com/services/political-services/, accessed 3 September 2015.
44. Ian Cioffi (23 June 2015), '"Rent a Crowd" Company Admits Politicians Are Using Their Service', *MintPress News*.
45. Teenie Matlock (November–December 2012), 'Framing Political Messages with Grammar and Metaphor', *American Scientist*.
46. See Lakoff (2003), Chapter 12 and Lakoff (2004), Chapter 1.
47. Lakoff (2004), p. 8.
48. *Ibid.*, p. 12.
49. *Ibid.*, p. 17.
50. *Ibid.*, p. 169.
51. *Ibid.*, p. 24.
52. Marc Cooper (April 2005), 'Thinking of Jackasses: The grand delusions of the Democratic Party', *The Atlantic*.
53. Steven Pinker (9 October 2006), 'Block That Metaphor!', *New Republic*.
54. Kahneman (2011), p. 368ff.
55. *Ibid.*, p. 370.
56. Larry M. Bartels (2003), 'Is "Popular Rule" Possible? Polls, political psychology, and democracy', *Brookings Review*, p. 2.
57. 'Robo – Ed Miliband: Gives Bizarre Identical Answers to EVERY Question', youtu.be/lRHZOL9O0UQ.

58. Damon Green's account can be found at www.twitlonger.com/show/bfensm.

59. See Kahneman (2011), p. 59ff.

60. Bush made the remark in a speech at the Athena Performing Arts Center at Greece Athena Middle and High School, Tuesday, 24 May 2005 in Rochester, NY. It was reported widely. See Dan Froomkin (25 May 2005), 'The Ostrich Approach', *The Washington Post*.

Chapter 6: Retail Therapy

1. Michel de Montaigne (2003), 'Of One Defect in Our Government', *The Complete Essays*, trans. M.A. Screech (London: Penguin).

2. I am guided here particularly by good discussions of the origins of advertising in Winston Fletcher (2008), *Powers of Persuasion: The Inside Story of British Advertising: 1951–2000* (Oxford: Oxford University Press), p. 10ff; and Henry Sampson (1875), *A History of Advertising From the Earliest Times* (London: Chatto and Windus).

3. Sampson (1875), p. 2.

4. William Blades (2014), *The Life and Typography of William Caxton, England's First Printer* (Cambridge: Cambridge University Press), p. 101.

5. Bob M. Fennis and Wolfgang Stroebe (2010), *The Psychology of Advertising* (Hove and New York: Psychology Press), p. 4.

6. *Printers' Ink*, October 1895. Also quoted by Scott himself in Walter Dill Scott (1903), *The Theory and Practice of Advertising: A Simple Exposition of the Principles of Psychology in Their Relation to Successful Advertising* (Boston: Small, Maynard and Co.), p. 3.

7. Scott (1903), p. 1.

8. *Ibid.*, p. 4.

9. Walter Dill Scott (1908), *The Psychology of Advertising: A Simple Exposition of The Principles of Psychology In Their Relation To Successful Advertising* (Boston: Small, Maynard and Co.), p. 18.

10. *Ibid.*, p. 20.

11. *Ibid.*, pp. 20–21.

12. Walter Dill Scott (1911), *Influencing Men in Business: The Psychology of Argument and Suggestion* (New York: The Ronald Press Company), p. 35.

13. Scott (1908), pp. 81–2.

14. *Ibid.*, p. 83.

15. Scott (1903), p. 233ff.

16. Vance Packard (1957), *The Hidden Persuaders* (originally New York: David McKay, now Ig Publishing), p. 31ff.

17. *Ibid.*, p. 32.
18. *Ibid.*, p. 37.
19. *Ibid.*, p. 38.
20. *Ibid.*, p. 39.
21. *Ibid.*, p. 42.
22. *Ibid.*, pp. 42–3.
23. *Ibid.*, pp. 42–4.
24. *Ibid.*, p. 165.
25. As cited in David Lewis (2013), *The Brain Sell: When Science Meets Shopping* (London: Nicholas Brealey Publishing), p. 23.
26. Packard (1957), p. 45.
27. *Ibid.*, p. 87. The following examples are Packard's.
28. climatizeuk.com/air-conditioning/benefits-of-airconditioning/.
29. Packard (1957), p. 90.
30. Some elements of the egg story have no doubt been overcooked; see Laura Shapiro (2005), *Something from the Oven: Reinventing Dinner in 1950s America* (New York: Penguin).
31. Packard (1957), p. 92.
32. *Ibid.*, p. 92.
33. *Ibid.*, Chapter 8.
34. Lawrence R. Samuel (2010), *Freud on Madison Avenue: Motivation Research and Subliminal Advertising in America* (Philadelphia: University of Pennsylvania Press), p. 14.
35. *Ibid.*, p. 52.
36. *Ibid.*, p. 44.
37. *Ibid.*, p. 23. This discussion of Lazarsfeld draws on Samuel too.
38. Facts of Dichter's life can be found in Samuel (2010); Ernest Dichter (1979), *Getting Motivated: The Secret Behind Individual Motivations by the Man Who Was Not Afraid to Ask 'Why?'* (Oxford: Pergamon); and 'Biographical Note', Ernest Dichter Papers, Hagley Museum and Library.
39. 'Science: Psychoanalysis in Advertising' (1940), *Time* magazine.
40. See Samuel (2010), pp. 40–1 and 68ff.
41. Ernest Dichter (1964), *Handbook of Consumer Motivations: The Psychology of the World of Objects* (New York: McGraw Hill), p. 1.
42. Dichter (1964), Chapter 2.
43. As cited by Samuel (2010), p. 34.
44. Packard (1957), pp. 97–8.
45. *Ibid.*, pp. 97–8.
46. See 'Biographical Note', Ernest Dichter Papers, Hagley Museum and Library.

47. Packard (1957), p. 101.
48. Lynne Ames (2 August 1998), 'The View From Peekskill: Tending the Flame of the Motivator', *The New York Times*.
49. Betty Friedan (1963), *The Feminine Mystique* (New York: W.W. Norton), pp. 91–2.
50. *Ibid.*, p. 181.
51. *Ibid.*, p 182.
52. *Ibid.*
53. *Ibid.*
54. Robert Graham (13 October 1953), 'Adman's Nightmare: Is the Prune a Witch?', *The Reporter*, p. 30.
55. Packard (1957), p. 34.
56. Graham (1953), p. 30.
57. Packard (1957), 'The Question of Morality', see especially p. 233.
58. Ernest Dichter (2012), *The Strategy of Desire*.
59. David G. Myers (2000), 'The funds, friends, and faith of happy people', *American Psychologist*, Vol. 55, No. 1, pp. 56–67.
60. Tim Kasser (2002), *The High Price of Materialism* (London: MIT Press), p. 9.
61. Kasser (2002), p. 22.
62. Monika A. Bauer, James E.B. Wilkie, Jung K. Kim, and Galen V. Bodenhausen (2012), 'Cueing Consumerism: Situational Materialism Undermines Personal and Social Well-Being', *Psychological Science*, 23, pp. 517–23.
63. Bauer *et al.* (2012), p. 522.
64. *Ibid.*, p. 522.
65. This is MagnaGlobal's prediction; see also Nathalie Tadena (8 December 2014), 'Ad Companies Slightly Lower 2015 Global Ad Forecasts', *The Wall Street Journal*, CMO Today.

Chapter 7: Left to Our Devices

1. I'm relying for information about the incident and Target on Charles Duhigg (16 February 2012), 'How Companies Learn Your Secrets', *The New York Times*.
2. Duhigg (2012).
3. David Lewis (2013), *The Brain Sell: When Science Meets Shopping* (London: Nicholas Brealey Publishing), p. 124. I am also helped here especially by Paco Underhill (1999), *Why We Buy: The Science of Shopping* (New York: Simon & Schuster), p. 45ff.
4. John T. Cacioppo, Joseph R. Priester, and Gary G. Berntson (1993), 'Rudimentary Determinants of Attitudes. II: Arm Flexion and Extension

Have Differential Effects on Attitudes', *Journal of Personality and Social Psychology*, Vol. 65, No. 1, pp. 5–17.

5. F. Strack, L.L. Martin and S. Stepper (1988), 'Inhibiting and facilitating conditions of the human smile: a nonobtrusive test of the facial feedback hypothesis', *Journal of Personality and Social Psychology*, 54(5), pp. 768–77.

6. Bran van den Bergh, Julien Schmitt, and Luk Warlop (2011), 'Embodied myopia', *Journal of Marketing Research*, 48.6, pp. 1033–44.

7. Van den Bergh *et al.* (2011), pp. 30–31.

8. Rebecca Smithers (17 July 2015), 'UK Supermarkets criticised over misleading pricing tactics', *The Guardian*; Simon Neville (19 August 2013), 'Tesco "half-price strawberries" deal prompts red faces and £300,000 fine', *The Guardian*.

9. *Which?* (21 April 2015), 'Which? super-complaint to the Competition and Markets Authority: misleading and opaque pricing practices in the grocery market', p. 1.

10. *Which?* (2015), p. 6.

11. Michael Brown, Daniel K. Farmer, Nilam Ganenthiran (2013), 'Recasting the Retail Store in Today's Omnichannel World', A.T. Kearney.

12. Underhill (1999), p. 101.

13. Npower (2011), 'Brits haven't lost the urge to splurge', npowermedia centre.com/Press-Releases/Brits-haven-t-lost-the-urge-to-splurge-1005.

14. Survey conducted by the National Employment Savings Trust (2013), 'Impulse-buy Brits spend £6.2 billion on things they don't use'.

15. Underhill (1999) p. 12.

16. *Ibid.*, p. 62.

17. *Ibid.*, p. 17.

18. *Ibid.*, p. 102.

19. *Ibid.*, p. 76.

20. *Ibid.*, p. 79.

21. *Ibid.*, p. 18.

22. Levine (2006), p. 28.

23. Samuel M. McClure, Jian Li, Damon Tomlin, Kim S. Cypert, Latané M. Montague and P. Read Montague (2004), 'Neural Correlates of Behavioral Preference for Culturally Familiar Drinks', *Neuron*, Vol. 44, Issue 2, p. 379.

24. McClure *et al.* (2004), p. 380.

25. Lewis (2013), p. 17; H. Plassmann, T.Z. Ramsøy, and M. Milosavljevic (2012), 'Branding the brain: A critical review and outlook', *Journal of Consumer Psychology*, 22(1), pp. 18–36.

26. On the methods of neuromarketing, I'm helped by clear accounts in Lewis (2013), p. 64ff and Leon Zurawicki (2010), *Neuromarketing: Exploring the Brain of the Consumer* (Heidelberg: Springer), p. 42ff.

27. Lewis (2013), p. 34.

28. *Ibid.*

29. *Ibid.*, p. 127.

30. *Ibid.*, p. 128.

31. *Ibid.*, p. 126.

32. *Ibid.*, p. 129.

33. Jonathan Levav and Jennifer J. Argo (2010), 'Physical Contact and Financial Risk Taking', *Psychological Science* 21(6), pp. 804–10.

34. As discussed in Lewis (2013), p. 87; the original study is J.D. Fisher, M. Rytting and R. Heslin (1976), 'Hands Touching Hands: Affective and Evaluative Effects of Interpersonal Touch', *Sociometry* 39 (4), pp. 416–21.

35. Phil Barden (2013), *Decoded: The Science Behind Why We Buy* (Chichester: John Wiley and Sons), p. 38ff; the original study can be found in B. Knutson, S. Rick, E. Wimmer, D. Prelec and G. Lowenstein (2007), 'Neural Predictors of Purchase', *Neuron*, 53, pp. 147–56.

36. Knutson *et al.* (2007), p. 152.

37. Barden (2013), p. 40.

38. *Ibid.*, p. 14.

39. *Ibid.*, p. 15.

40. *Ibid.*, p. 27.

41. B. Wansink, K. van Itterrsum and J.M. Painter (2005), 'How Descriptive Food Names Bias Sensory Perceptions in Restaurants', *Food Quality and Preference*, 16.5, pp. 393–400; discussed in Barden (2013).

42. Sybil S. Yang, Sheryl E. Kimes and Mauro M. Sessarego (2009), '$ or Dollars: Effects of Menu-Price Formats on Restaurant Checks', *Cornell Hospitality Reports*, 9.8.

43. Barden (2013), p. 49.

44. Dan Ariely (2009), *Predictably Irrational: The Hidden Forces that Shape Our Decisions* (London: HarperCollins), Chapter 1.

45. I'm guided by a good discussion in Leigh Caldwell (2012), *The Psychology of Price: How to Use price to Increase Demand, Profit and Customer Satisfaction* (Richmond: Crimson Publishing) p. 91ff.

46. Raymond Tallis (2012), *Aping Mankind: Neuromania, Darwinitis and the Misrepresentation of Humanity* (London: Routledge).

47. Hilary Putnam (1967), 'The Nature of Mental States', in W.H. Capitan and D.D. Merrill (eds), *Art, Mind, and Religion* (Pittsburgh: Pittsburgh University Press).

48. Pete Etchells (5 December 2013), 'Does neuromarketing live up to the hype?', *The Guardian* – worryingly, the otherwise sober David Lewis's name is attached to these findings.

49. See www.nmsba.com/Ethics.

50. Lewis (2013), p. 138.

51. Gemma Calvert (30 June 2014), 'The Cyber Age of "Moodvertising"', www.12ahead.com/cyber-age-moodvertising.

52. Adam D.I. Kramer, Jamie E. Guillory, and Jeffrey T. Hancock (2014), 'Experimental evidence of massive-scale emotional contagion through social networks', *Proceedings of the National Academy of Sciences of the United States of America*, 11.24, pp. 8788–90.

53. Robert Booth (30 June 2014), 'Facebook reveals news feed experiment to control emotions', *The Guardian*.

54. Robert M. Bond, Christopher J. Fariss, Jason J. Jones, Adam D.I. Kramer, Cameron Marlow, Jaime E. Settle and James H. Fowler (2012), 'A 61-million-person experiment in social influence and political mobilization', *Nature*, 489, pp. 295–8.

55. Robert Epstein (19 August 2015), 'How Google Could Rig the 2016 Election', *Politico* magazine.

56. Robert Epstein and Ronald E. Robertson (2015), 'The search engine manipulation effect (SEME) and its possible impact on the outcomes of elections', *Proceedings of the National Academy of Sciences of the United States of America*, Vol. 112, No. 33.

57. Zygmunt Bauman and David Lyon (2013), *Liquid Surveillance: A Conversation* (Cambridge, Polity Press).

Chapter 8: The Lost Art of Argument

1. See Walter J. Ong (1982), *Orality and Literacy: The Technologizing of the World* (London: Methuen, 1982), p. 5ff. I learned much from a good discussion in Nicholas Carr (2010), *The Shallows: How the Internet is Changing the Way We Read, Think and Remember* (London: Atlantic Books), Chapter 3.

2. Milman Parry (Adam Parry, ed.) (1971), *The Making of Homeric Verse: The Collected Papers of Milman Parry* (Oxford: Oxford University Press), and Ong (1982), p. 18ff.

3. Ong (1982), p. 24. Ong also informs the following discussion.

4. Ong (1982), p. 23.

5. G.S. Kirk, J.E. Raven, and M. Schofield (eds) (1983), *The Presocratic Philosophers* (Cambridge: Cambridge University Press), fragment 291, pp. 2–5.

6. Anthony Kenny (2010), *A New History of Western Philosophy* (Oxford: Oxford University Press), p. 21.

7. John Burnet (1892), *Poem of Parmenides*.

8. Diogenes Laertius, *Lives and Opinions of Eminent Philosophers*, Book IX.

9. Kirk *et al.* (1983), fragment 346.

10. Xenophon, *Memorabilia*, 1.2.14.

11. Plato, *Theaetetus*, 171a.

12. John Locke (1836), *An Essay Concerning Human Understanding* (London: T. Tegg and Son), p. 513.

13. Kenny (2010), p. 784.

14. Aristotle, *Prior Analytics*, I.2, 24b, 18–20.

15. Aristotle, *Rhetoric*, Book 1.

16. *Ibid.*

17. *Ibid.*

18. *Ibid.*

19. Sam Leith (2011), *You Talkin' to Me: Rhetoric from Aristotle to Obama* (London: Profile Books), p. 59.

20. Carl I. Hovland, Arthur A. Lumsdaine, Fred D. Sheffield (1949), *Experiments on Mass Communications*, Vol. III (Princeton: Princeton University Press), p. 22ff.

21. Carl I. Hovland, Irving L. Janis and Harold H. Kelley (1953), *Communication and Persuasion: Psychology Studies in Opinion Change* (New Haven and London: Yale University Press), p. 100ff.

22. Hovland (1953), p. 140.

23. *Ibid.*, p. 21.

24. For an extended discussion, see Richard Wilkinson and Kate Pickett (2010), *The Spirit Level: Why Equality is Better for Everyone* (London: Penguin Books).

25. Ruth W. Grant (2012), *Strings Attached: Untangling the Ethics of Incentives* (Princeton: Princeton University Press), p. 112ff. This book helped me get clear on a number of sorts of non-rational persuasion, and I'm grateful to the author for the many insights in it.

26. *Ibid.*, p. 115.

27. *Ibid.*, p. 131.

28. *Ibid.*, p. 136.

29. Martha C. Nussbaum (2010), *Not For Profit: Why Democracy Needs The Humanities* (Princeton: Princeton University Press), p. 1.

30. *Ibid.*, p. 2.

31. Nussbaum (2010), p. 51.

32. Aldous Huxley (2004), *Brave New World Revisited* (New York: HarperCollins), Chapter 11.

33. Anca M. Miron and Jack W. Brehm (2006), 'Reactance Theory – 40 Years Later', *ZFSP*, 37(1), p. 4.

34. Grant (2012), p. 136.

35. Leonard Bickman (1974), 'The Social Power of a Uniform', *Journal of Applied Social Psychology*, 4, pp. 47–61.

36. See Levine (2006), Chapter 7.

37. Joseph C. Nunes and Xavier Drèze (2006), 'The Endowed Progress Effect: How Artificial Advancement Increases Effort', *Journal of Consumer Research*, 32, pp. 504–12.

38. Mark Muraven and Roy F. Baumeister (2000), 'Self Regulation and Depletion of Limited Resources: Does Self-Control Resemble a Muscle?', *Psychological Bulletin*, 126.

39. Roy E. Baumeister, Ellen Bratslavsky, Mark Muraven and Dianne M. Tice (1998), 'Ego Depletion: Is the Active Self a Limited Resource?', *Journal of Personality and Social Psychology*, 74, pp. 1252–65.

40. Erik G. Helzer and David A. Pizarro (2010), 'Dirty Liberals! Reminders of Physical Cleanliness Influence Moral and Political Attitudes', *Psychological Science*, pp. 1–6.

41. J.M. Burger, N. Messian, S. Patel, A. del Prado and C. Anderson (2004), 'What a coincidence! The effects of incidental similarity on compliance', *Personality and Social Psychology Bulletin*, 30, pp. 35–43.

42. Kathleen D. Vohs, Nicole L. Mead, Miranda R. Goode (2006), 'The Psychological Consequences of Money', *Science*, 314, pp. 1154–56.

43. Daniele Marzoli and Luca Tommasi (2009), 'Side biases in humans (*Homo sapiens*): three ecological studies on hemispheric asymmetries', *Naturwissenschaften*, 96.9, pp. 1099–1106.

44. Joshua M. Ackerman, Christopher C. Nocera, John A. Bargh (2010), 'Incidental Haptic Sensations Influence Social Judgments and Decisions', *Science*, 328, pp. 1712–15.

45. M.S. McGlone and J. Tofighbakhsh (2000), 'Birds of a Feather Flock Conjointly (?): Rhyme as Reason in Aphorisms', *Psychological Science*, 11.5, pp. 424–8.

46. Another fine title: Daniel M. Oppenheimer (2006), 'Consequences of Erudite Vernacular Utilized Irrespective of Necessity: Problems with Using Long Words Needlessly', *Applied Cognitive Psychology*, 20, pp. 139–56. See the discussion in Kahneman (2011), p. 62ff.

Epilogue

1. David Remnick (9 November 2016), 'An American Tragedy', *The New Yorker*.

2. Jonathan Freedland (10 November 2016), 'Will Donald Trump Destroy America?', *The Guardian*.

3. Jasmine C. Lee and Kevin Quealy (18 October 2016), 'The 279 People, Places and Things Donald Trump Has Insulted on Twitter', *The New York Times*.

4. Patrick Healy and Matt Flegenheimer (29 August 2016), 'Hillary Clinton Piles Up Research in Bid to Needle Donald Trump at First Debate', *The New York Times*.

5. Politifact, 'Comparing Hillary Clinton, Donald Trump on the Truth-O-Meter', accessed 25 October 2016, www.politifact.com.

6. Glenn Kessler (22 March 2016), 'All of Donald Trump's Four-Pinocchio Ratings in One Place', *The Washington Post*.

7. Kyle Cheney, Isaac Arnsdorf, Daniel Lippman, Daniel Strauss, and Brent Griffiths (25 September 2016), 'Donald Trump's Week of Misrepresentations, Exaggerations and Half-Truths' and Kyle Cheney, Isaac Arnsdorf, Daniel Lippman, and Daniel Strauss (25 September 2016), 'Hillary Clinton Struggles Most With Truth About Herself', both in www.politico.com, accessed 27 October 2016.

8. David Roberts (1 April 2010), 'Post-truth Politics', *Grist*.

9. Dan P. McAdams (June 2016), 'The Mind of Donald Trump', *The Atlantic*.

10. Larry Wilmore, 'Complete Remarks at 2016 White House Correspondents' Dinner, youtu.be/1IDFt3BL7FA.

11. 'Art of the Lie' (10 September 2016), *The Economist*.

12. John Connor (17 July 2014), 'Tony Abbott's Carbon Tax Outrage Signals Nadir of Post-Truth Politics', *The Age*.

13. Yannis Kourtoglou (13 June 2016), 'Brexit Could Threaten Western Political Civilization, says EU's Tusk', *Reuters*.

14. Philip Inman (27 October 2016), 'UK Economy Shrugs Off Brexit Uncertainty with 0.5% Growth', *The Guardian*.

15. Interview with Faisal Islam of Sky News, published on 21 June 2016.

16. Manuel Funke, Moritz Schularick, and Christoph Trebesch, 'Politics in the Slump: Polarization and Extremism after Financial Crises, 1870–2014', 21 November 2015, Vox.org.

17. Steve Nelson (6 March 2016), 'Donald Trump: Death Rattle of Angry, Fearful White Men', *Huffington Post*.

Bibliography

Andrew, Donna T. *London Debating Societies 1776–1799*. London: London Record Society, 1994

Andrew, Donna T. 'Popular Culture and Public Debate: London 1780', *The Historical Journal* (1996): 405–23

Ariely, Dan. *Predictably Irrational: The Hidden Forces that Shape Our Decisions*. London: HarperCollins, 2009

Asch, Solomon. 'Opinions and Social Pressure', in Elliott Aronson, ed. *Readings About the Social Animal*. New York: W.H. Freeman, 1995

Barden, Phil. *Decoded: The Science Behind Why We Buy*. Chichester: John Wiley and Sons, 2013

Baumeister, Roy E., Ellen Bratslavsky, Mark Muraven, and Dianne M. Tice. 'Ego Depletion: Is the Active Self a Limited Resource?', *Journal of Personality and Social Psychology* (1998): 1252–65

Berlin, Isaiah. *Liberty*. Oxford: Oxford University Press, 2002

Bernays, Edward L. *Propaganda*. Brooklyn: Ig Publishing, 1928

Bernays, Edward L. *Biography of an Idea: Memoirs of Public Relations Counsel Edward L. Bernays*. New York: Simon & Schuster, 1965

Bush, George H.W. *Speaking of Freedom: The Collected Speeches*. New York: Simon & Schuster, 2009

Cabinet Office Behavioural Insights Team. 'Applying Behavioural Insights to Organ Donation', 2013. www.gov.uk/government/uploads/system/uploads/attachment_data/file/267100/Applying_Behavioural_Insights_to_Organ_Donation.pdf

Caldwell, Leigh. *The Psychology of Price: How to Use Price to Increase Demand, Profit and Customer Satisfaction*. Richmond: Crimson Publishing, 2012

Cameron, David. 'The Next Age of Government', video, TED, February 2010, www.ted.com/talks/david_cameron

Carr, Nicholas. *The Shallows: How the Internet is Changing the Way We Read, Think and Remember*. London: Atlantic Books, 2010

Cavanaugh, John and Jerry Mander, eds. *Alternatives to Global Capitalism: A Better World is Possible*. San Francisco: Berrett-Koehler, 2002

Cialdini, Robert B. *Influence: Science and Practice*. Boston: Pearson, 2009

Crutchfield, Richard S. 'Conformity and Character', *American Psychologist* (1995): 191–98

Dichter, Ernest. *Handbook of Consumer Motivations: The Psychology of the World of Objects*. New York: McGraw Hill, 1964

Dichter, Ernest. *Getting Motivated: The Secret Behind Individual Motivations by the Man Who Was Not Afraid to Ask 'Why?'* Oxford: Pergamon, 1979

Dinan, William and David Miller, eds. *Thinker, Faker, Spinner, Spy: Corporate PR and the Assault on Democracy*. London: Pluto Press, 2007

Docherty, Neil. *To Sell A War*. Canada Broadcasting Corporation, 1992

Ewen, Stuart. *PR! A Social History of Spin*. New York: Basic Books, 1996

'Faked Kuwaiti Girl Testimony', YouTube video, viewed 26 March 2014, youtu.be/LmfVs3WaE9Y

Fennis, Bob M. and Wolfgang Stroebe. *The Psychology of Advertising*. Hove and New York: Psychology Press, 2010

Festinger, Leon. *A Theory of Cognitive Dissonance*. Stanford: Stanford University Press, 1957

Friedan, Betty. *The Feminine Mystique*. New York: W.W. Norton, 1963

Gigerenzer, Gerd. *Risk Savvy: How to Make Good Decisions*. New York: Penguin, 2014

Gouldner, Alvin W. 'The Norm of Reciprocity: A Preliminary Statement', *American Sociological Review* (1960): 161–78

Grant, Ruth W. *Strings Attached: Untangling the Ethics of Incentives*. Princeton: Princeton University Press, 2012

Grimshaw, Chris. 'A Tour of the United Kingdom's Public Relations Industry', in *Thinker, Faker, Spinner, Spy: Corporate PR and the Assault on Democracy*. William Dinan and David Miller, eds. London: Pluto Press, 2007

Haynes, Laura, Owain Service, Ben Goldacre, and David Torgerson, 'Test, Learn, Adapt: Developing Public Policy with Randomised Controlled Trials', Cabinet Office, 2013. www.gov.uk/government/uploads/system/uploads/attachment_data/file/62529/TLA-1906126.pdf

Hiebert, Ray Eldon. *Courtier to the Crowd: the Story of Ivy Lee and the Development of Public Relations*. Ames: Iowa State University Press, 1966

Hovland, Carl I., Arthur A. Lumsdaine, Fred D. Sheffield. *Experiments on Mass Communications*. Princeton: Princeton University Press, 1949

Hovland, Carl I., Irving L. Janis, and Harold H. Kelley. *Communication and Persuasion: Psychology Studies in Opinion Change*. New Haven and London: Yale University Press, 1953

Kahneman, D. and A. Tversky. 'The Framing of Decisions and the Psychology of Choice', *Science* (1981): 453–8

Kahneman, Daniel. *Thinking, Fast and Slow*. London: Penguin, 2011

Kasser, Tim. *The High Price of Materialism*. London: MIT Press, 2002

Kelly, Jamie Terrence. *Framing Democracy: A Behavioral Approach to Democratic Theory*. Princeton: Princeton University Press, 2012

Kirk, G.S., J.E. Raven, and M. Schofield, eds. *The Presocratic Philosophers*. Cambridge: Cambridge University Press, 1983

Kramer, Adam D.I., Jamie E. Guillory, and Jeffrey T. Hancock. 'Experimental evidence of massive-scale emotional contagion through social networks', *Proceedings of the National Academy of Sciences of the United States of America* (2014): 8788–90

Lakoff, George and Mark Johnson. *The Metaphors We Live By*. Chicago: University of Chicago Press, 1980

Lakoff, George and Mark Johnson. *Philosophy in the Flesh: The Embodied Mind and Its Challenge to Western Philosophy*. New York: Basic Books, 1999

Lakoff, George. *Moral Politics*. Chicago: University of Chicago Press, 2003

Lakoff, George. *Don't Think of an Elephant: Know Your Values and Frame the Debate*. White River Junction: Chelsea Green Publishing, 2004

Lakoff, George. *Whose Freedom? The Battle Over America's Most Important Idea*. New York: Farrar, Straus & Giroux, 2006

Le Bon, Gustave. *The Crowd: A Study of the Popular Mind*. Mineola, NY: Dover Publications, 2002

Leith, Sam. *You Talkin' to Me: Rhetoric from Aristotle to Obama*. London: Profile Books, 2011

Levine, Robert. *The Power of Persuasion: How We're Bought and Sold*. Oxford: Oneworld, 2006

Lewis, David. *The Brain Sell: When Science Meets Shopping.* London: Nicholas Brealey Publishing, 2013

Lippmann, Walter. *The Phantom Public.* New York: Harcourt Brace and Co., 1927

Lippmann, Walter. *Public Opinion.* Mineola, NY: Dover Publications, 2004

MacArthur, John R. *Second Front: Censorship and Propaganda in the 1991 Gulf War.* Berkeley: University of California Press, 2004

Marlin, Randal. *Propaganda and the Ethics of Persuasion.* Peterborough: Broadview Press, 2013

McCalman, Iain. 'Ultra-Radicalism and Convivial Debating-Clubs in London, 1795–1838', *The English Historical Review* (1987): 309–33

McGlone, M.S. and J. Tofighbakhsh. 'Birds of a Feather Flock Conjointly (?): Rhyme as Reason in Aphorisms', *Psychological Science* (2000): 424–8

Miller, David and William Dinan. *A Century of Spin: How Public Relations Became the Cutting Edge of Corporate Power.* London: Pluto Press, 2008

Nussbaum, Martha C. *Not For Profit: Why Democracy Needs The Humanities.* Princeton: Princeton University Press, 2010

Ong, Walter J. *Orality and Literacy: The Technologizing of the World.* London: Methuen, 1982

Oppenheimer, Daniel M. 'Consequences of Erudite Vernacular Utilized Irrespective of Necessity: Problems with Using Long Words Needlessly', *Applied Cognitive Psychology* (2006): 139–56

Packard, Vance. *The Hidden Persuaders.* Brooklyn: Ig Publishing, 1957

Russell, Bertrand. *The Problems of Philosophy.* Rockville, MD: Arc Manor, 2008

Samuel, Lawrence R. *Freud on Madison Avenue: Motivation Research and Subliminal Advertising in America.* Philadelphia: University of Pennsylvania Press, 2010

Scott, Walter Dill. *The Theory and Practice of Advertising: A Simple Exposition of the Principles of Psychology in Their Relation to Successful Advertising.* Boston: Small, Maynard and Co., 1903

Scott, Walter Dill. *Influencing Men in Business: The Psychology of Argument and Suggestion.* New York: The Ronald Press Company, 1911

Stauber, John and Sheldon Rampton. *Toxic Sludge is Good for You! Lies,*

Damn Lies, and the Public Relations Industry. Monroe, ME: Common Courage Press, 1995

Sunstein, Cass. 'The Storrs Lectures: Behavioral Economics and Paternalism', *Yale Law Journal* (2012): 1826–99

Sunstein, Cass. *Simpler: The Future of Government*. New York: Simon & Schuster, 2013

Sunstein, Cass. *Why Nudge?: The Politics of Libertarian Paternalism*. Yale: Yale University Press, 2014

Thale, Mary. 'London Debating Societies in the 1790s', *The Historical Journal* (1989): 57–86

Thaler, Richard H. and Cass R. Sunstein. *Nudge: Improving Decisions about Health, Wealth, and Happiness*. London: Penguin, 2008

Trotter, Wilfred. *Instincts of the Herd in Peace and War*. New York: Macmillan, 1919

Tversky, A. and D. Kahneman. 'Availability: A heuristic for judging frequency and probability', *Cognitive Psychology* (1972): 207–33

Tversky, A. and D. Kahneman. 'Loss Aversion in Riskless Choice: A Reference-Dependent Model', *The Quarterly Journal of Economics* (1991): 1039–61

Tye, Larry. *The Father of Spin: Edward L. Bernays and the Birth of Public Relations*. New York: Henry Holt and Co., 1998

Underhill, Paco. *Why We Buy: The Science of Shopping*. New York: Simon & Schuster, 1999

Unger, Craig. *House of Bush, House of Saud: The Secret Relationship Between the World's Two Most Powerful Dynasties*. London: Scribner, 2004

Wilkinson, Richard and Kate Pickett. *The Spirit Level: Why Equality is Better for Everyone*. London: Penguin Books, 2010

Williams, Bernard. *Truth and Truthfulness: An Essay in Genealogy*. Princeton: Princeton University Press, 2011

Wilson, T.D. and C.E. Houston, K.M. Etling, and N. Brekke. 'A New Look at Anchoring Effects: Basic Anchoring and Its Antecedents', *Journal of Experimental Psychology* (1996): 387–402

Fletcher, Winston. *Powers of Persuasion: The Inside Story of British Advertising: 1951–2000*. Oxford: Oxford University Press, 2008

Zurawicki, Leon. *Neuromarketing: Exploring the Brain of the Consumer*. Heidelberg: Springer, 2010

Index